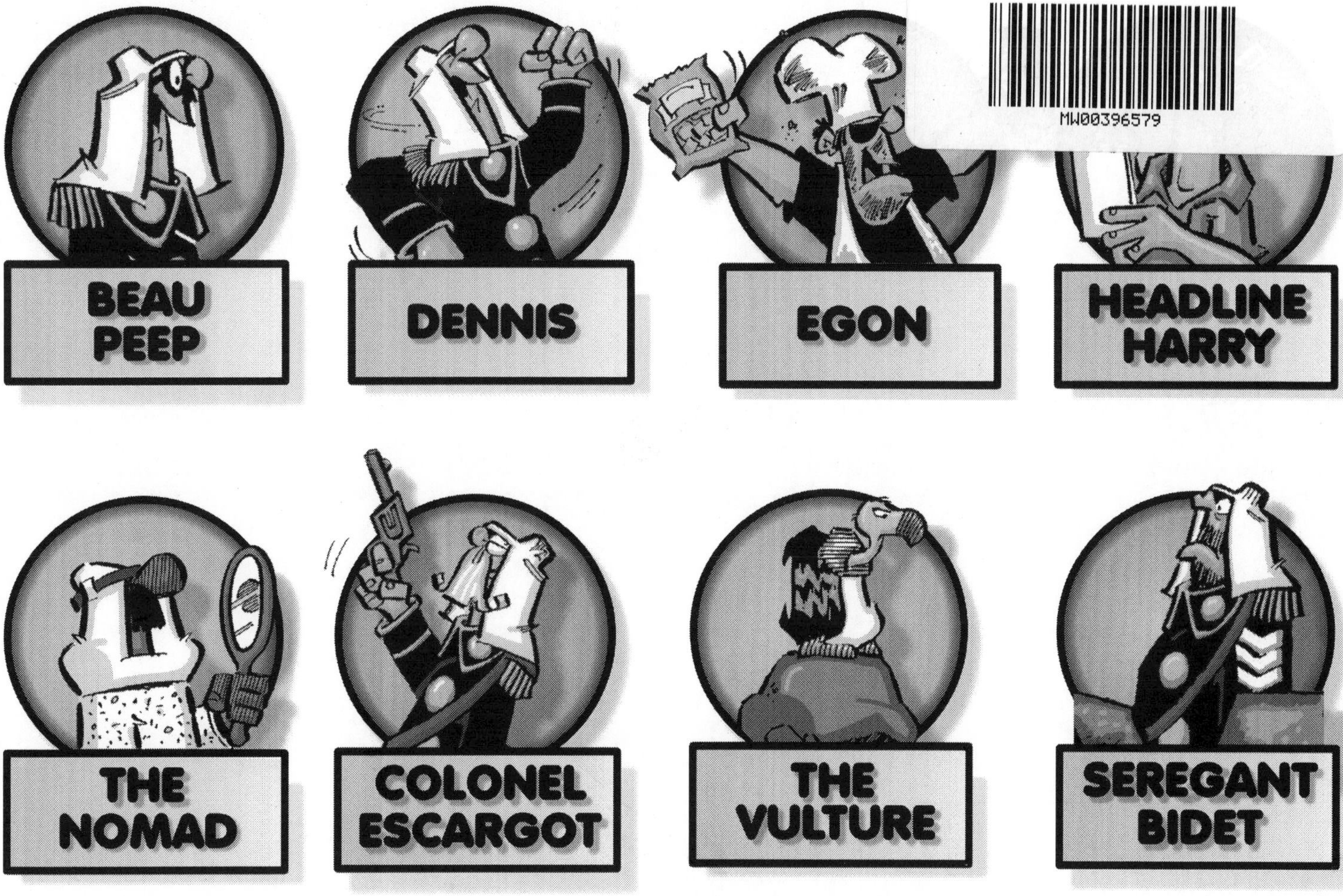
BEAU PEEP
DENNIS
EGON
HEADLINE HARRY
THE NOMAD
COLONEL ESCARGOT
THE VULTURE
SEREGANT BIDET

www.beaupeep.com

Beau Peep Book 20. v1.00. Jan 2012. Typesetting, Graphics and Assorted Technical Jiggery Pokery by Steve Hammond and Mike Dailly.

THE ADVENTURES OF THE LEGIONNAIRE
BEAU PEEP

The return of Beau Peep...

Beau Peep has been running since 1978 and, after taking off our socks and shoes, we've worked out that this comes to 33 years or one third of a century. And we're still both 28 years of age. Remarkable. Hope you enjoy this latest collection of strips.

Roger Kettle and Andrew Christine.

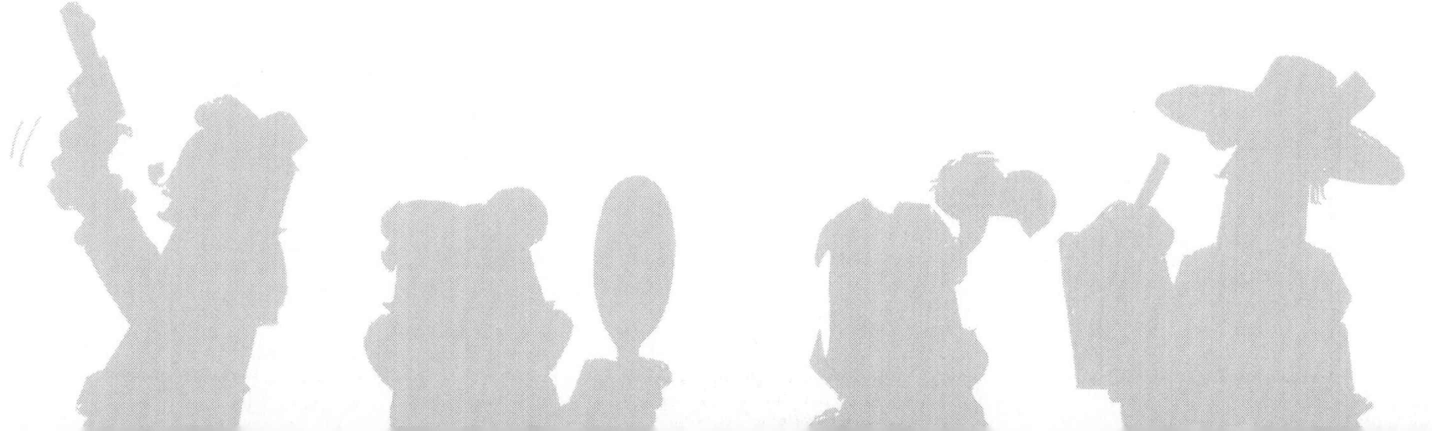

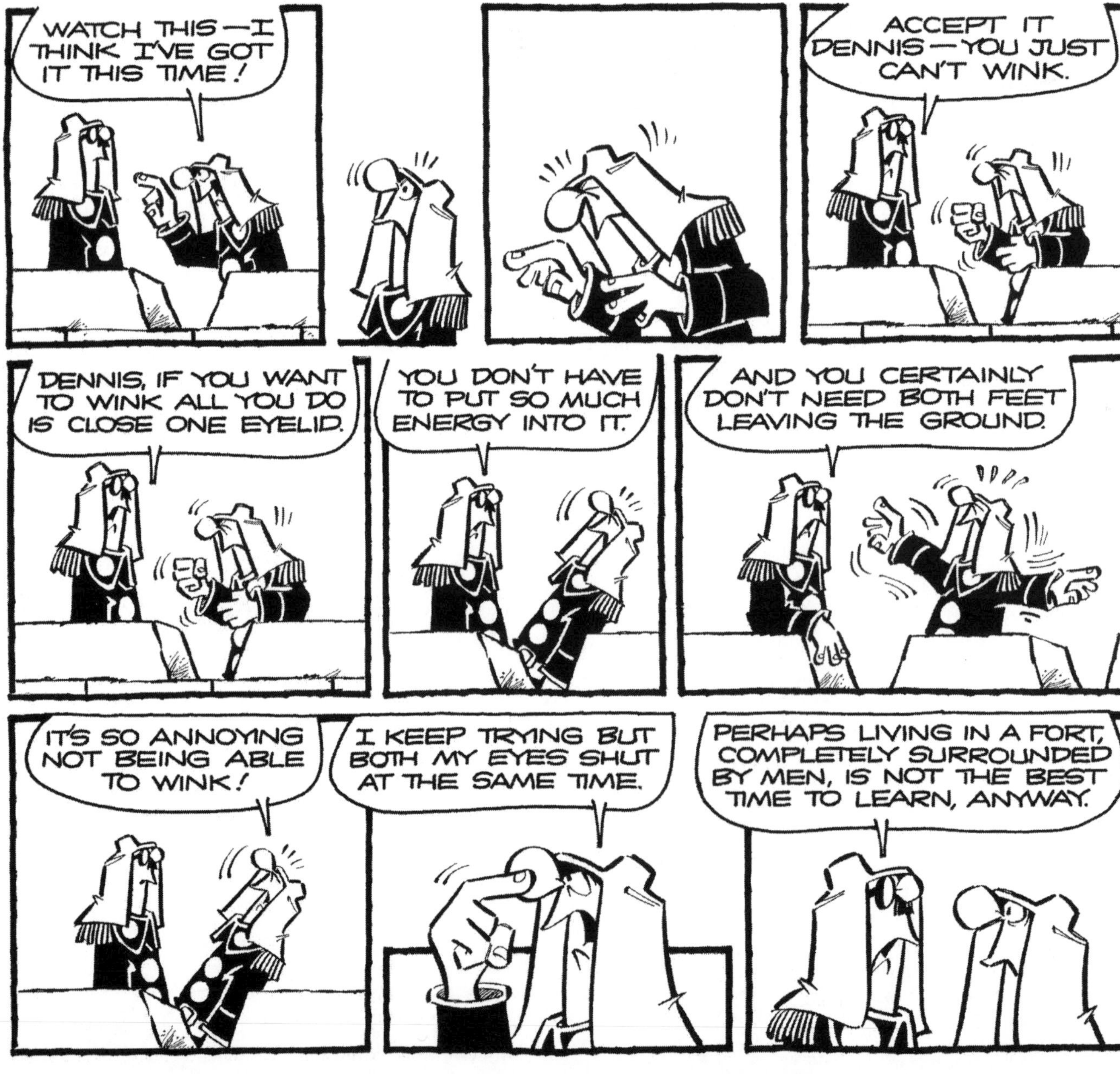
WATCH THIS—I THINK I'VE GOT IT THIS TIME!
ACCEPT IT DENNIS—YOU JUST CAN'T WINK.
DENNIS, IF YOU WANT TO WINK ALL YOU DO IS CLOSE ONE EYELID.
YOU DON'T HAVE TO PUT SO MUCH ENERGY INTO IT.
AND YOU CERTAINLY DON'T NEED BOTH FEET LEAVING THE GROUND.
IT'S SO ANNOYING NOT BEING ABLE TO WINK!
I KEEP TRYING BUT BOTH MY EYES SHUT AT THE SAME TIME.
PERHAPS LIVING IN A FORT, COMPLETELY SURROUNDED BY MEN, IS NOT THE BEST TIME TO LEARN, ANYWAY.

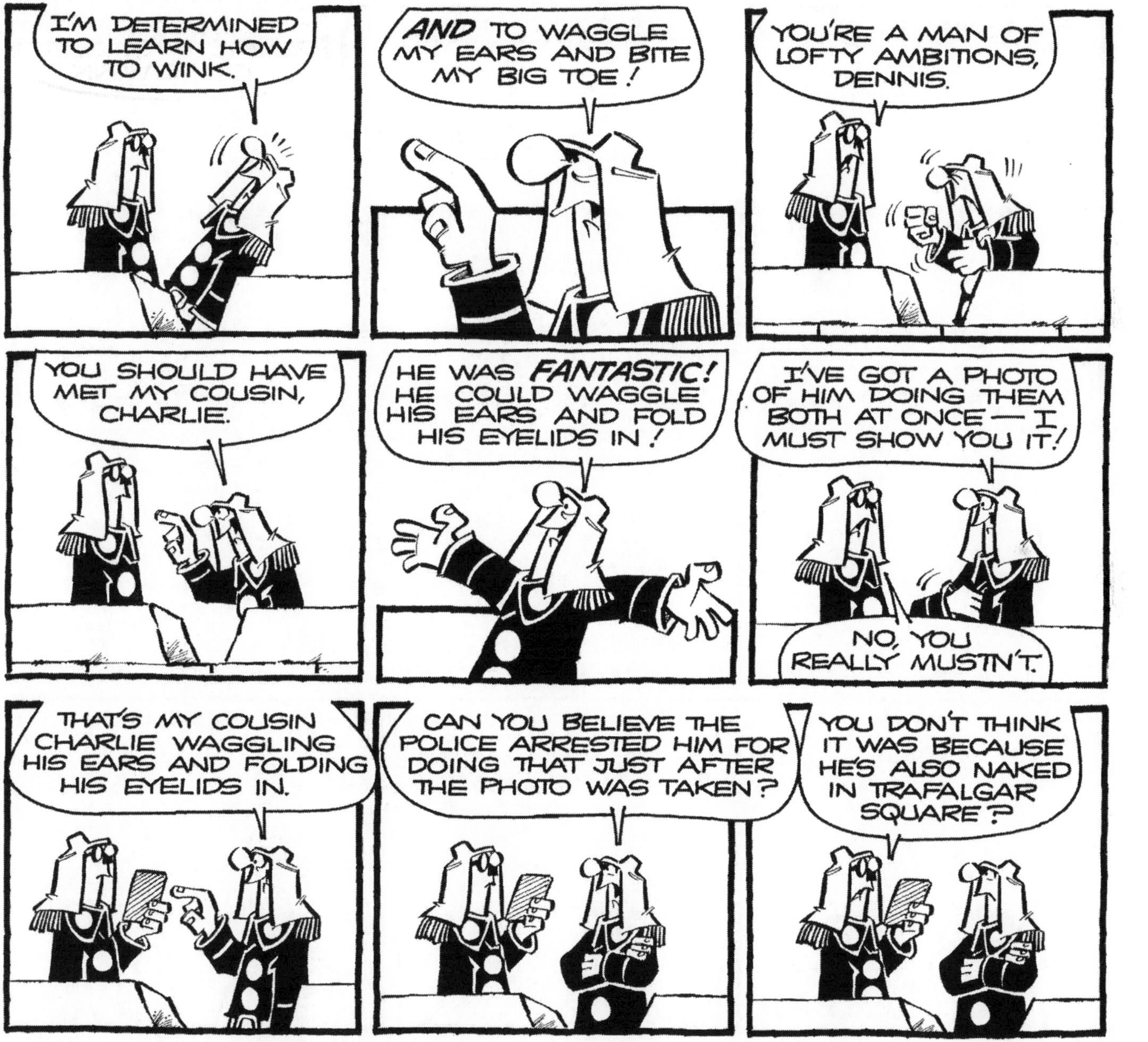
I'M DETERMINED TO LEARN HOW TO WINK.
AND TO WAGGLE MY EARS AND BITE MY BIG TOE!
YOU'RE A MAN OF LOFTY AMBITIONS, DENNIS.
YOU SHOULD HAVE MET MY COUSIN, CHARLIE.
HE WAS FANTASTIC! HE COULD WAGGLE HIS EARS AND FOLD HIS EYELIDS IN!
I'VE GOT A PHOTO OF HIM DOING THEM BOTH AT ONCE — I MUST SHOW YOU IT!
NO, YOU REALLY MUSTN'T.
THAT'S MY COUSIN CHARLIE WAGGLING HIS EARS AND FOLDING HIS EYELIDS IN.
CAN YOU BELIEVE THE POLICE ARRESTED HIM FOR DOING THAT JUST AFTER THE PHOTO WAS TAKEN?
YOU DON'T THINK IT WAS BECAUSE HE'S ALSO NAKED IN TRAFALGAR SQUARE?

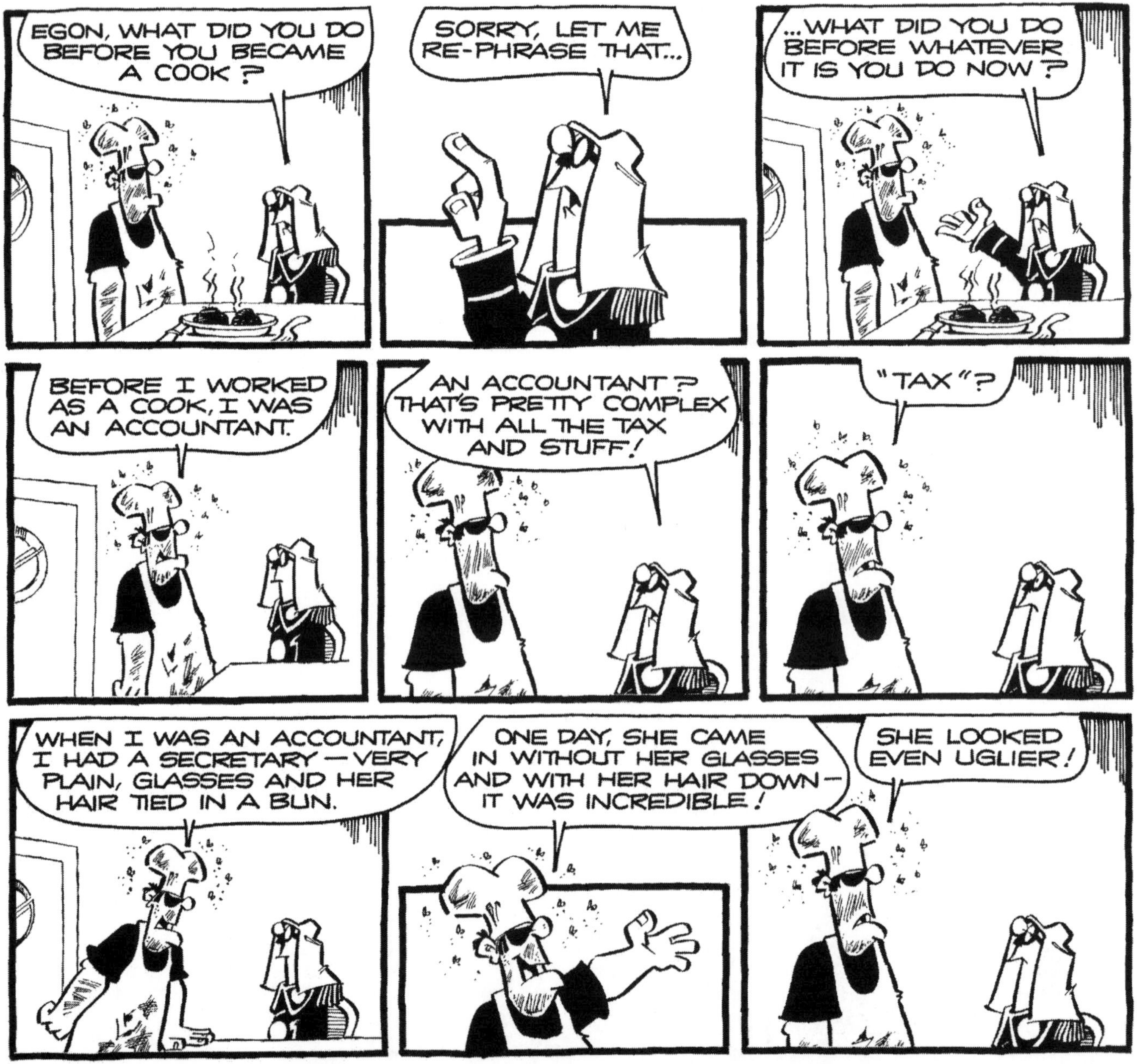
EGON, WHAT DID YOU DO BEFORE YOU BECAME A COOK ?
SORRY, LET ME RE-PHRASE THAT...
...WHAT DID YOU DO BEFORE WHATEVER IT IS YOU DO NOW ?
BEFORE I WORKED AS A COOK, I WAS AN ACCOUNTANT.
AN ACCOUNTANT ? THAT'S PRETTY COMPLEX WITH ALL THE TAX AND STUFF!
"TAX"?
WHEN I WAS AN ACCOUNTANT, I HAD A SECRETARY — VERY PLAIN, GLASSES AND HER HAIR TIED IN A BUN.
ONE DAY, SHE CAME IN WITHOUT HER GLASSES AND WITH HER HAIR DOWN — IT WAS INCREDIBLE!
SHE LOOKED EVEN UGLIER!

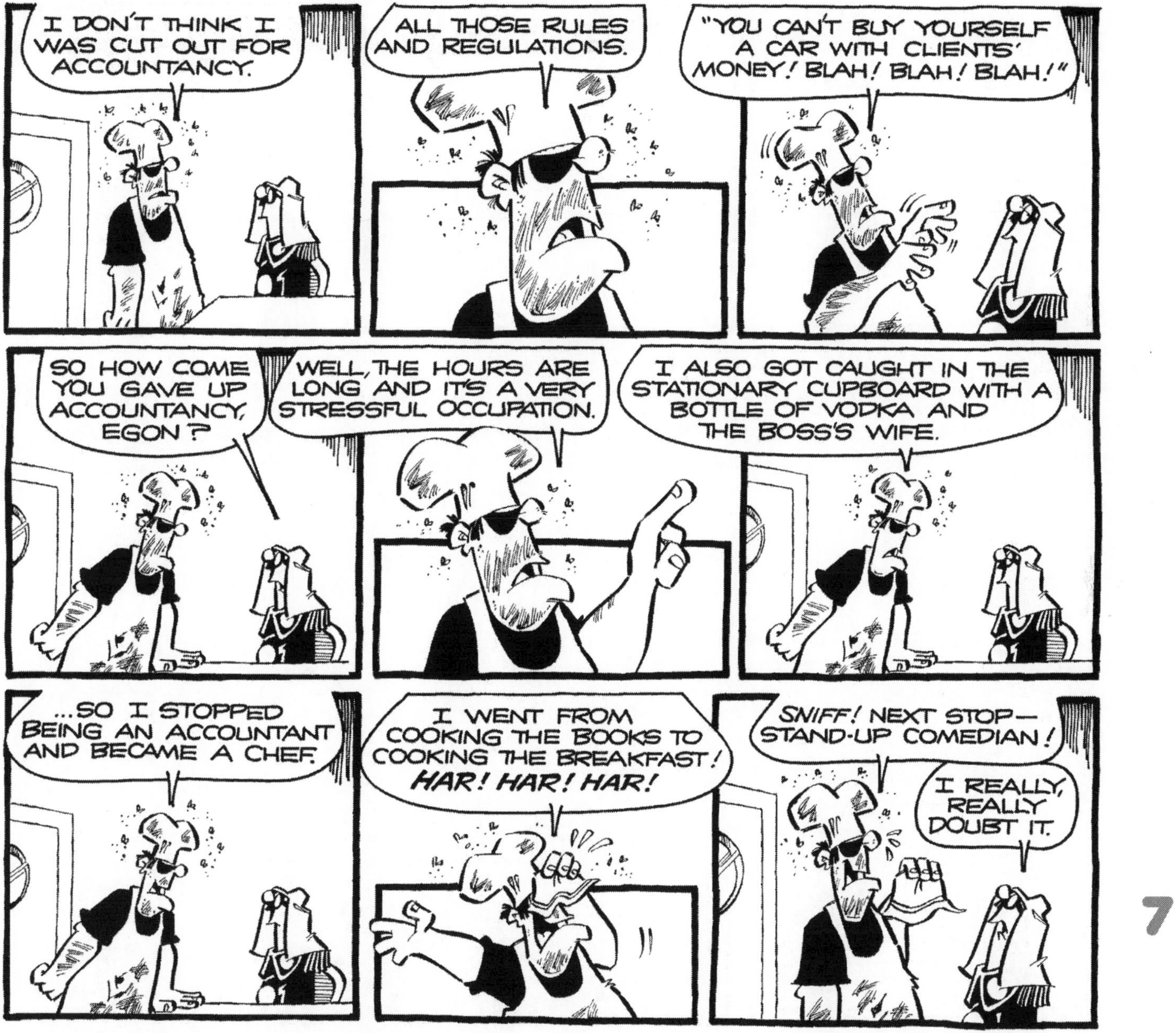

I DON'T THINK I WAS CUT OUT FOR ACCOUNTANCY.
ALL THOSE RULES AND REGULATIONS.
"YOU CAN'T BUY YOURSELF A CAR WITH CLIENTS' MONEY! BLAH! BLAH! BLAH!"
SO HOW COME YOU GAVE UP ACCOUNTANCY, EGON?
WELL, THE HOURS ARE LONG AND IT'S A VERY STRESSFUL OCCUPATION.
I ALSO GOT CAUGHT IN THE STATIONARY CUPBOARD WITH A BOTTLE OF VODKA AND THE BOSS'S WIFE.
...SO I STOPPED BEING AN ACCOUNTANT AND BECAME A CHEF.
I WENT FROM COOKING THE BOOKS TO COOKING THE BREAKFAST! *HAR! HAR! HAR!*
SNIFF! NEXT STOP— STAND-UP COMEDIAN!
I REALLY, REALLY DOUBT IT.

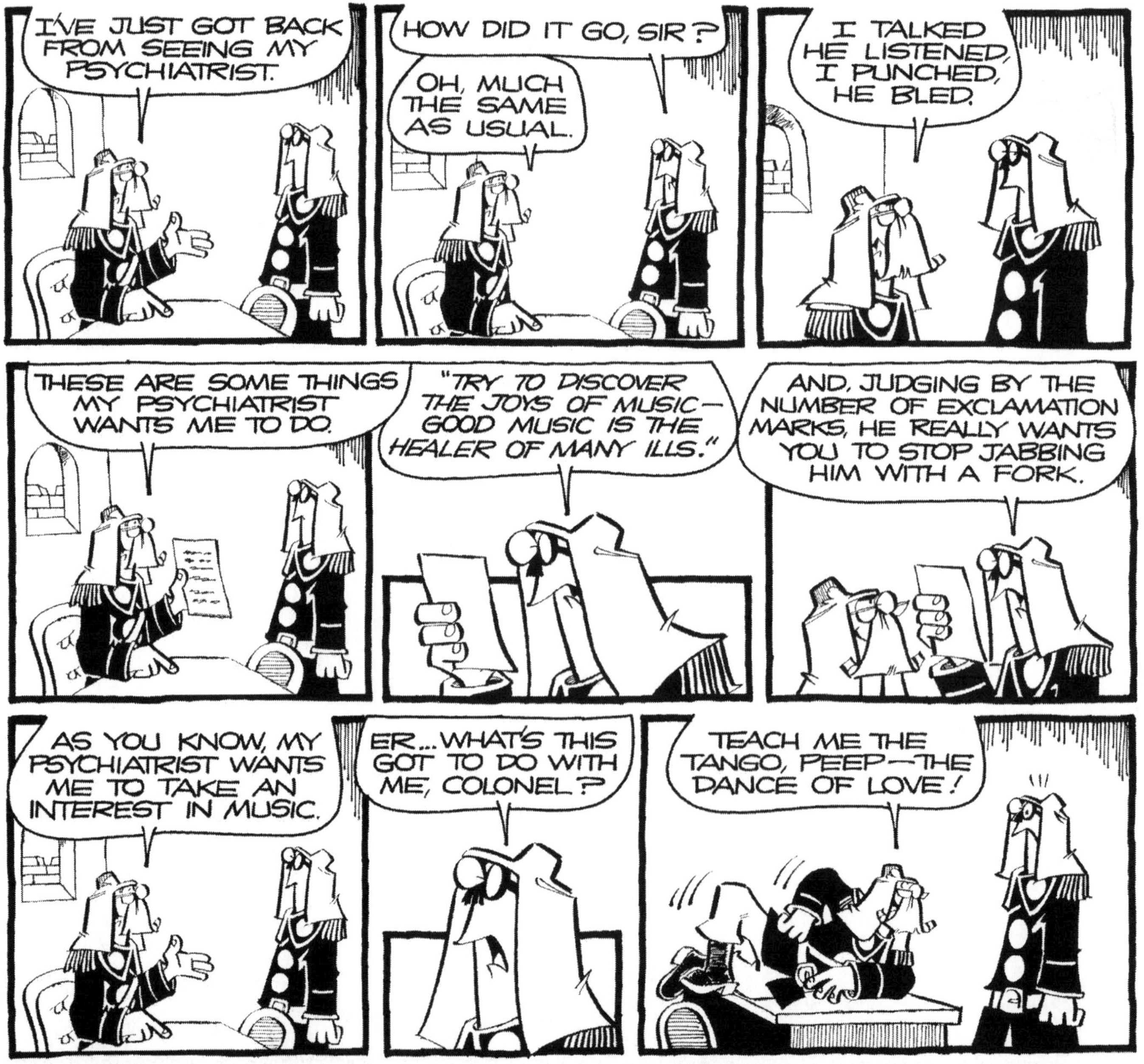
I'VE JUST GOT BACK FROM SEEING MY PSYCHIATRIST.
HOW DID IT GO, SIR?
OH, MUCH THE SAME AS USUAL.
I TALKED HE LISTENED, I PUNCHED, HE BLED.
THESE ARE SOME THINGS MY PSYCHIATRIST WANTS ME TO DO.
"TRY TO DISCOVER THE JOYS OF MUSIC— GOOD MUSIC IS THE HEALER OF MANY ILLS."
AND, JUDGING BY THE NUMBER OF EXCLAMATION MARKS, HE REALLY WANTS YOU TO STOP JABBING HIM WITH A FORK.
AS YOU KNOW, MY PSYCHIATRIST WANTS ME TO TAKE AN INTEREST IN MUSIC.
ER...WHAT'S THIS GOT TO DO WITH ME, COLONEL?
TEACH ME THE TANGO, PEEP—THE DANCE OF LOVE!

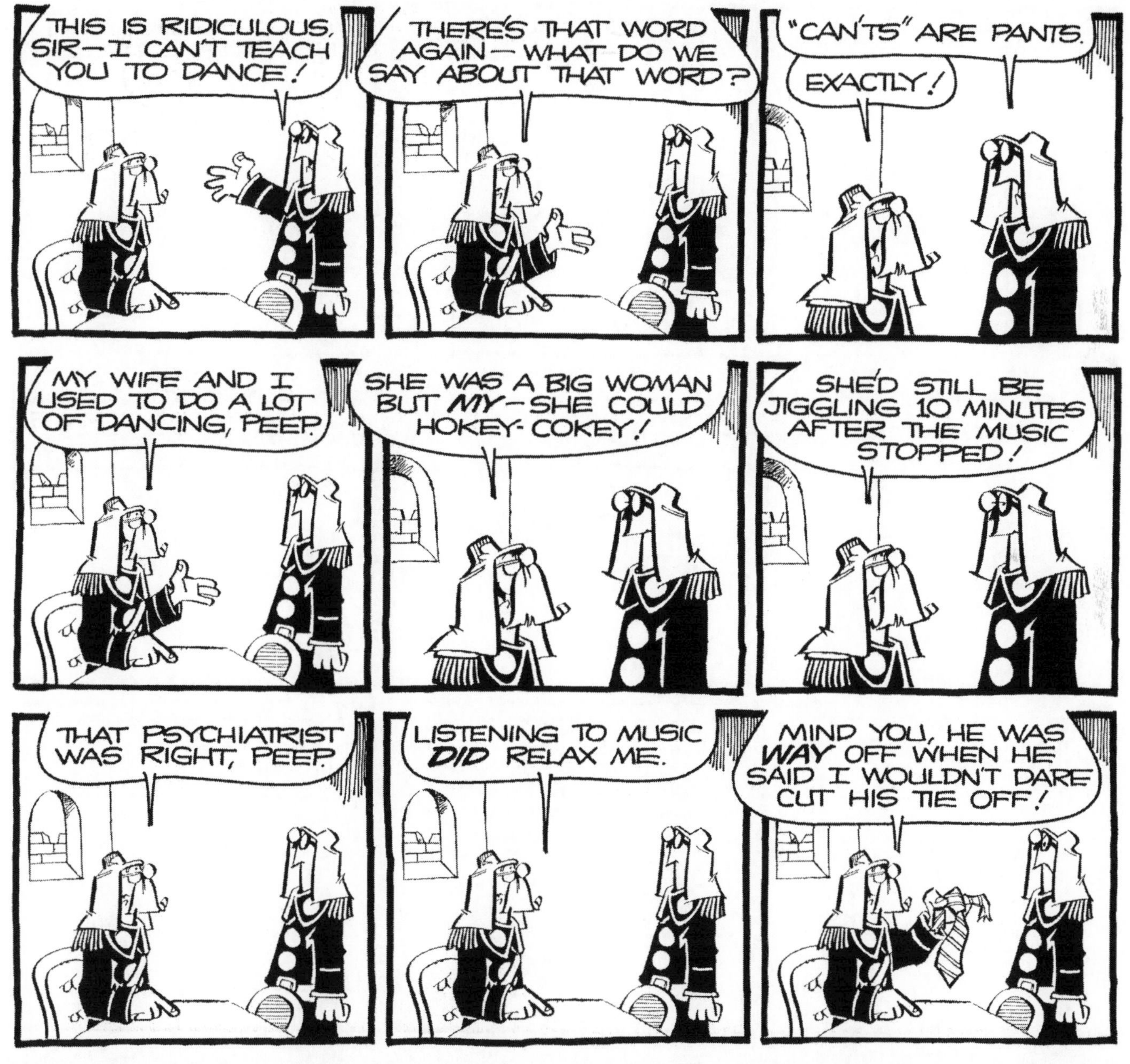
THIS IS RIDICULOUS, SIR—I CAN'T TEACH YOU TO DANCE!
THERE'S THAT WORD AGAIN—WHAT DO WE SAY ABOUT THAT WORD?
"CAN'TS" ARE PANTS.
EXACTLY!
MY WIFE AND I USED TO DO A LOT OF DANCING, PEEP.
SHE WAS A BIG WOMAN BUT *MY*—SHE COULD HOKEY-COKEY!
SHE'D STILL BE JIGGLING 10 MINUTES AFTER THE MUSIC STOPPED!
THAT PSYCHIATRIST WAS RIGHT, PEEP.
LISTENING TO MUSIC *DID* RELAX ME.
MIND YOU, HE WAS *WAY* OFF WHEN HE SAID I WOULDN'T DARE CUT HIS TIE OFF!

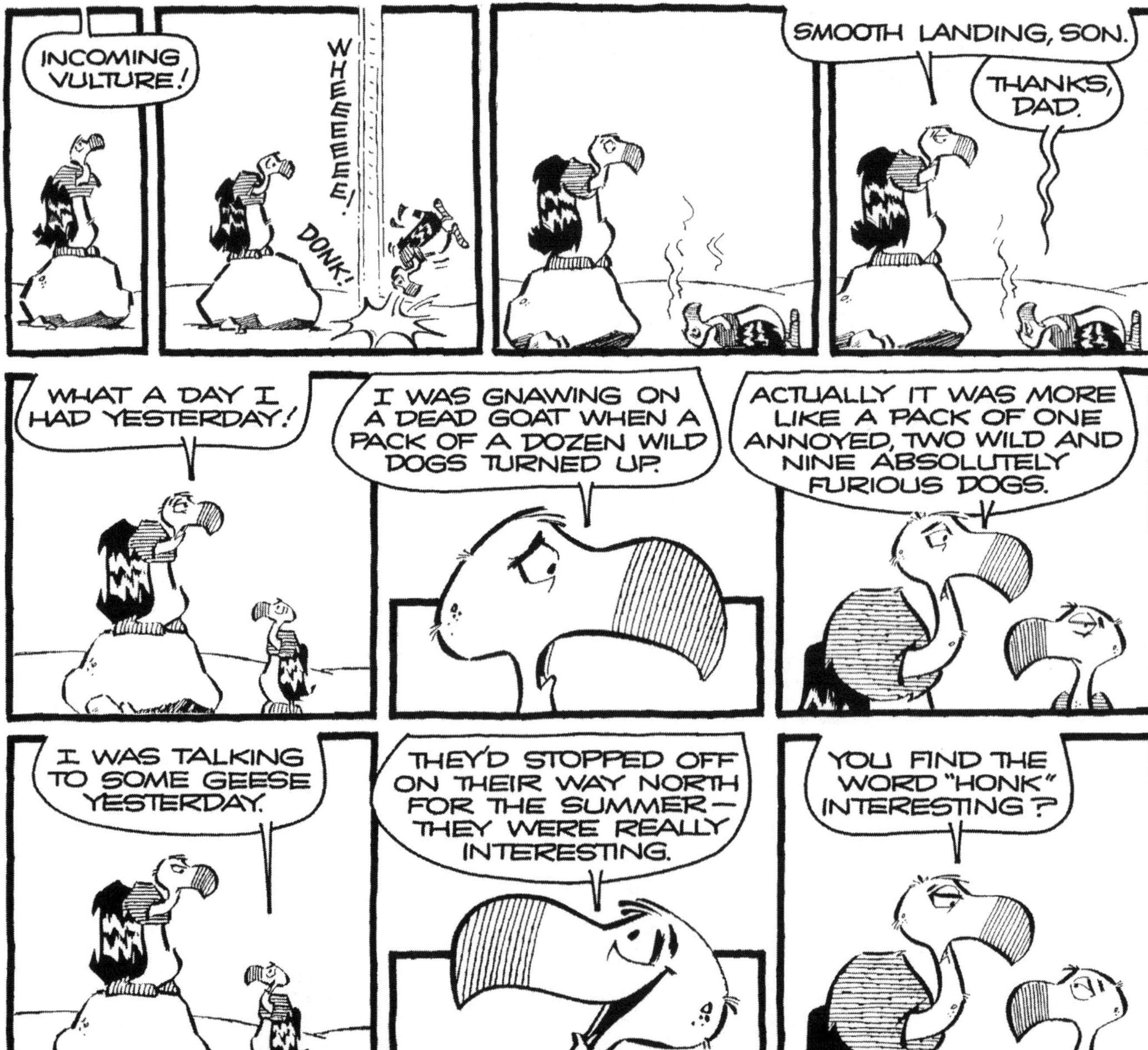
INCOMING VULTURE!
WHEEEEEEE!
DONK!
SMOOTH LANDING, SON.
THANKS, DAD.
WHAT A DAY I HAD YESTERDAY!
I WAS GNAWING ON A DEAD GOAT WHEN A PACK OF A DOZEN WILD DOGS TURNED UP.
ACTUALLY IT WAS MORE LIKE A PACK OF ONE ANNOYED, TWO WILD AND NINE ABSOLUTELY FURIOUS DOGS.
I WAS TALKING TO SOME GEESE YESTERDAY.
THEY'D STOPPED OFF ON THEIR WAY NORTH FOR THE SUMMER— THEY WERE REALLY INTERESTING.
YOU FIND THE WORD "HONK" INTERESTING?

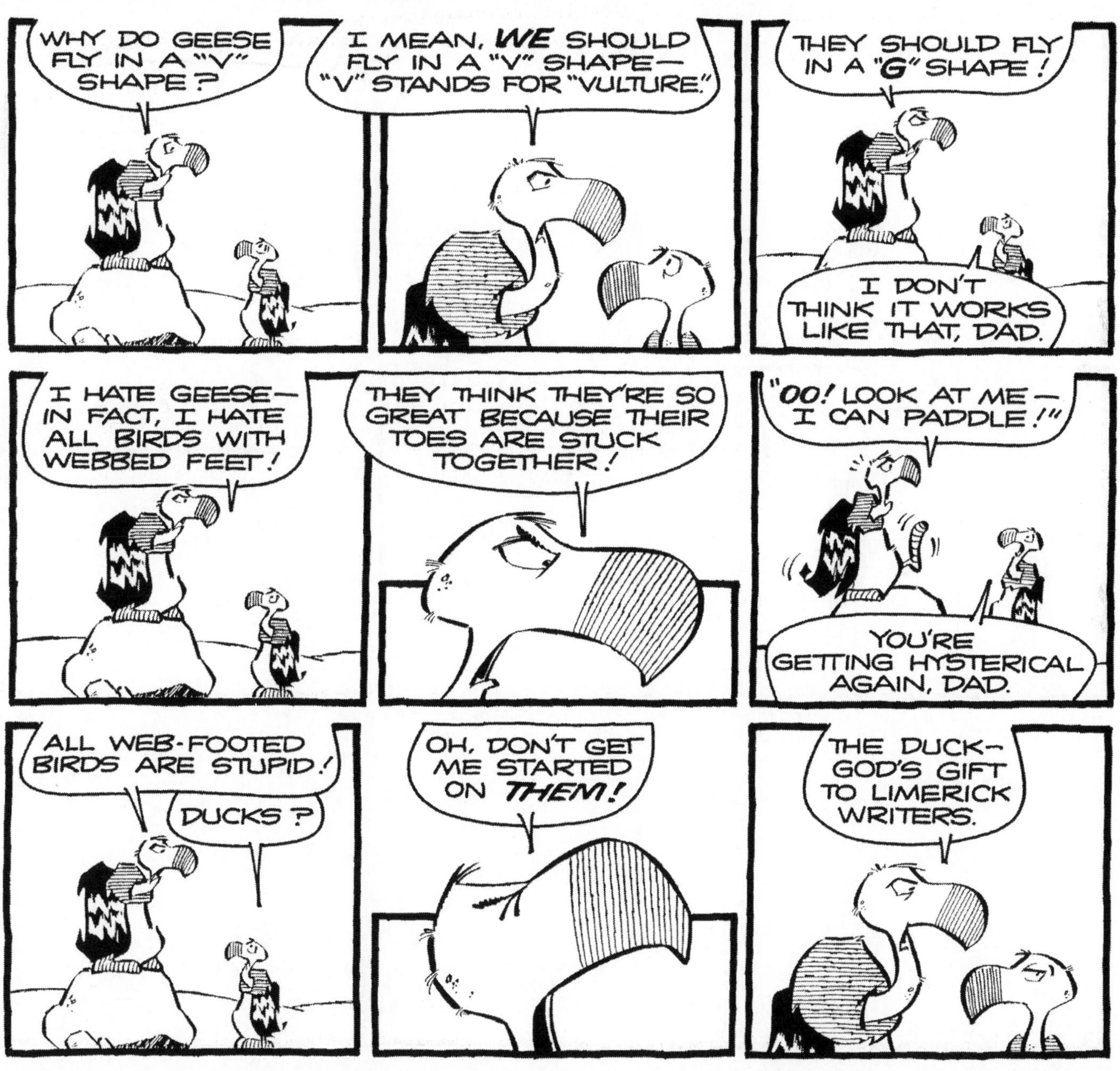
WHY DO GEESE FLY IN A "V" SHAPE?
I MEAN, WE SHOULD FLY IN A "V" SHAPE— "V" STANDS FOR "VULTURE."
THEY SHOULD FLY IN A "G" SHAPE!
I DON'T THINK IT WORKS LIKE THAT, DAD.
I HATE GEESE— IN FACT, I HATE ALL BIRDS WITH WEBBED FEET!
THEY THINK THEY'RE SO GREAT BECAUSE THEIR TOES ARE STUCK TOGETHER!
"OO! LOOK AT ME— I CAN PADDLE!"
YOU'RE GETTING HYSTERICAL AGAIN, DAD.
ALL WEB-FOOTED BIRDS ARE STUPID!
DUCKS?
OH, DON'T GET ME STARTED ON THEM!
THE DUCK— GOD'S GIFT TO LIMERICK WRITERS.

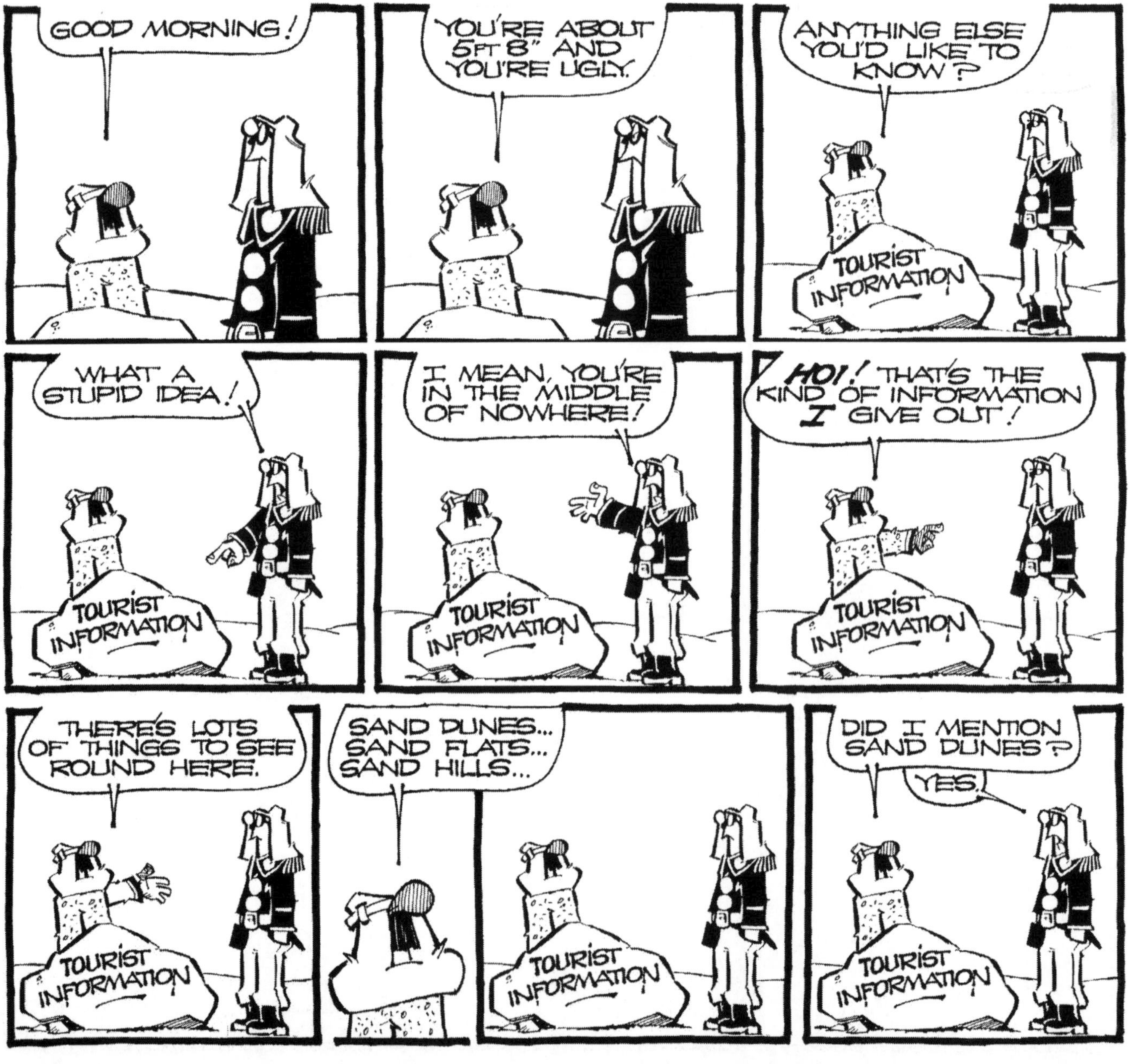
GOOD MORNING!
YOU'RE ABOUT 5FT 8" AND YOU'RE UGLY.
ANYTHING ELSE YOU'D LIKE TO KNOW?
TOURIST INFORMATION
WHAT A STUPID IDEA!
TOURIST INFORMATION
I MEAN, YOU'RE IN THE MIDDLE OF NOWHERE!
TOURIST INFORMATION
HO!! THAT'S THE KIND OF INFORMATION I GIVE OUT!
TOURIST INFORMATION
THERE'S LOTS OF THINGS TO SEE ROUND HERE.
TOURIST INFORMATION
SAND DUNES... SAND FLATS... SAND HILLS...
TOURIST INFORMATION
DID I MENTION SAND DUNES?
YES.
TOURIST INFORMATION

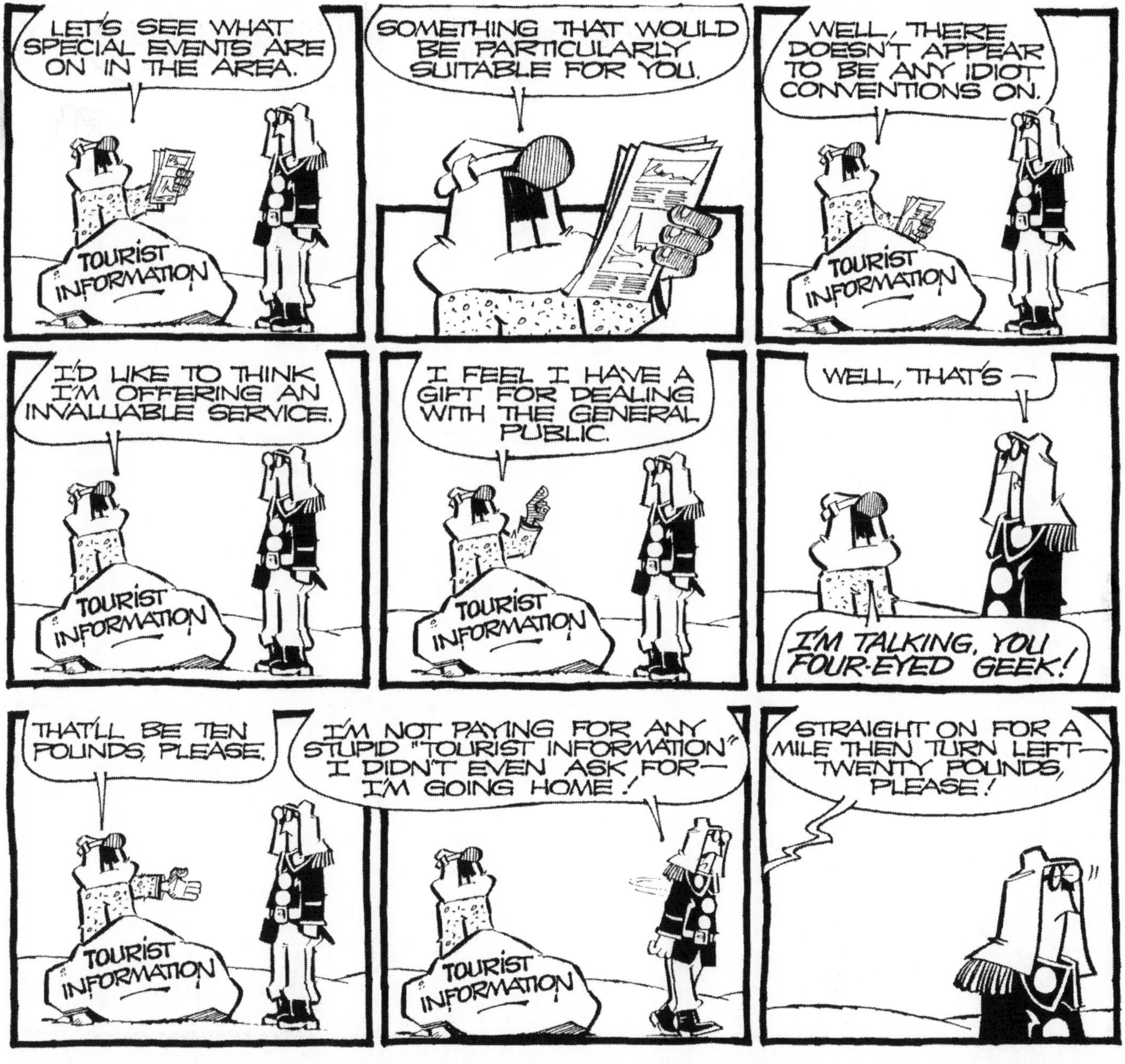
LET'S SEE WHAT SPECIAL EVENTS ARE ON IN THE AREA.
SOMETHING THAT WOULD BE PARTICULARLY SUITABLE FOR YOU.
WELL, THERE DOESN'T APPEAR TO BE ANY IDIOT CONVENTIONS ON.
TOURIST INFORMATION
I'D LIKE TO THINK I'M OFFERING AN INVALUABLE SERVICE.
I FEEL I HAVE A GIFT FOR DEALING WITH THE GENERAL PUBLIC.
WELL, THAT'S —
I'M TALKING, YOU FOUR-EYED GEEK!
THAT'LL BE TEN POUNDS, PLEASE.
I'M NOT PAYING FOR ANY STUPID "TOURIST INFORMATION" I DIDN'T EVEN ASK FOR— I'M GOING HOME!
STRAIGHT ON FOR A MILE THEN TURN LEFT— TWENTY POUNDS, PLEASE!

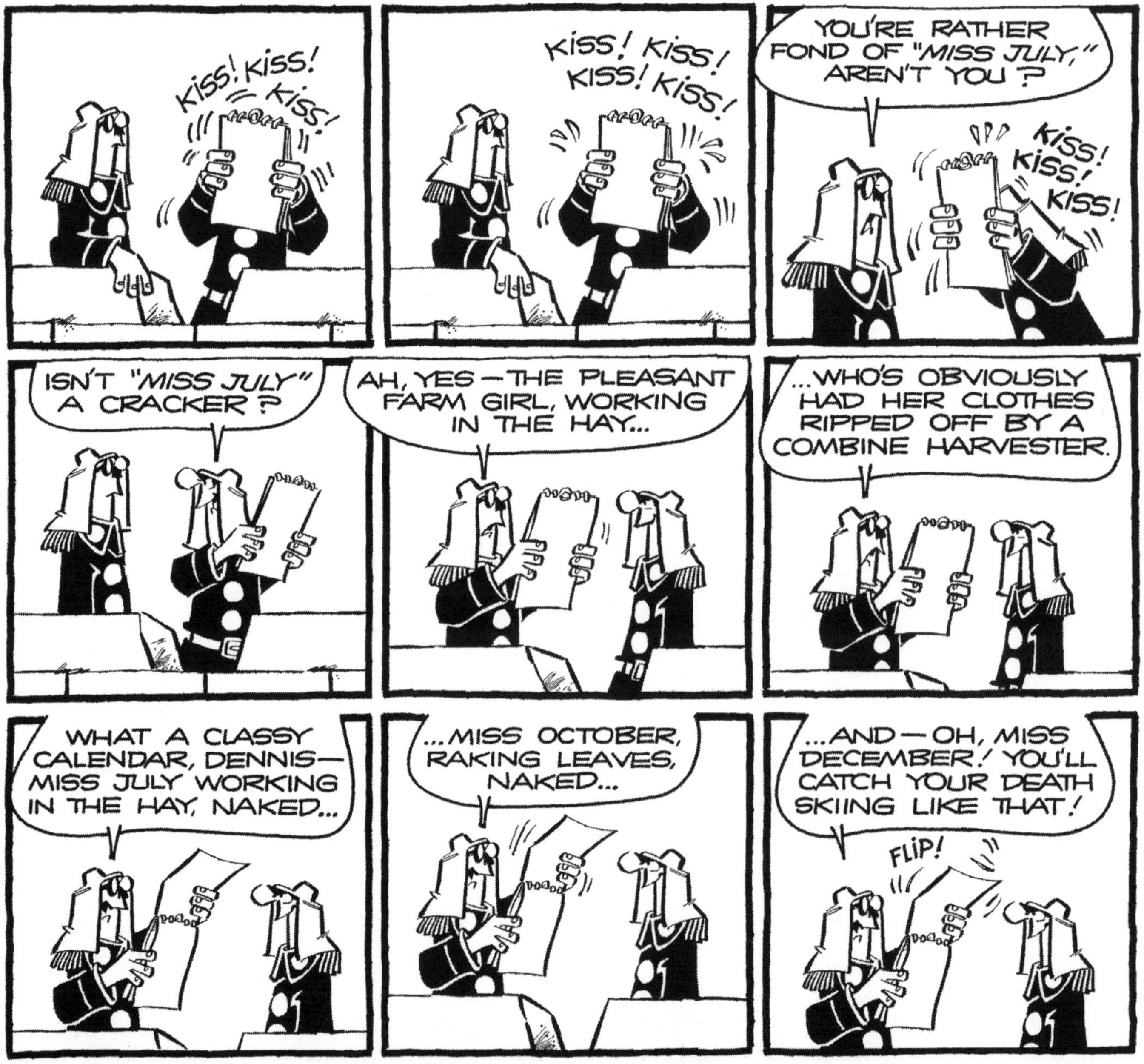
KISS! KISS! KISS! KISS!
KISS! KISS! KISS! KISS!
YOU'RE RATHER FOND OF "MISS JULY," AREN'T YOU?
KISS! KISS! KISS!
ISN'T "MISS JULY" A CRACKER?
AH, YES — THE PLEASANT FARM GIRL, WORKING IN THE HAY...
...WHO'S OBVIOUSLY HAD HER CLOTHES RIPPED OFF BY A COMBINE HARVESTER.
WHAT A CLASSY CALENDAR, DENNIS — MISS JULY WORKING IN THE HAY, NAKED...
...MISS OCTOBER, RAKING LEAVES, NAKED...
...AND — OH, MISS DECEMBER! YOU'LL CATCH YOUR DEATH SKIING LIKE THAT!
FLIP!

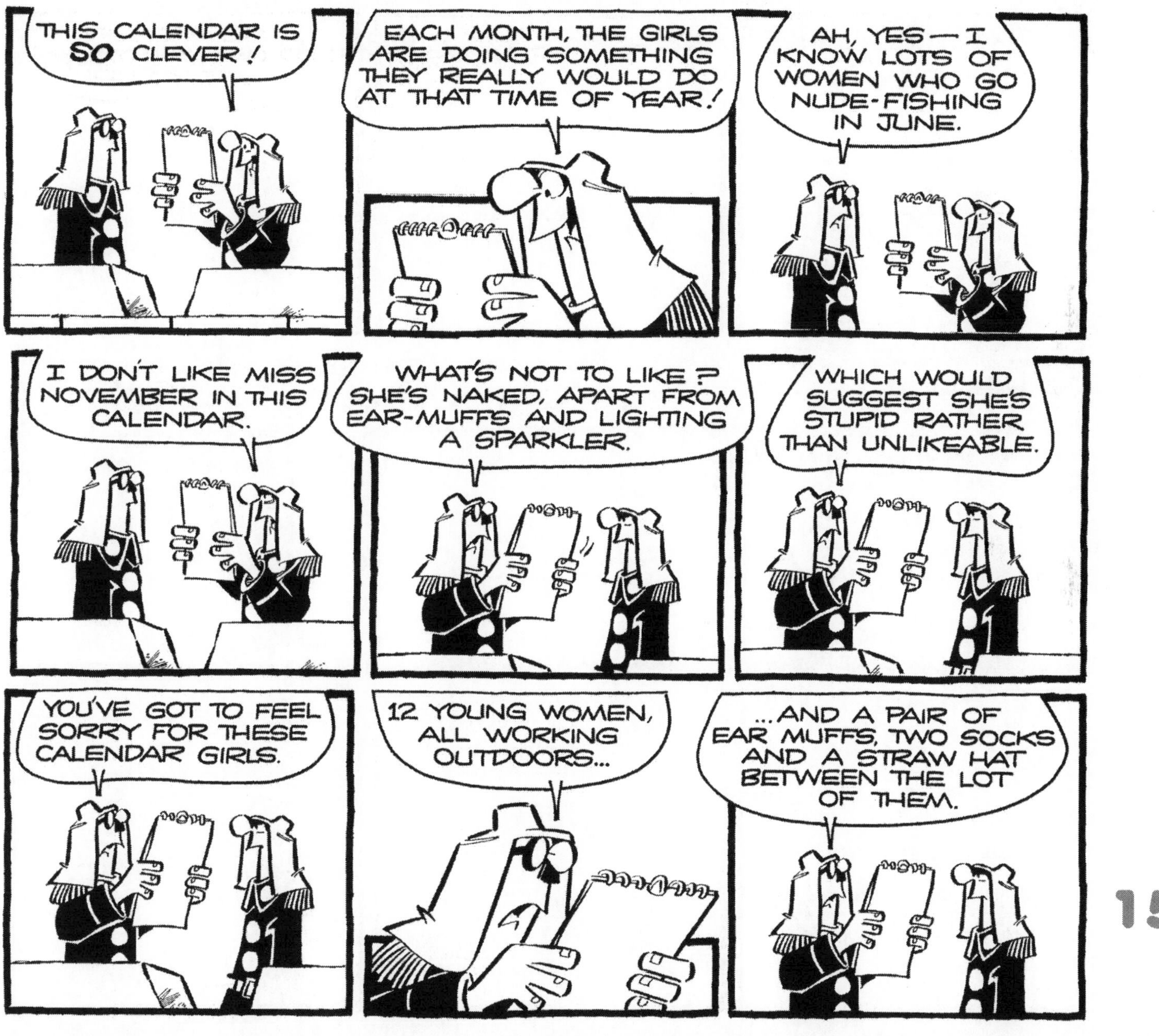
THIS CALENDAR IS SO CLEVER!
EACH MONTH, THE GIRLS ARE DOING SOMETHING THEY REALLY WOULD DO AT THAT TIME OF YEAR!
AH, YES — I KNOW LOTS OF WOMEN WHO GO NUDE-FISHING IN JUNE.
I DON'T LIKE MISS NOVEMBER IN THIS CALENDAR.
WHAT'S NOT TO LIKE? SHE'S NAKED, APART FROM EAR-MUFFS AND LIGHTING A SPARKLER.
WHICH WOULD SUGGEST SHE'S STUPID RATHER THAN UNLIKEABLE.
YOU'VE GOT TO FEEL SORRY FOR THESE CALENDAR GIRLS.
12 YOUNG WOMEN, ALL WORKING OUTDOORS...
...AND A PAIR OF EAR MUFFS, TWO SOCKS AND A STRAW HAT BETWEEN THE LOT OF THEM.

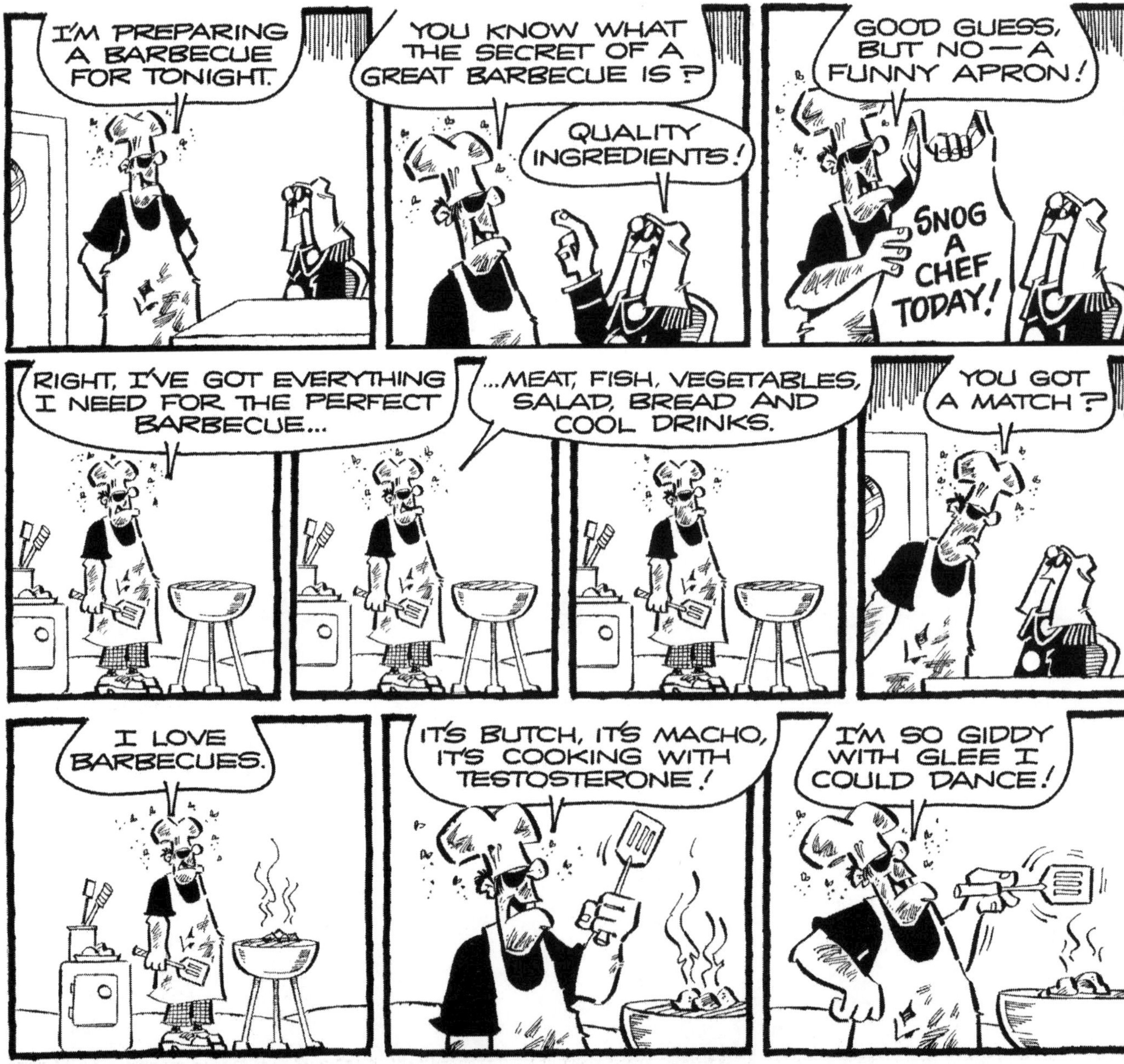
I'M PREPARING A BARBECUE FOR TONIGHT.
YOU KNOW WHAT THE SECRET OF A GREAT BARBECUE IS?
QUALITY INGREDIENTS!
GOOD GUESS, BUT NO — A FUNNY APRON!
SNOG A CHEF TODAY!
RIGHT, I'VE GOT EVERYTHING I NEED FOR THE PERFECT BARBECUE...
...MEAT, FISH, VEGETABLES, SALAD, BREAD AND COOL DRINKS.
YOU GOT A MATCH?
I LOVE BARBECUES.
IT'S BUTCH, IT'S MACHO, IT'S COOKING WITH TESTOSTERONE!
I'M SO GIDDY WITH GLEE I COULD DANCE!

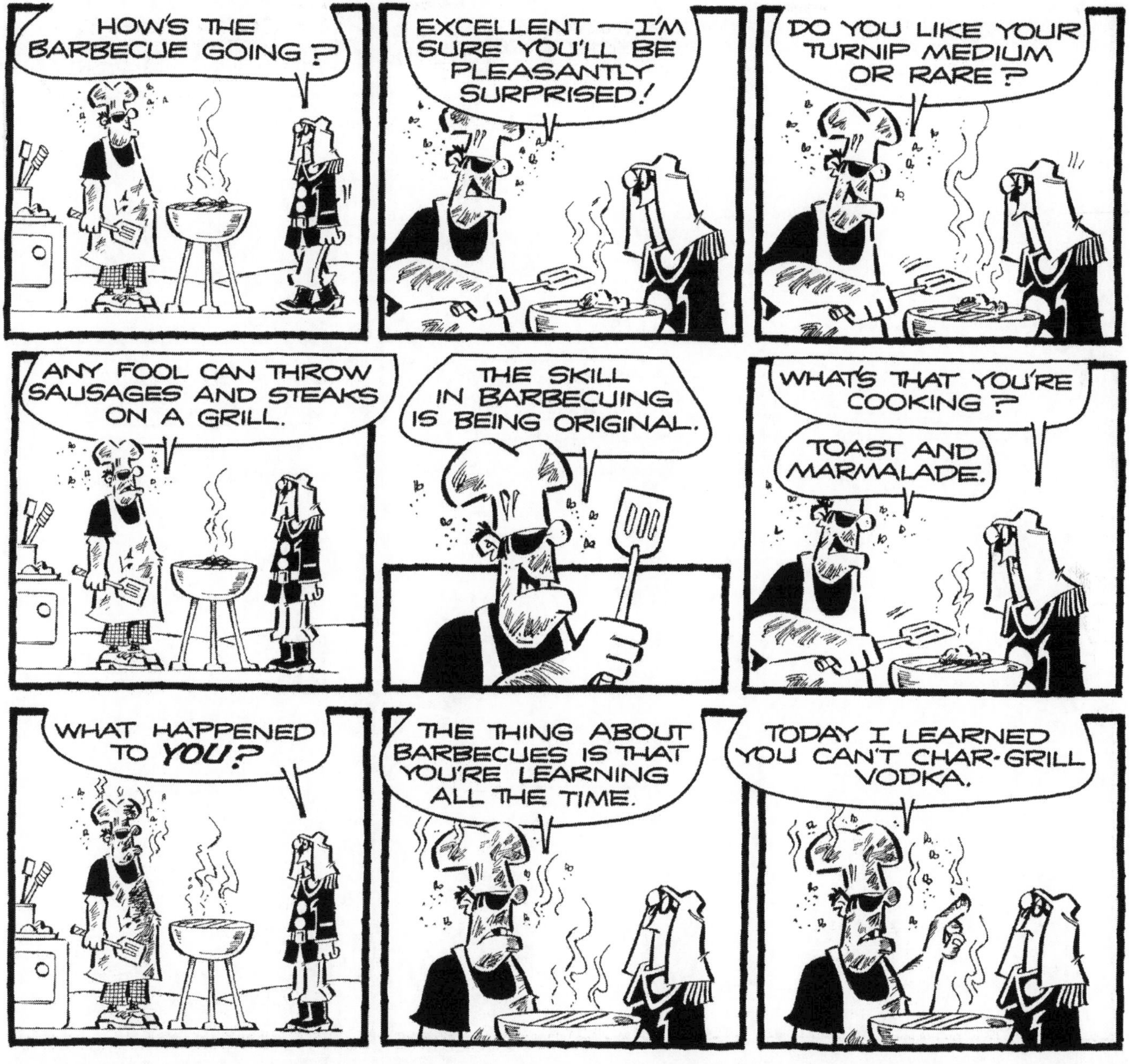
HOW'S THE BARBECUE GOING?
EXCELLENT — I'M SURE YOU'LL BE PLEASANTLY SURPRISED!
DO YOU LIKE YOUR TURNIP MEDIUM OR RARE?
ANY FOOL CAN THROW SAUSAGES AND STEAKS ON A GRILL.
THE SKILL IN BARBECUING IS BEING ORIGINAL.
WHAT'S THAT YOU'RE COOKING?
TOAST AND MARMALADE.
WHAT HAPPENED TO *YOU*?
THE THING ABOUT BARBECUES IS THAT YOU'RE LEARNING ALL THE TIME.
TODAY I LEARNED YOU CAN'T CHAR-GRILL VODKA.

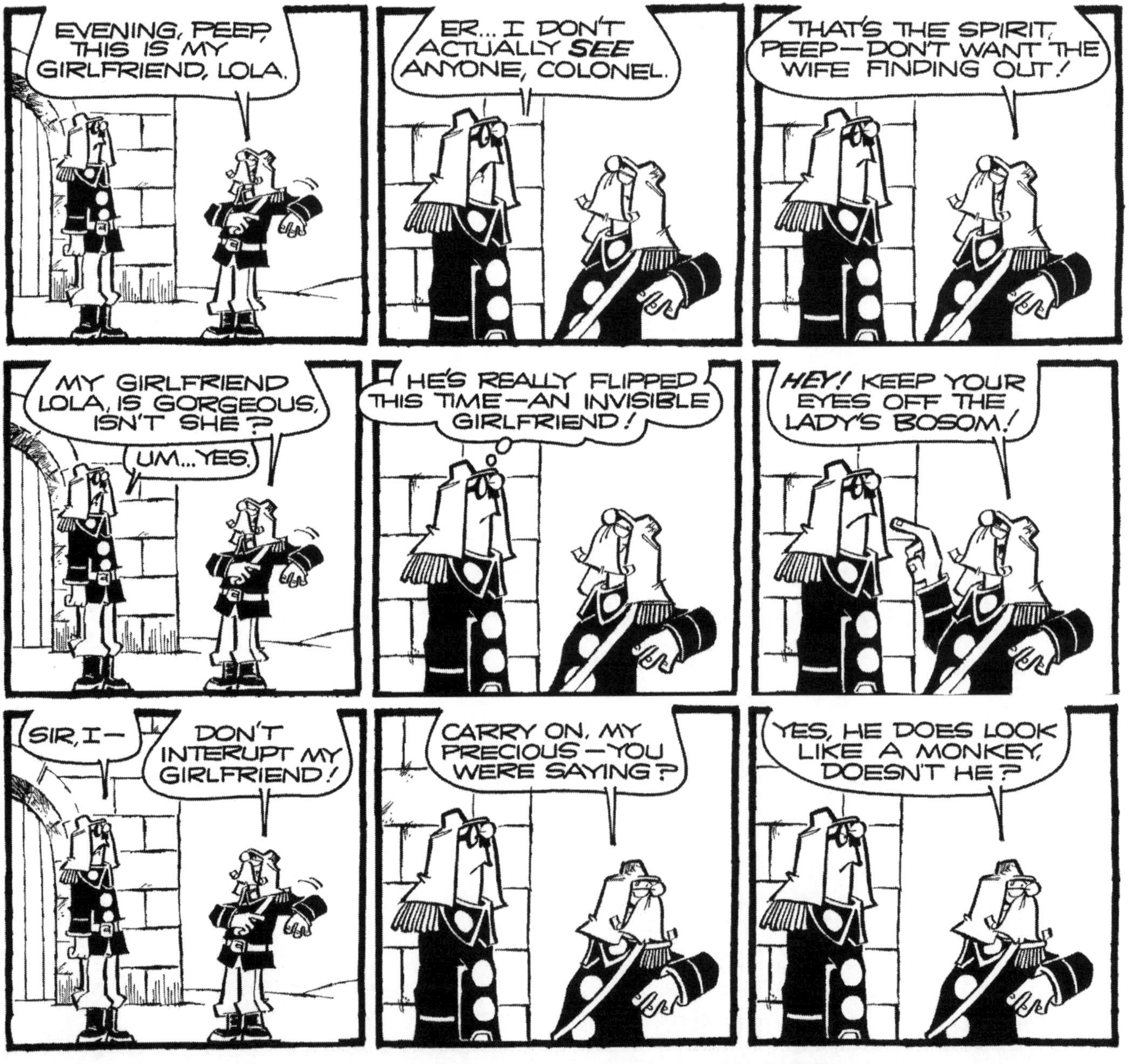
EVENING, PEEP, THIS IS MY GIRLFRIEND, LOLA.
ER... I DON'T ACTUALLY SEE ANYONE, COLONEL.
THAT'S THE SPIRIT, PEEP—DON'T WANT THE WIFE FINDING OUT!
MY GIRLFRIEND LOLA, IS GORGEOUS, ISN'T SHE?
UM... YES.
HE'S REALLY FLIPPED THIS TIME—AN INVISIBLE GIRLFRIEND!
HEY! KEEP YOUR EYES OFF THE LADY'S BOSOM!
SIR, I—
DON'T INTERUPT MY GIRLFRIEND!
CARRY ON, MY PRECIOUS—YOU WERE SAYING?
YES, HE DOES LOOK LIKE A MONKEY, DOESN'T HE?

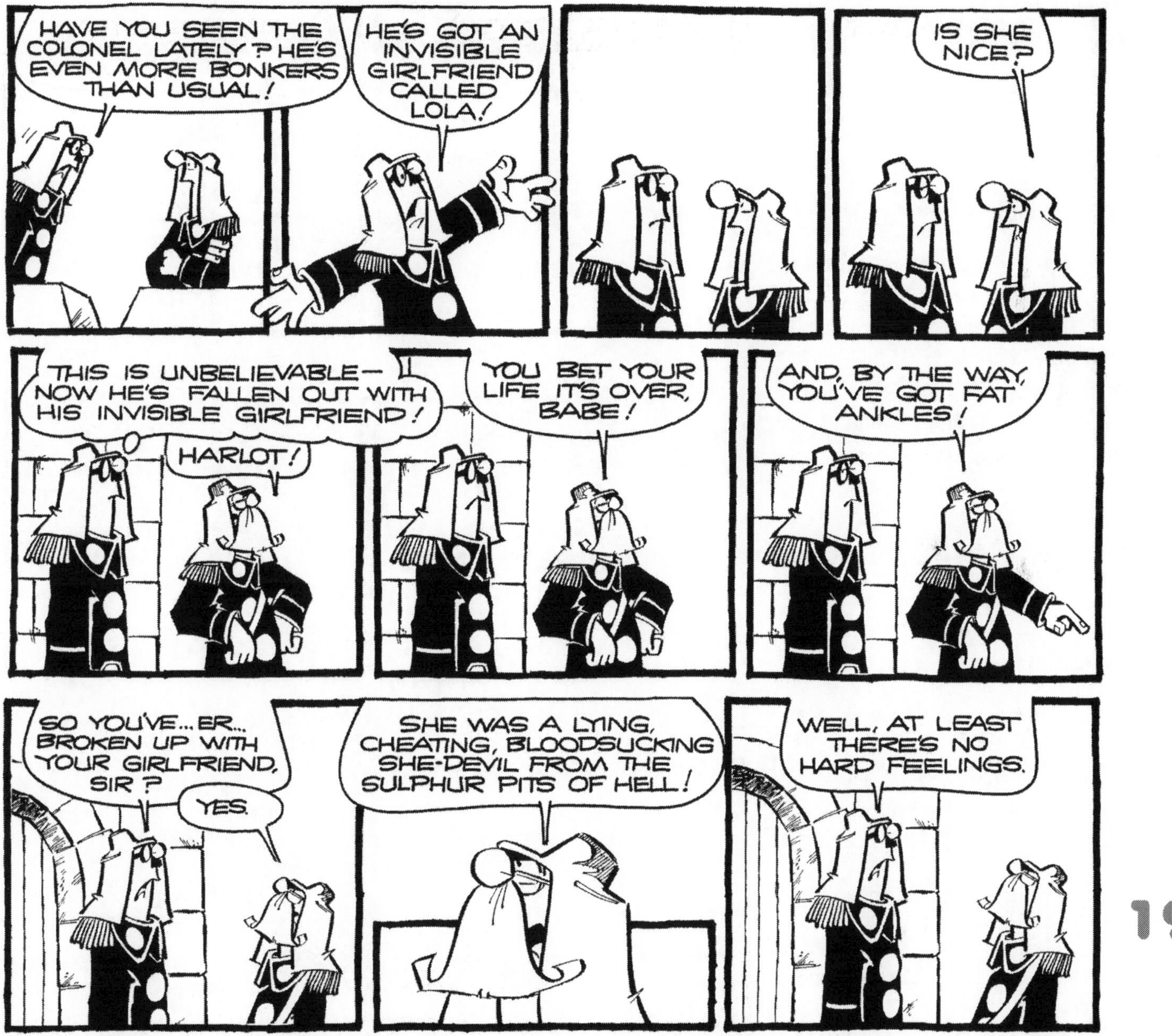
HAVE YOU SEEN THE COLONEL LATELY? HE'S EVEN MORE BONKERS THAN USUAL!
HE'S GOT AN INVISIBLE GIRLFRIEND CALLED LOLA!
IS SHE NICE?
THIS IS UNBELIEVABLE— NOW HE'S FALLEN OUT WITH HIS INVISIBLE GIRLFRIEND!
HARLOT!
YOU BET YOUR LIFE IT'S OVER, BABE!
AND, BY THE WAY, YOU'VE GOT FAT ANKLES!
SO YOU'VE... ER... BROKEN UP WITH YOUR GIRLFRIEND, SIR?
YES.
SHE WAS A LYING, CHEATING, BLOODSUCKING SHE-DEVIL FROM THE SULPHUR PITS OF HELL!
WELL, AT LEAST THERE'S NO HARD FEELINGS.

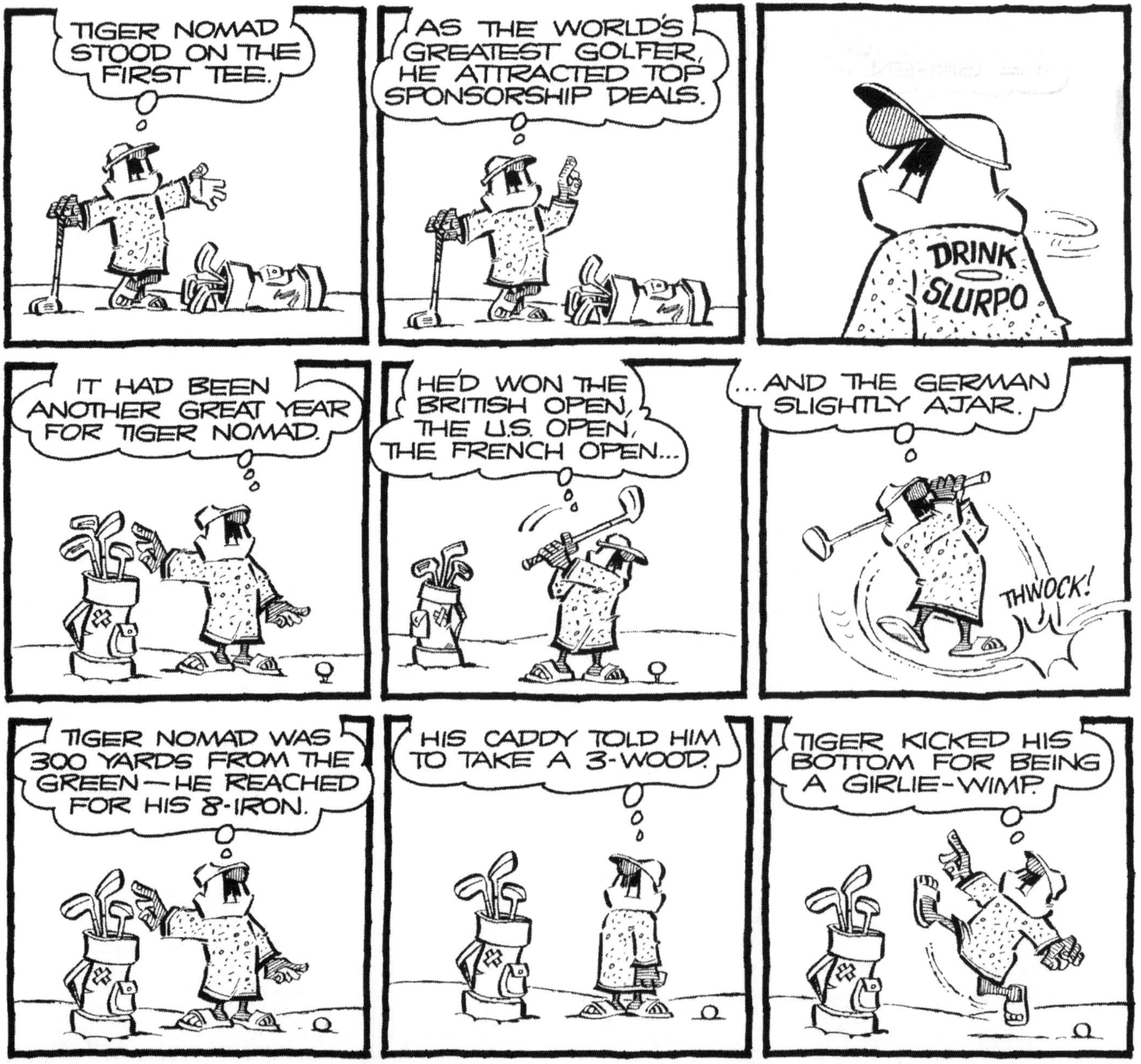
TIGER NOMAD STOOD ON THE FIRST TEE.
AS THE WORLD'S GREATEST GOLFER, HE ATTRACTED TOP SPONSORSHIP DEALS.
DRINK SLURPO
IT HAD BEEN ANOTHER GREAT YEAR FOR TIGER NOMAD.
HE'D WON THE BRITISH OPEN, THE U.S. OPEN, THE FRENCH OPEN...
...AND THE GERMAN SLIGHTLY AJAR.
THWOCK!
TIGER NOMAD WAS 300 YARDS FROM THE GREEN—HE REACHED FOR HIS 8-IRON.
HIS CADDY TOLD HIM TO TAKE A 3-WOOD.
TIGER KICKED HIS BOTTOM FOR BEING A GIRLIE-WIMP.

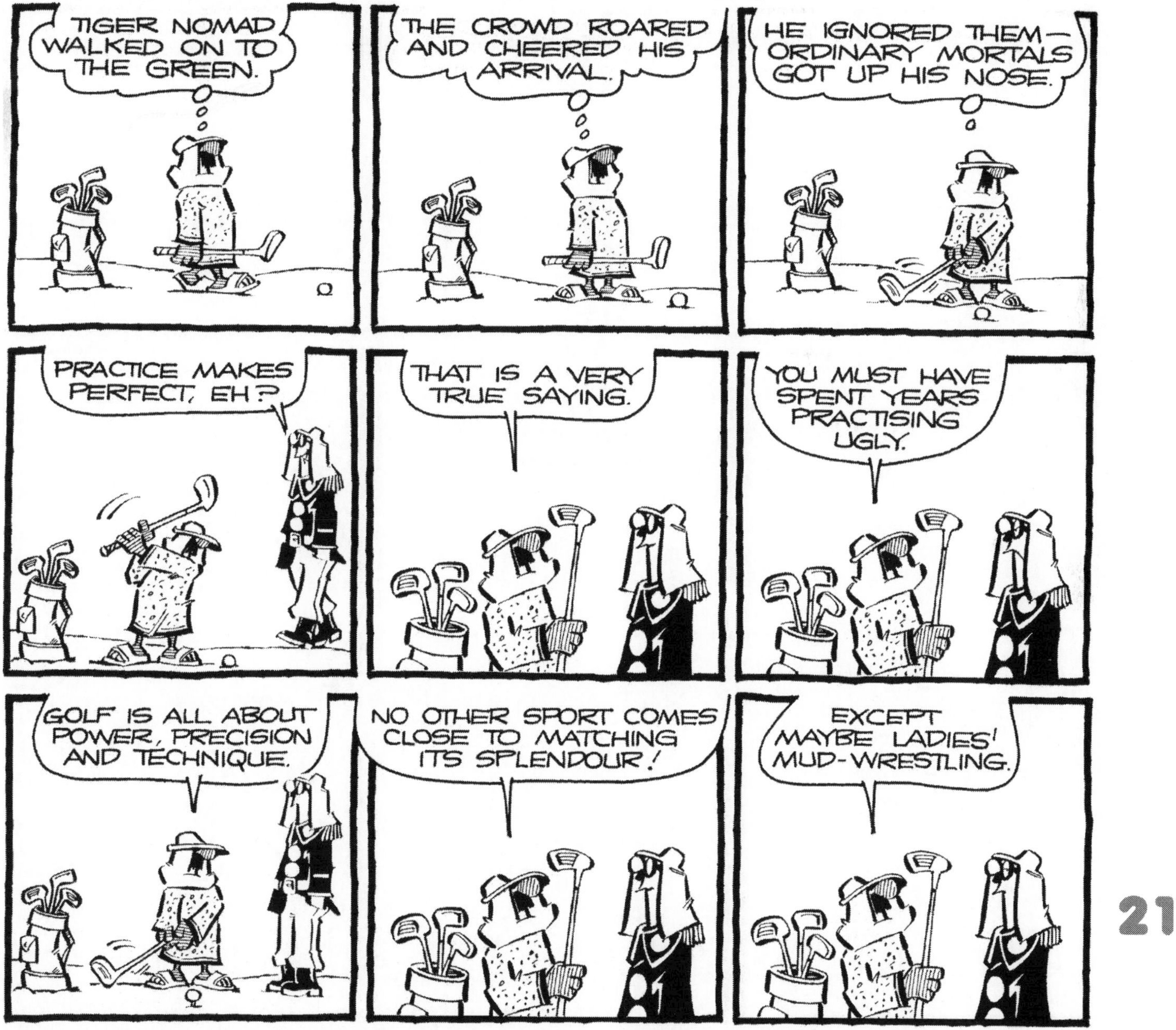
TIGER NOMAD WALKED ON TO THE GREEN.
THE CROWD ROARED AND CHEERED HIS ARRIVAL.
HE IGNORED THEM— ORDINARY MORTALS GOT UP HIS NOSE.
PRACTICE MAKES PERFECT, EH?
THAT IS A VERY TRUE SAYING.
YOU MUST HAVE SPENT YEARS PRACTISING UGLY.
GOLF IS ALL ABOUT POWER, PRECISION AND TECHNIQUE.
NO OTHER SPORT COMES CLOSE TO MATCHING ITS SPLENDOUR!
EXCEPT MAYBE LADIES' MUD-WRESTLING.

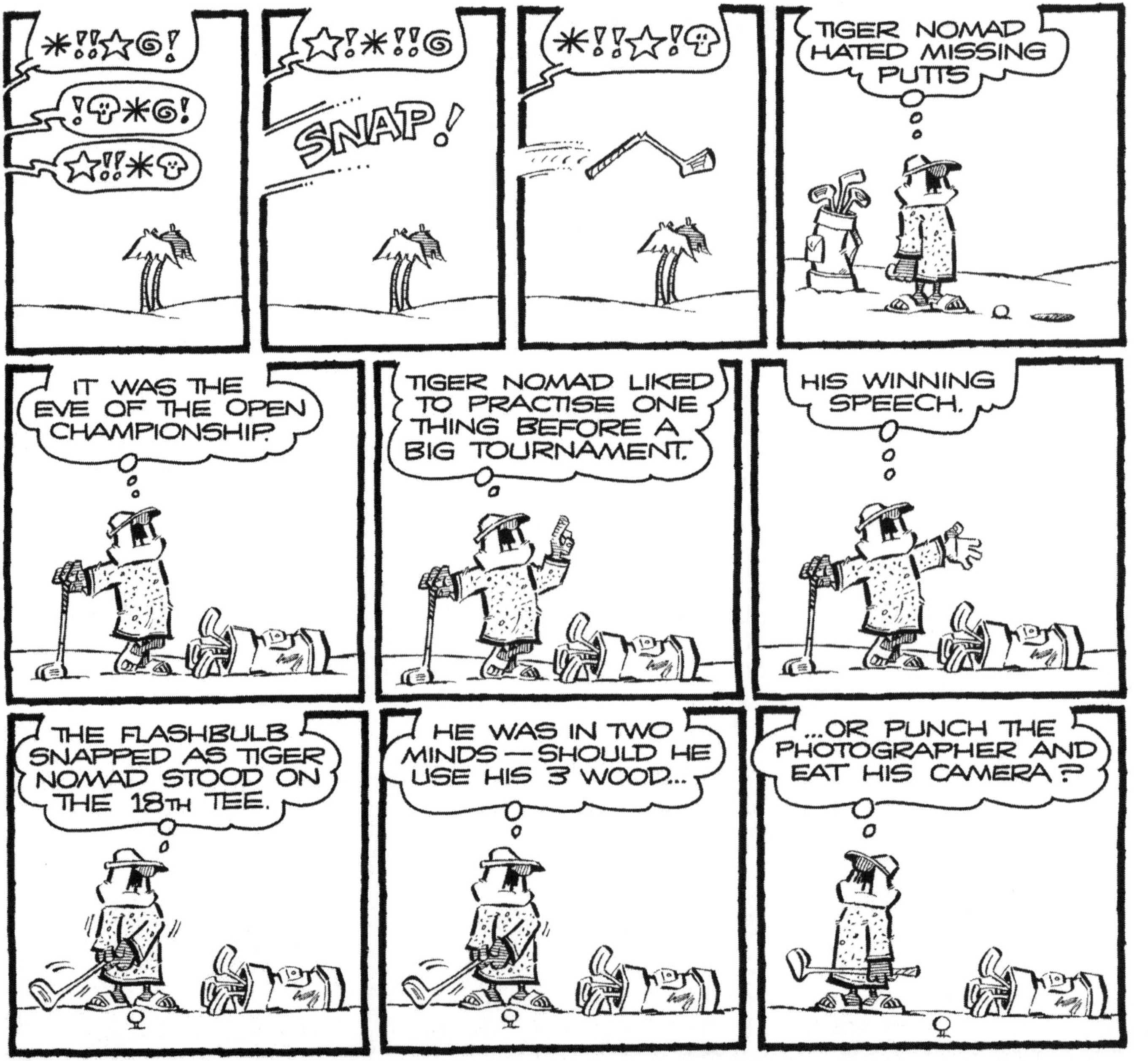
SNAP!
TIGER NOMAD HATED MISSING PUTTS
IT WAS THE EVE OF THE OPEN CHAMPIONSHIP.
TIGER NOMAD LIKED TO PRACTISE ONE THING BEFORE A BIG TOURNAMENT.
HIS WINNING SPEECH.
THE FLASHBULB SNAPPED AS TIGER NOMAD STOOD ON THE 18TH TEE.
HE WAS IN TWO MINDS — SHOULD HE USE HIS 3 WOOD...
...OR PUNCH THE PHOTOGRAPHER AND EAT HIS CAMERA?

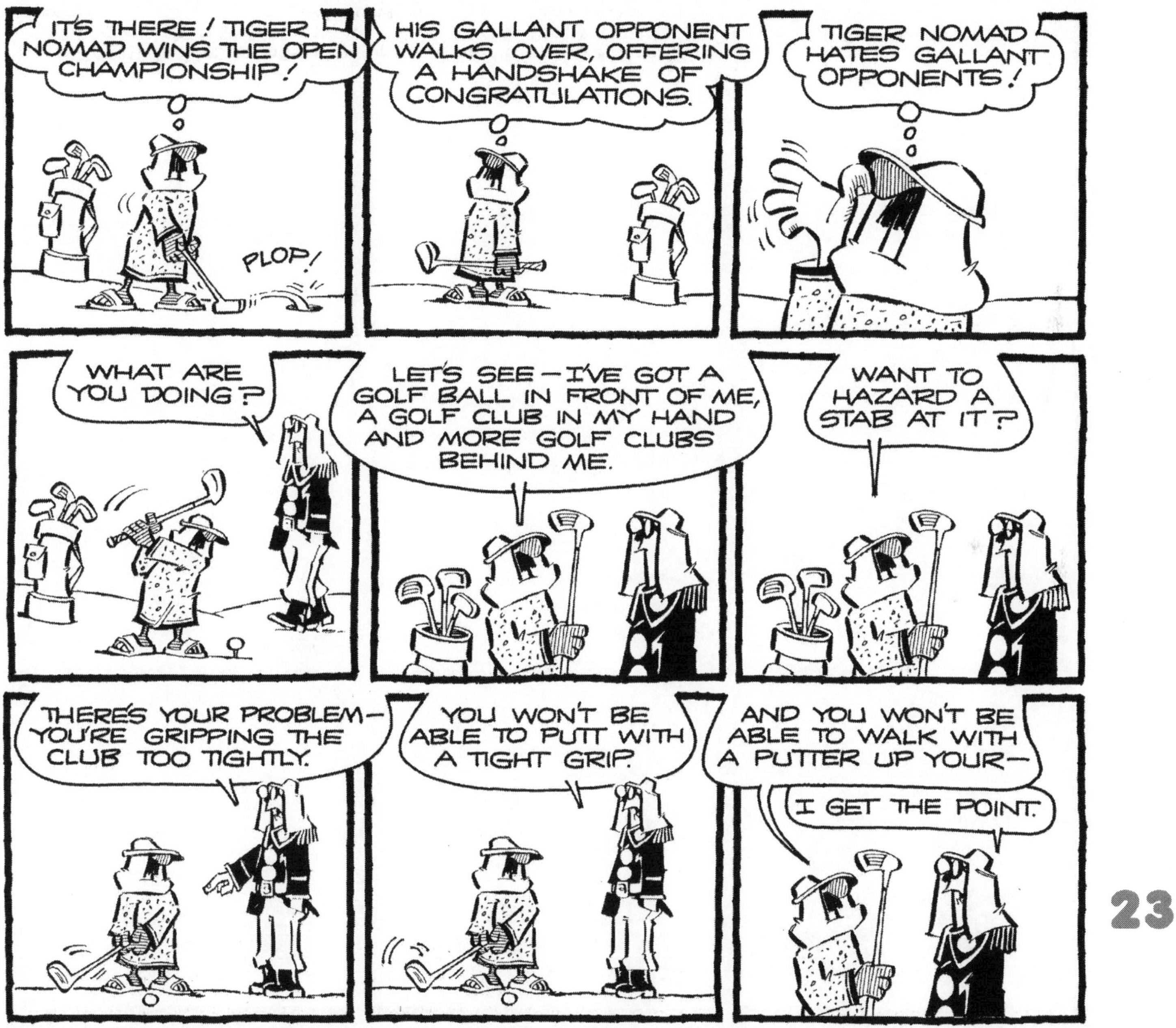
IT'S THERE! TIGER NOMAD WINS THE OPEN CHAMPIONSHIP!
PLOP!
HIS GALLANT OPPONENT WALKS OVER, OFFERING A HANDSHAKE OF CONGRATULATIONS.
TIGER NOMAD HATES GALLANT OPPONENTS!
WHAT ARE YOU DOING?
LET'S SEE—I'VE GOT A GOLF BALL IN FRONT OF ME, A GOLF CLUB IN MY HAND AND MORE GOLF CLUBS BEHIND ME.
WANT TO HAZARD A STAB AT IT?
THERE'S YOUR PROBLEM—YOU'RE GRIPPING THE CLUB TOO TIGHTLY.
YOU WON'T BE ABLE TO PUTT WITH A TIGHT GRIP.
AND YOU WON'T BE ABLE TO WALK WITH A PUTTER UP YOUR—
I GET THE POINT.

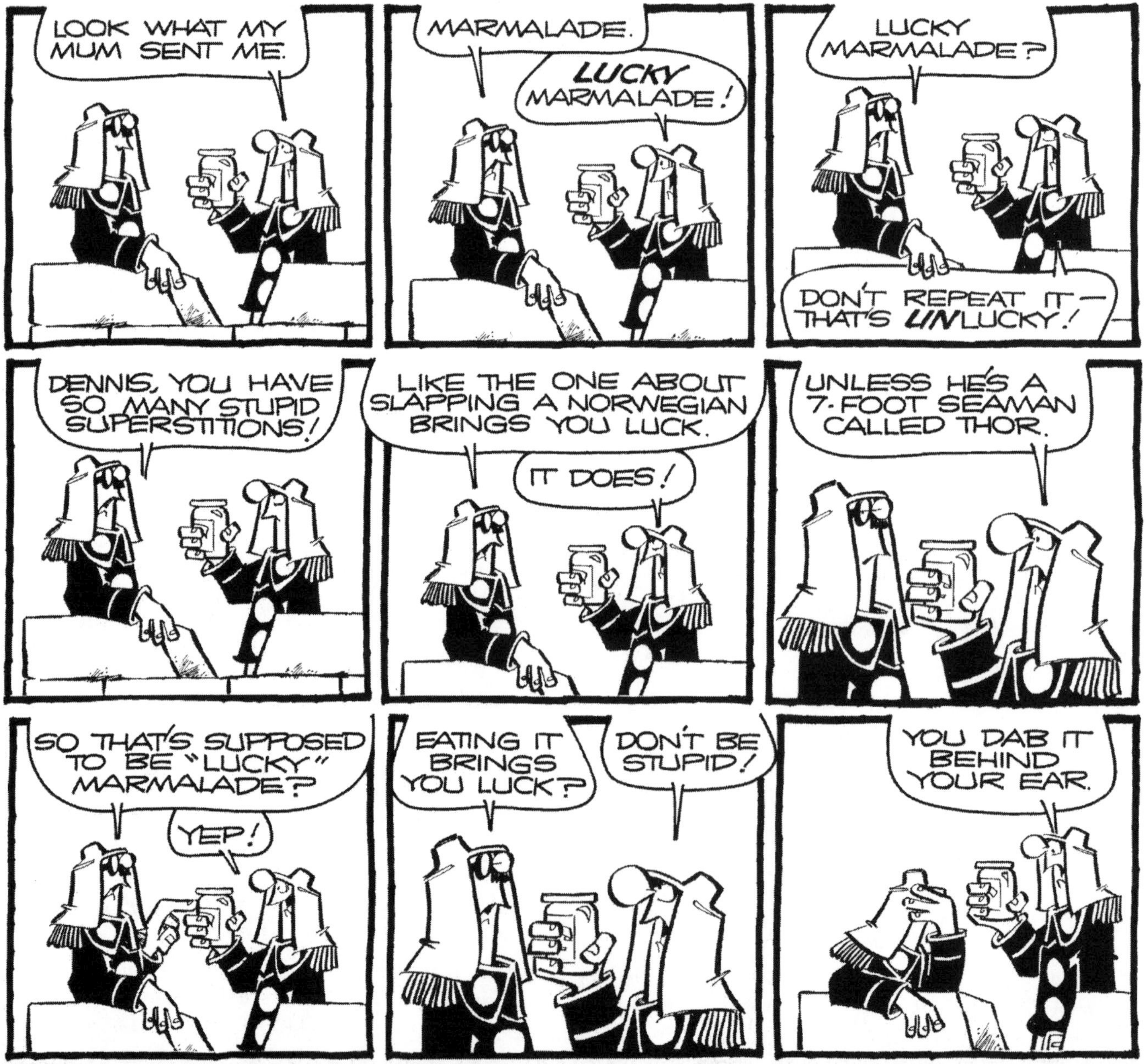
LOOK WHAT MY MUM SENT ME.
MARMALADE.
LUCKY MARMALADE!
LUCKY MARMALADE?
DON'T REPEAT IT — THAT'S *UN*LUCKY!
DENNIS, YOU HAVE SO MANY STUPID SUPERSTITIONS!
LIKE THE ONE ABOUT SLAPPING A NORWEGIAN BRINGS YOU LUCK.
IT DOES!
UNLESS HE'S A 7-FOOT SEAMAN CALLED THOR.
SO THAT'S SUPPOSED TO BE "LUCKY" MARMALADE?
YEP!
EATING IT BRINGS YOU LUCK?
DON'T BE STUPID!
YOU DAB IT BEHIND YOUR EAR.

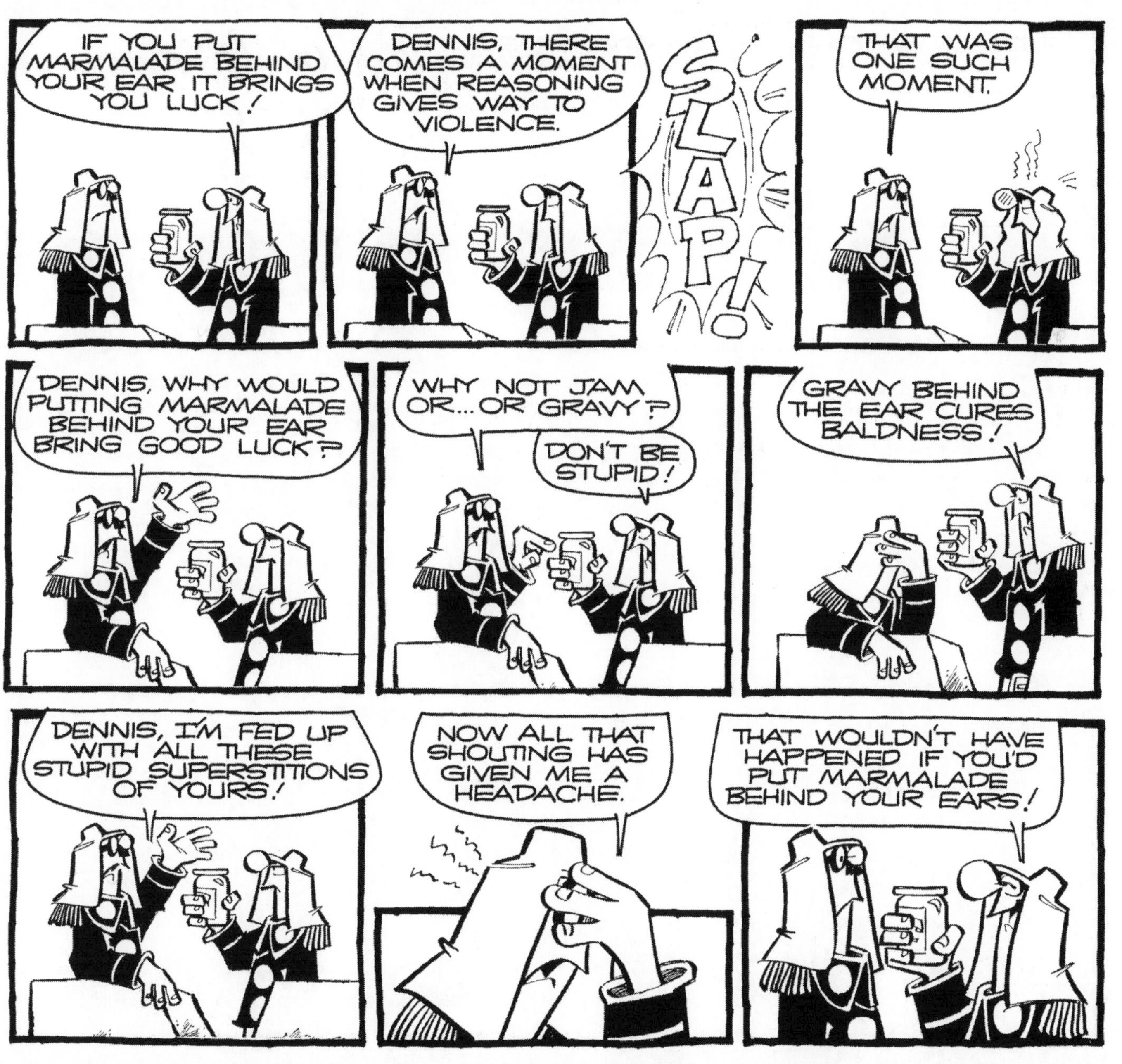
IF YOU PUT MARMALADE BEHIND YOUR EAR IT BRINGS YOU LUCK!
DENNIS, THERE COMES A MOMENT WHEN REASONING GIVES WAY TO VIOLENCE.
SLAP!
THAT WAS ONE SUCH MOMENT.
DENNIS, WHY WOULD PUTTING MARMALADE BEHIND YOUR EAR BRING GOOD LUCK?
WHY NOT JAM OR... OR GRAVY?
DON'T BE STUPID!
GRAVY BEHIND THE EAR CURES BALDNESS!
DENNIS, I'M FED UP WITH ALL THESE STUPID SUPERSTITIONS OF YOURS!
NOW ALL THAT SHOUTING HAS GIVEN ME A HEADACHE.
THAT WOULDN'T HAVE HAPPENED IF YOU'D PUT MARMALADE BEHIND YOUR EARS!

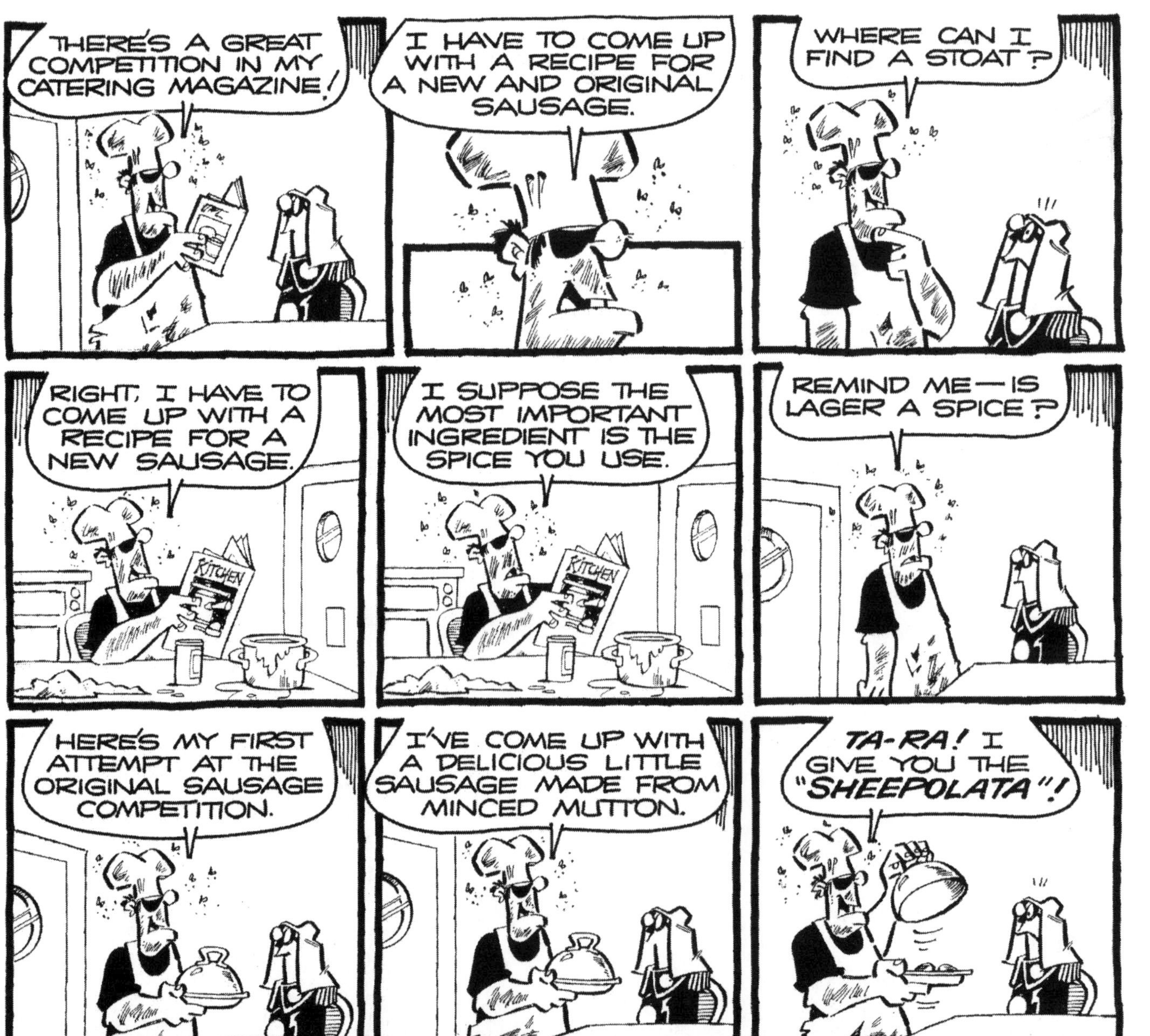
THERE'S A GREAT COMPETITION IN MY CATERING MAGAZINE!
I HAVE TO COME UP WITH A RECIPE FOR A NEW AND ORIGINAL SAUSAGE.
WHERE CAN I FIND A STOAT?
RIGHT; I HAVE TO COME UP WITH A RECIPE FOR A NEW SAUSAGE.
KITCHEN
I SUPPOSE THE MOST IMPORTANT INGREDIENT IS THE SPICE YOU USE.
KITCHEN
REMIND ME—IS LAGER A SPICE?
HERE'S MY FIRST ATTEMPT AT THE ORIGINAL SAUSAGE COMPETITION.
I'VE COME UP WITH A DELICIOUS LITTLE SAUSAGE MADE FROM MINCED MUTTON.
TA-RA! I GIVE YOU THE "*SHEEPOLATA*"!

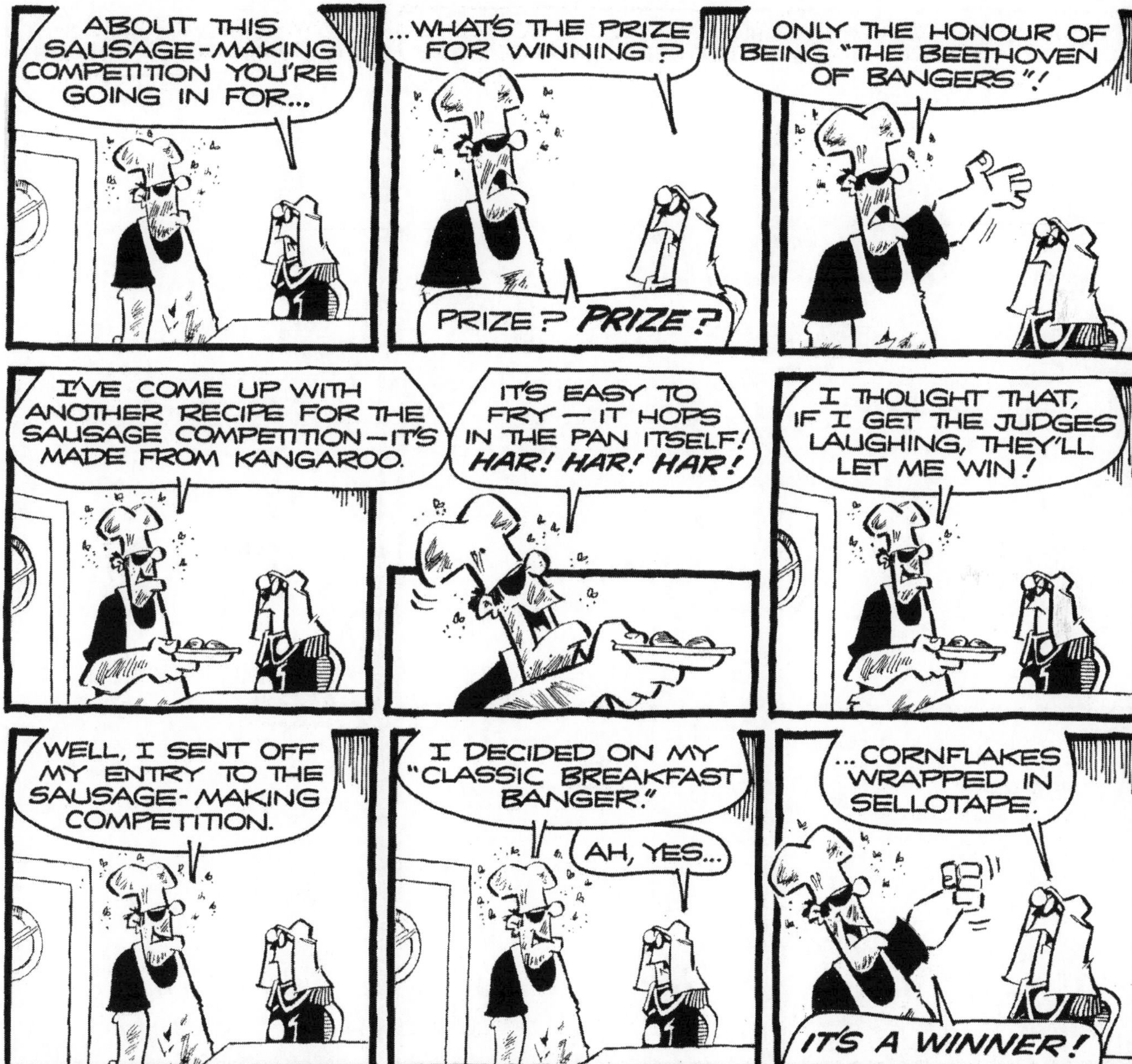
ABOUT THIS SAUSAGE-MAKING COMPETITION YOU'RE GOING IN FOR...
...WHAT'S THE PRIZE FOR WINNING?
PRIZE? PRIZE?
ONLY THE HONOUR OF BEING "THE BEETHOVEN OF BANGERS"!
I'VE COME UP WITH ANOTHER RECIPE FOR THE SAUSAGE COMPETITION—IT'S MADE FROM KANGAROO.
IT'S EASY TO FRY — IT HOPS IN THE PAN ITSELF! HAR! HAR! HAR!
I THOUGHT THAT, IF I GET THE JUDGES LAUGHING, THEY'LL LET ME WIN!
WELL, I SENT OFF MY ENTRY TO THE SAUSAGE-MAKING COMPETITION.
I DECIDED ON MY "CLASSIC BREAKFAST BANGER."
AH, YES...
...CORNFLAKES WRAPPED IN SELLOTAPE.
IT'S A WINNER!

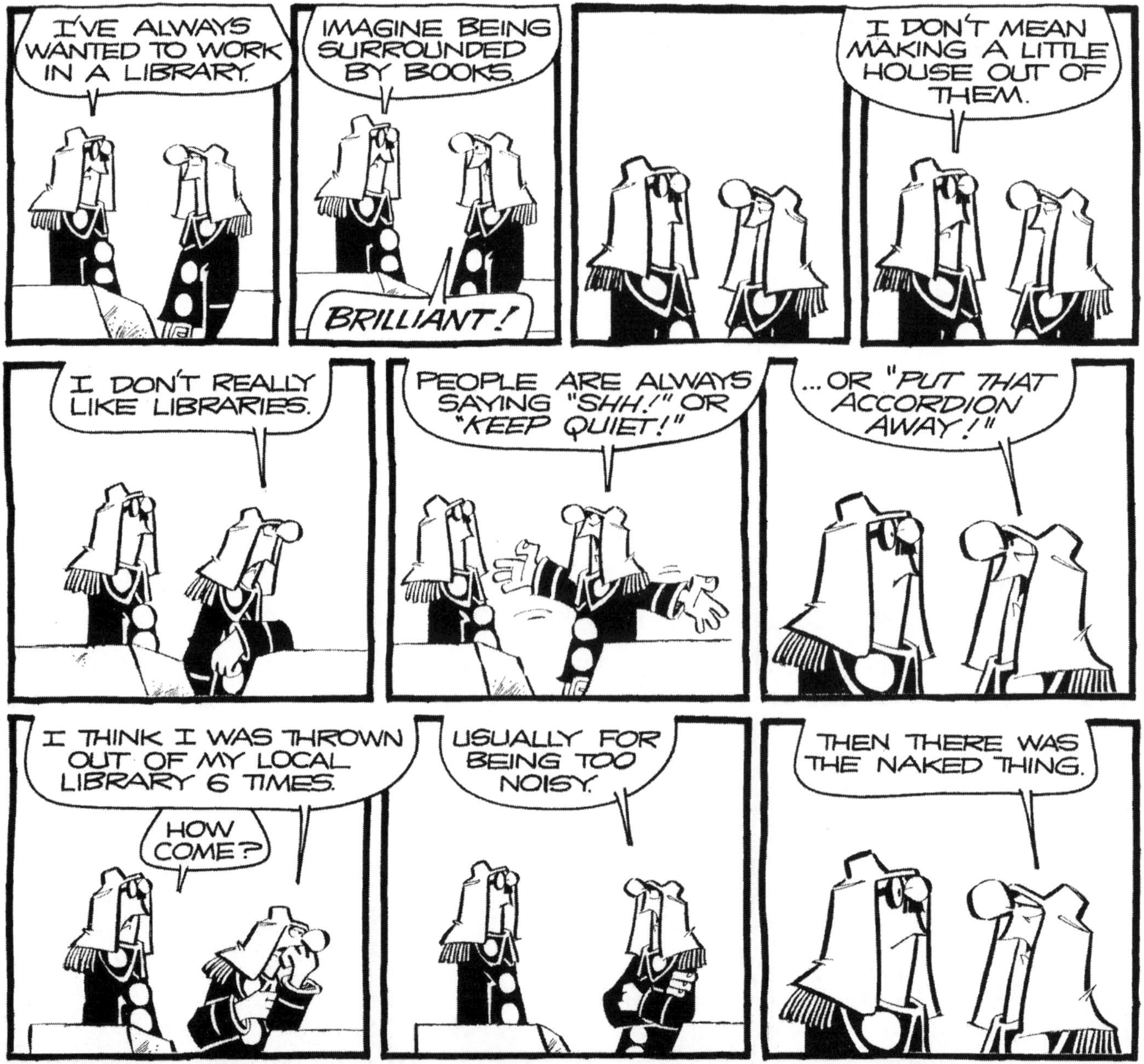
I'VE ALWAYS WANTED TO WORK IN A LIBRARY.
IMAGINE BEING SURROUNDED BY BOOKS.
BRILLIANT!
I DON'T MEAN MAKING A LITTLE HOUSE OUT OF THEM.
I DON'T REALLY LIKE LIBRARIES.
PEOPLE ARE ALWAYS SAYING "SHH!" OR "KEEP QUIET!"
...OR "PUT THAT ACCORDION AWAY!"
I THINK I WAS THROWN OUT OF MY LOCAL LIBRARY 6 TIMES.
HOW COME?
USUALLY FOR BEING TOO NOISY.
THEN THERE WAS THE NAKED THING.

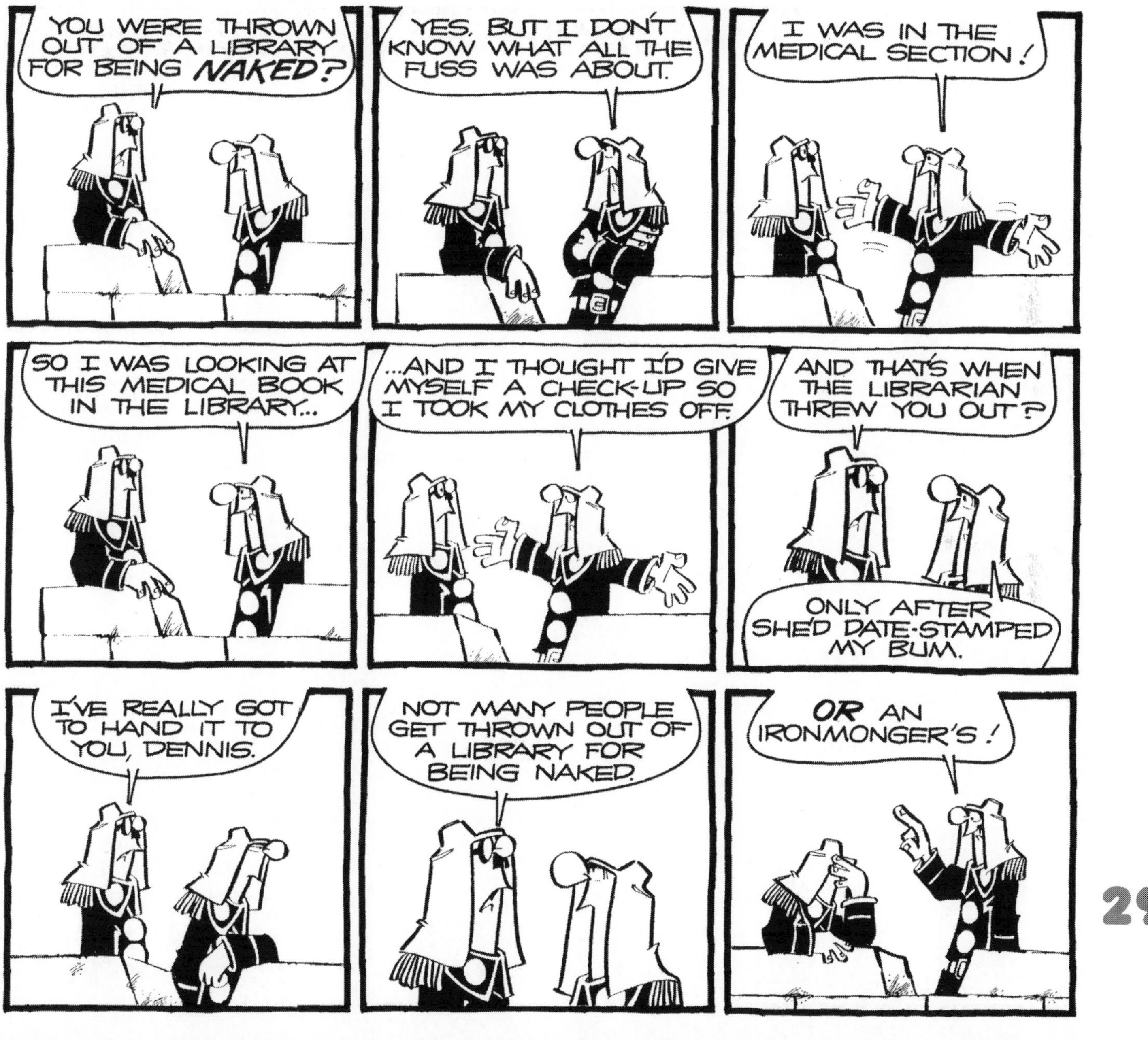
YOU WERE THROWN OUT OF A LIBRARY FOR BEING NAKED?
YES, BUT I DON'T KNOW WHAT ALL THE FUSS WAS ABOUT.
I WAS IN THE MEDICAL SECTION!
SO I WAS LOOKING AT THIS MEDICAL BOOK IN THE LIBRARY...
...AND I THOUGHT I'D GIVE MYSELF A CHECK-UP SO I TOOK MY CLOTHES OFF.
AND THAT'S WHEN THE LIBRARIAN THREW YOU OUT?
ONLY AFTER SHE'D DATE-STAMPED MY BUM.
I'VE REALLY GOT TO HAND IT TO YOU, DENNIS.
NOT MANY PEOPLE GET THROWN OUT OF A LIBRARY FOR BEING NAKED.
OR AN IRONMONGER'S!

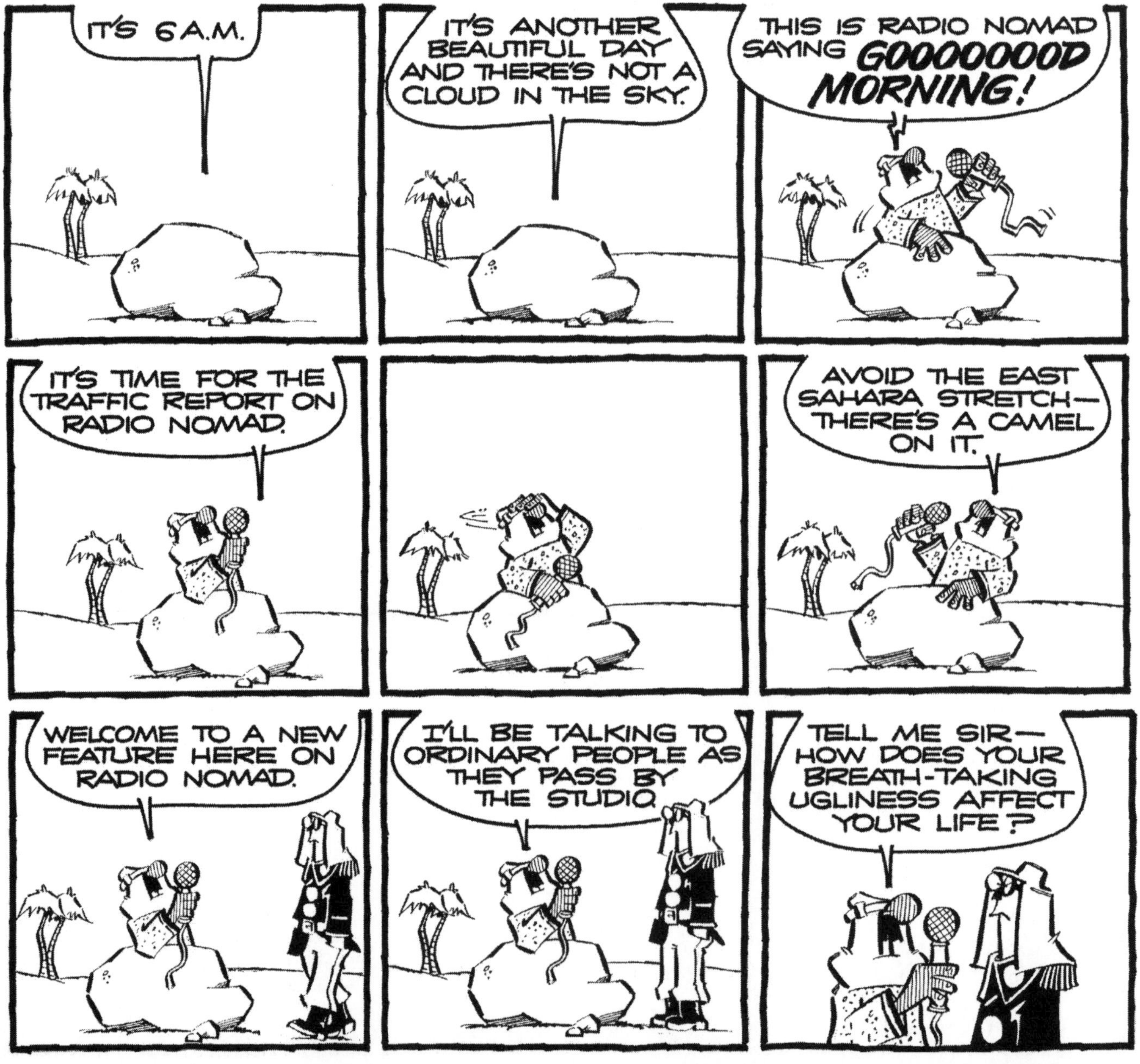
IT'S 6 A.M.
IT'S ANOTHER BEAUTIFUL DAY AND THERE'S NOT A CLOUD IN THE SKY.
THIS IS RADIO NOMAD SAYING GOOOOOOOD MORNING!
IT'S TIME FOR THE TRAFFIC REPORT ON RADIO NOMAD.
AVOID THE EAST SAHARA STRETCH— THERE'S A CAMEL ON IT.
WELCOME TO A NEW FEATURE HERE ON RADIO NOMAD.
I'LL BE TALKING TO ORDINARY PEOPLE AS THEY PASS BY THE STUDIO.
TELL ME SIR— HOW DOES YOUR BREATH-TAKING UGLINESS AFFECT YOUR LIFE?

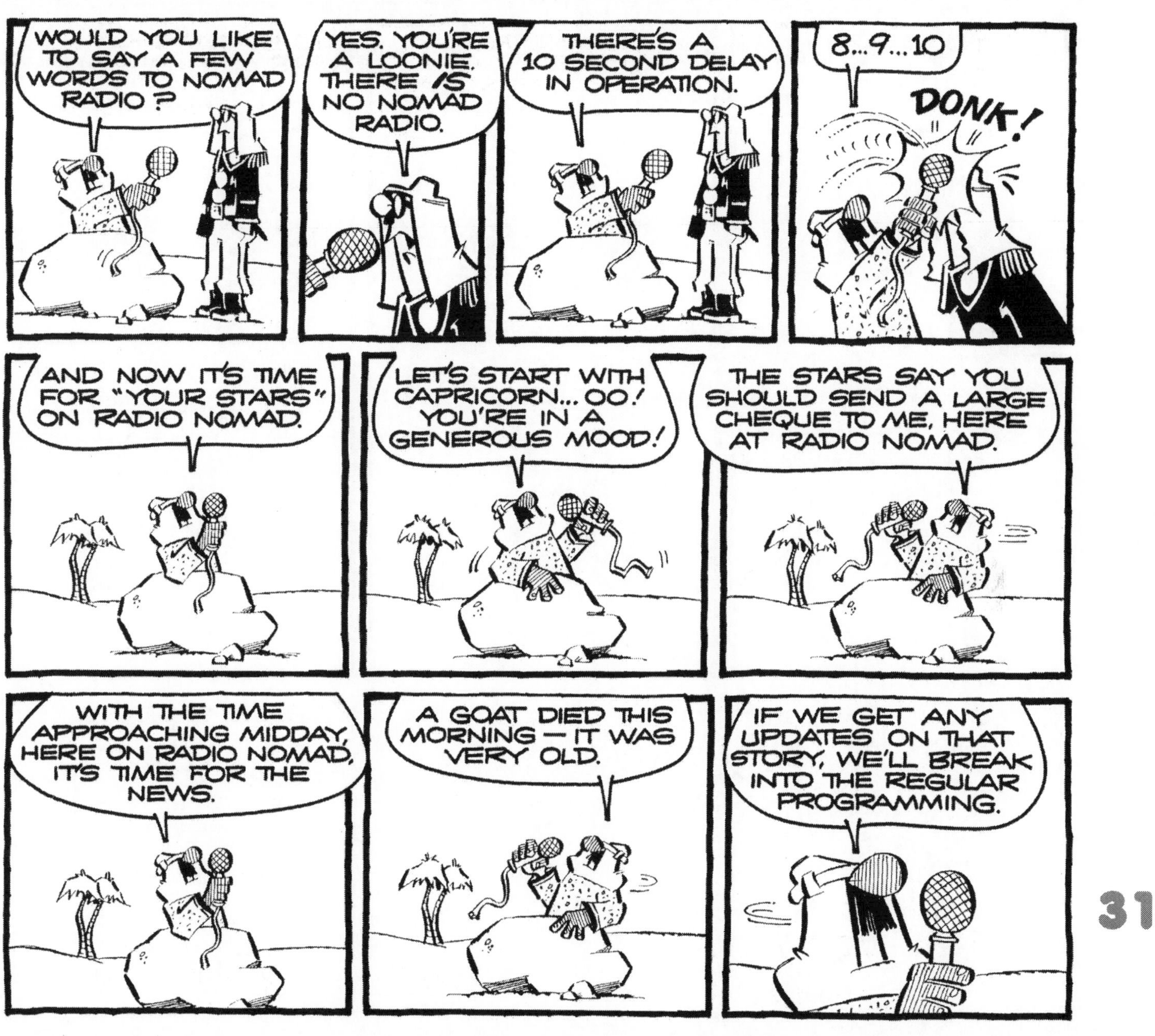
WOULD YOU LIKE TO SAY A FEW WORDS TO NOMAD RADIO ?
YES. YOU'RE A LOONIE. THERE IS NO NOMAD RADIO.
THERE'S A 10 SECOND DELAY IN OPERATION.
8...9...10
DONK!
AND NOW IT'S TIME FOR "YOUR STARS" ON RADIO NOMAD.
LET'S START WITH CAPRICORN... OO! YOU'RE IN A GENEROUS MOOD!
THE STARS SAY YOU SHOULD SEND A LARGE CHEQUE TO ME, HERE AT RADIO NOMAD.
WITH THE TIME APPROACHING MIDDAY, HERE ON RADIO NOMAD, IT'S TIME FOR THE NEWS.
A GOAT DIED THIS MORNING – IT WAS VERY OLD.
IF WE GET ANY UPDATES ON THAT STORY, WE'LL BREAK INTO THE REGULAR PROGRAMMING.

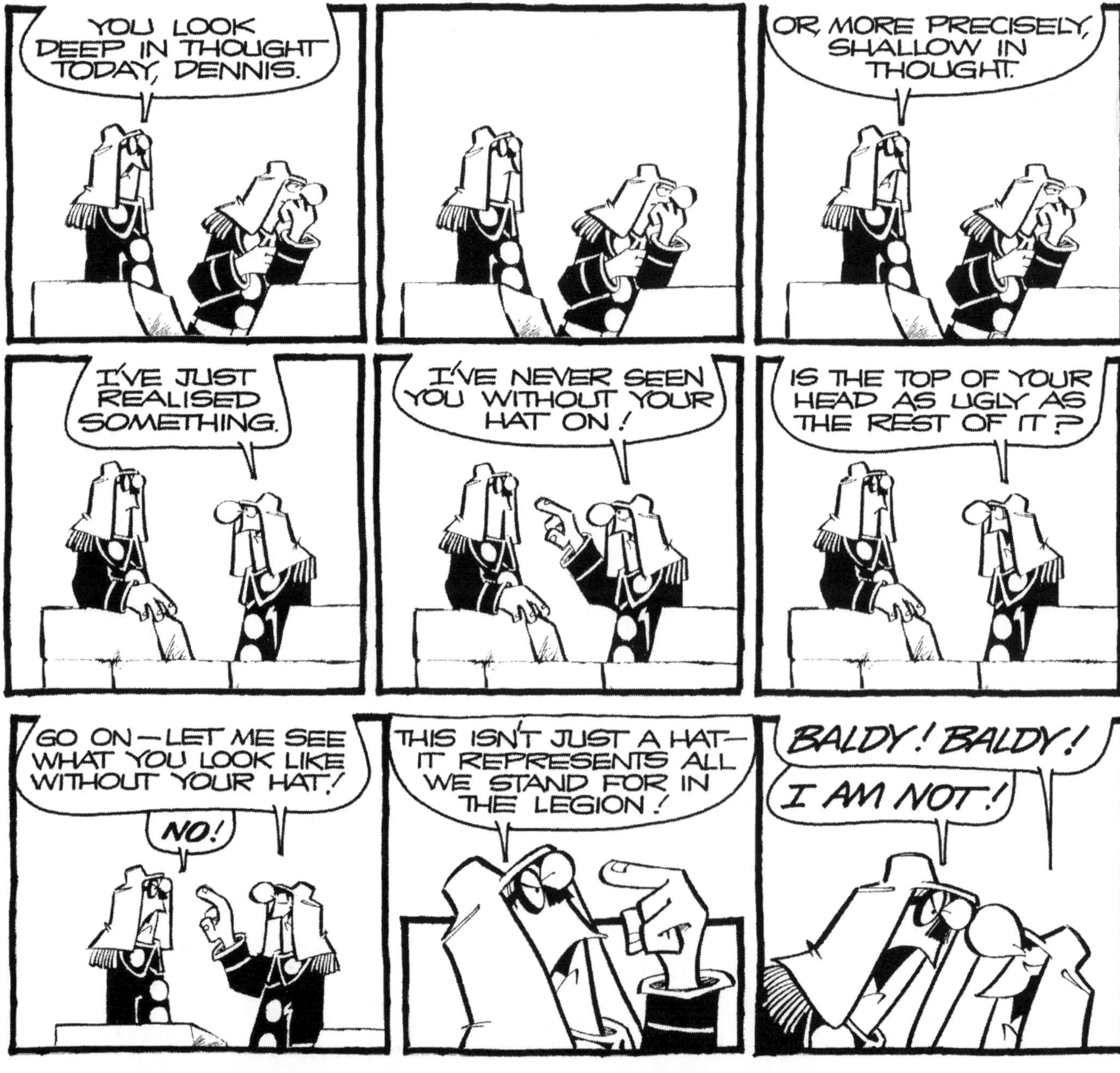
YOU LOOK DEEP IN THOUGHT TODAY, DENNIS.
OR, MORE PRECISELY, SHALLOW IN THOUGHT.
I'VE JUST REALISED SOMETHING.
I'VE NEVER SEEN YOU WITHOUT YOUR HAT ON!
IS THE TOP OF YOUR HEAD AS UGLY AS THE REST OF IT?
GO ON—LET ME SEE WHAT YOU LOOK LIKE WITHOUT YOUR HAT!
NO!
THIS ISN'T JUST A HAT—IT REPRESENTS ALL WE STAND FOR IN THE LEGION!
BALDY! BALDY!
I AM NOT!

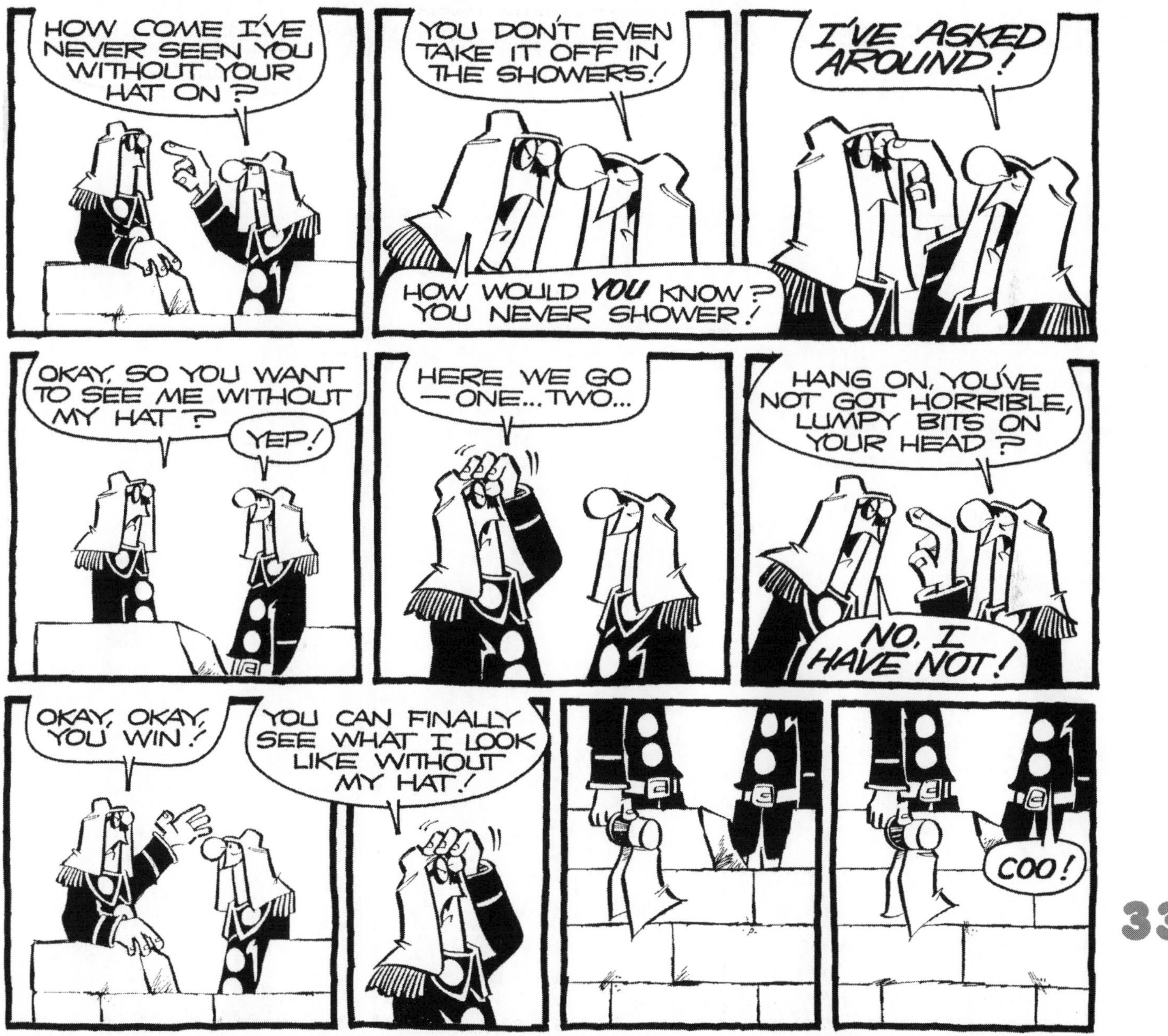
HOW COME I'VE NEVER SEEN YOU WITHOUT YOUR HAT ON?
YOU DON'T EVEN TAKE IT OFF IN THE SHOWERS!
HOW WOULD YOU KNOW? YOU NEVER SHOWER!
I'VE ASKED AROUND!
OKAY, SO YOU WANT TO SEE ME WITHOUT MY HAT?
YEP!
HERE WE GO —ONE... TWO...
HANG ON, YOU'VE NOT GOT HORRIBLE, LUMPY BITS ON YOUR HEAD?
NO, I HAVE NOT!
OKAY, OKAY, YOU WIN!
YOU CAN FINALLY SEE WHAT I LOOK LIKE WITHOUT MY HAT!
COO!

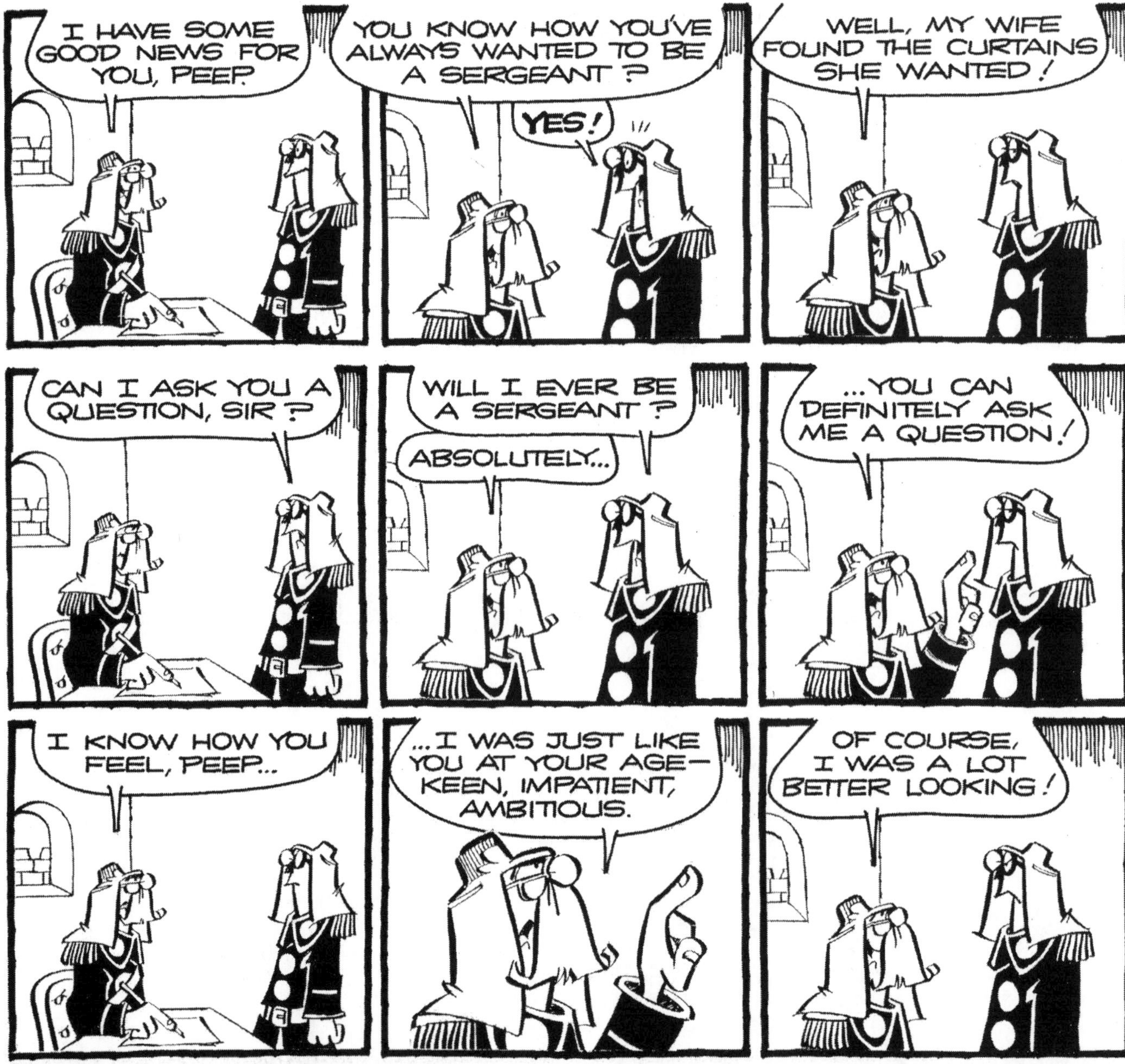
I HAVE SOME GOOD NEWS FOR YOU, PEEP.
YOU KNOW HOW YOU'VE ALWAYS WANTED TO BE A SERGEANT ?
YES !
WELL, MY WIFE FOUND THE CURTAINS SHE WANTED !
CAN I ASK YOU A QUESTION, SIR ?
WILL I EVER BE A SERGEANT ?
ABSOLUTELY...
...YOU CAN DEFINITELY ASK ME A QUESTION !
I KNOW HOW YOU FEEL, PEEP...
...I WAS JUST LIKE YOU AT YOUR AGE— KEEN, IMPATIENT, AMBITIOUS.
OF COURSE, I WAS A LOT BETTER LOOKING !

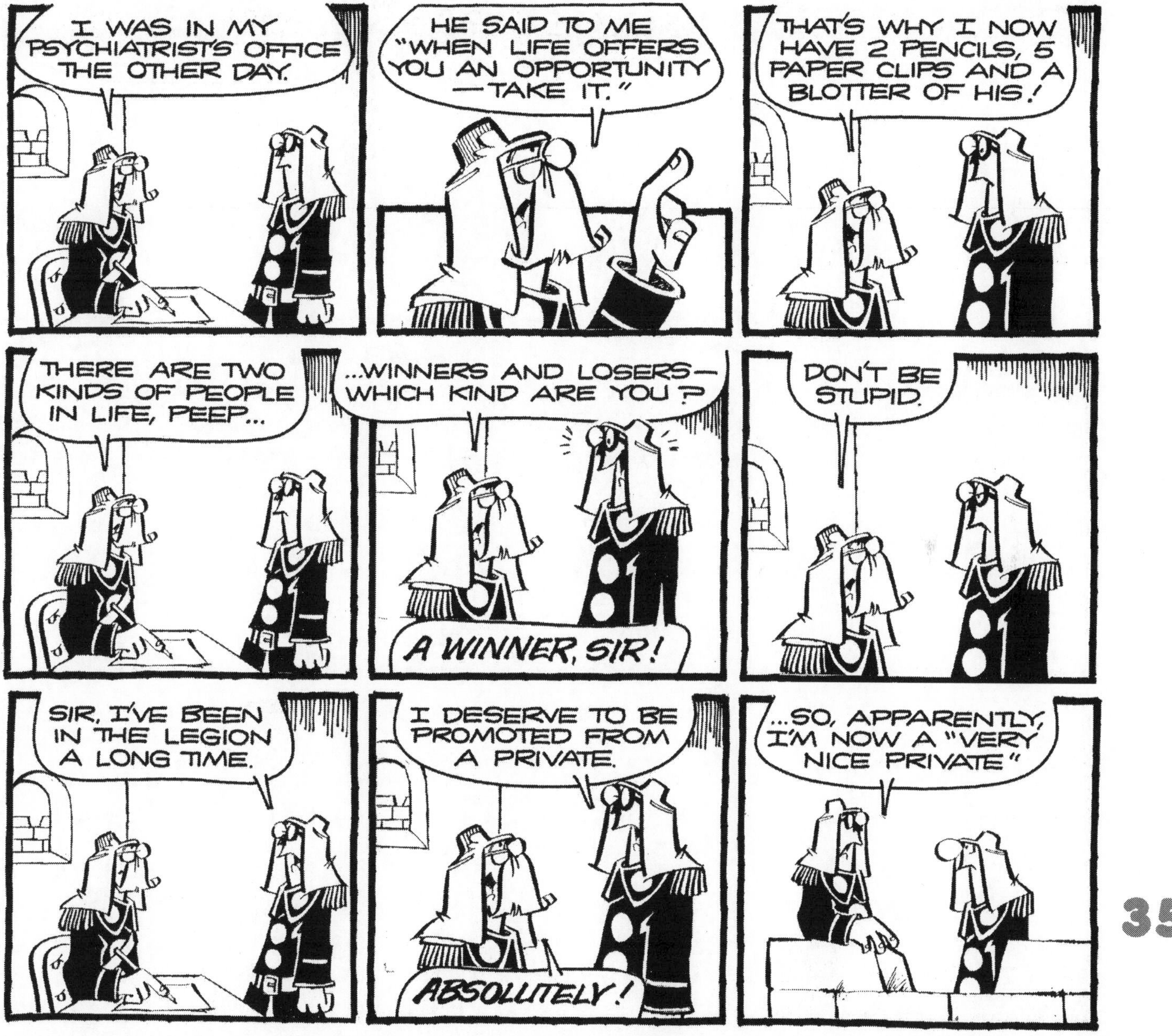
I WAS IN MY PSYCHIATRIST'S OFFICE THE OTHER DAY.
HE SAID TO ME "WHEN LIFE OFFERS YOU AN OPPORTUNITY —TAKE IT."
THAT'S WHY I NOW HAVE 2 PENCILS, 5 PAPER CLIPS AND A BLOTTER OF HIS!
THERE ARE TWO KINDS OF PEOPLE IN LIFE, PEEP...
...WINNERS AND LOSERS— WHICH KIND ARE YOU?
A WINNER, SIR!
DON'T BE STUPID.
SIR, I'VE BEEN IN THE LEGION A LONG TIME.
I DESERVE TO BE PROMOTED FROM A PRIVATE.
ABSOLUTELY!
...SO, APPARENTLY, I'M NOW A "VERY NICE PRIVATE"

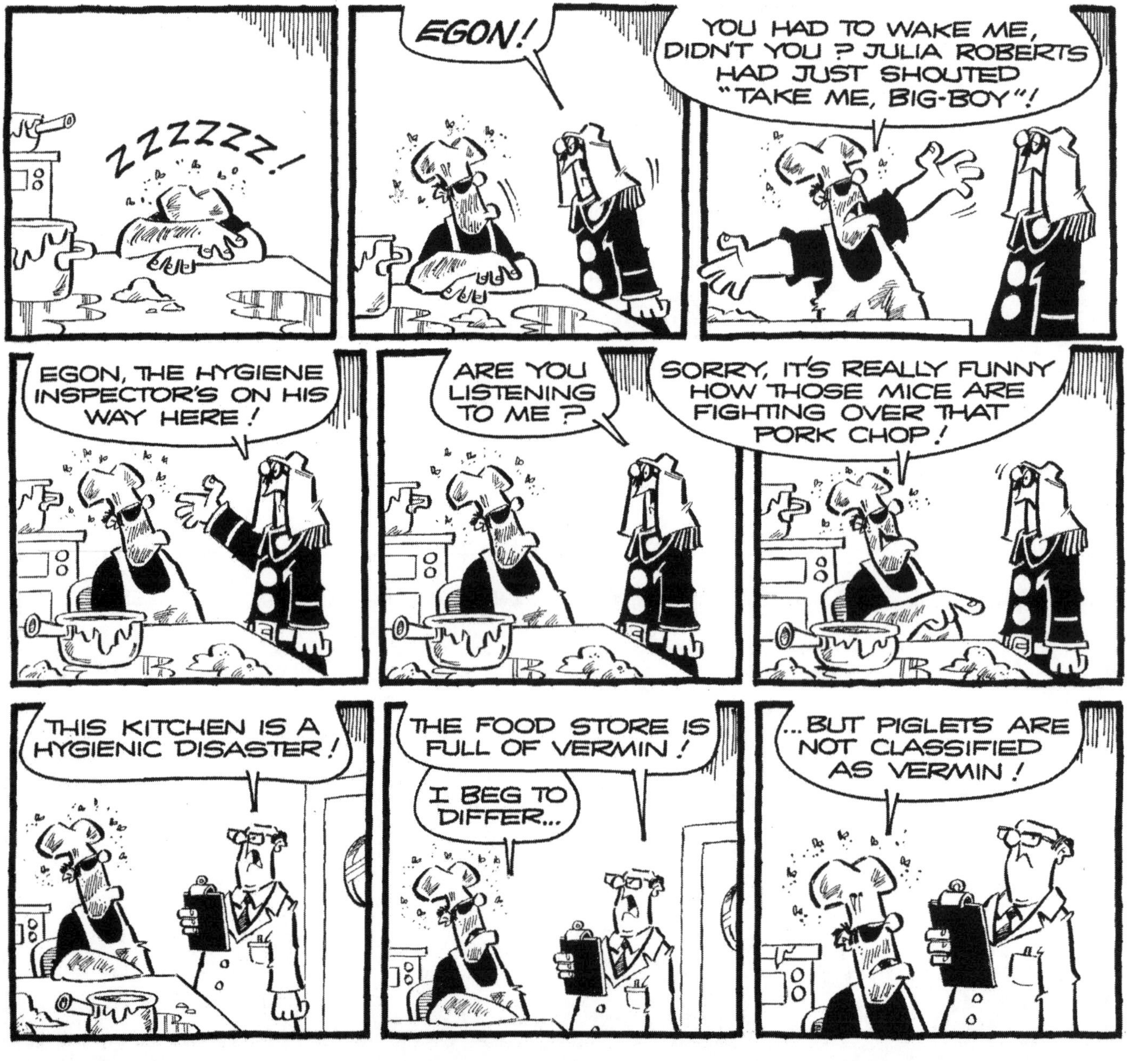
ZZZZZZ!
EGON!
YOU HAD TO WAKE ME, DIDN'T YOU ? JULIA ROBERTS HAD JUST SHOUTED "TAKE ME, BIG-BOY"!
EGON, THE HYGIENE INSPECTOR'S ON HIS WAY HERE !
ARE YOU LISTENING TO ME ?
SORRY, IT'S REALLY FUNNY HOW THOSE MICE ARE FIGHTING OVER THAT PORK CHOP !
THIS KITCHEN IS A HYGIENIC DISASTER !
THE FOOD STORE IS FULL OF VERMIN !
I BEG TO DIFFER...
...BUT PIGLETS ARE NOT CLASSIFIED AS VERMIN !

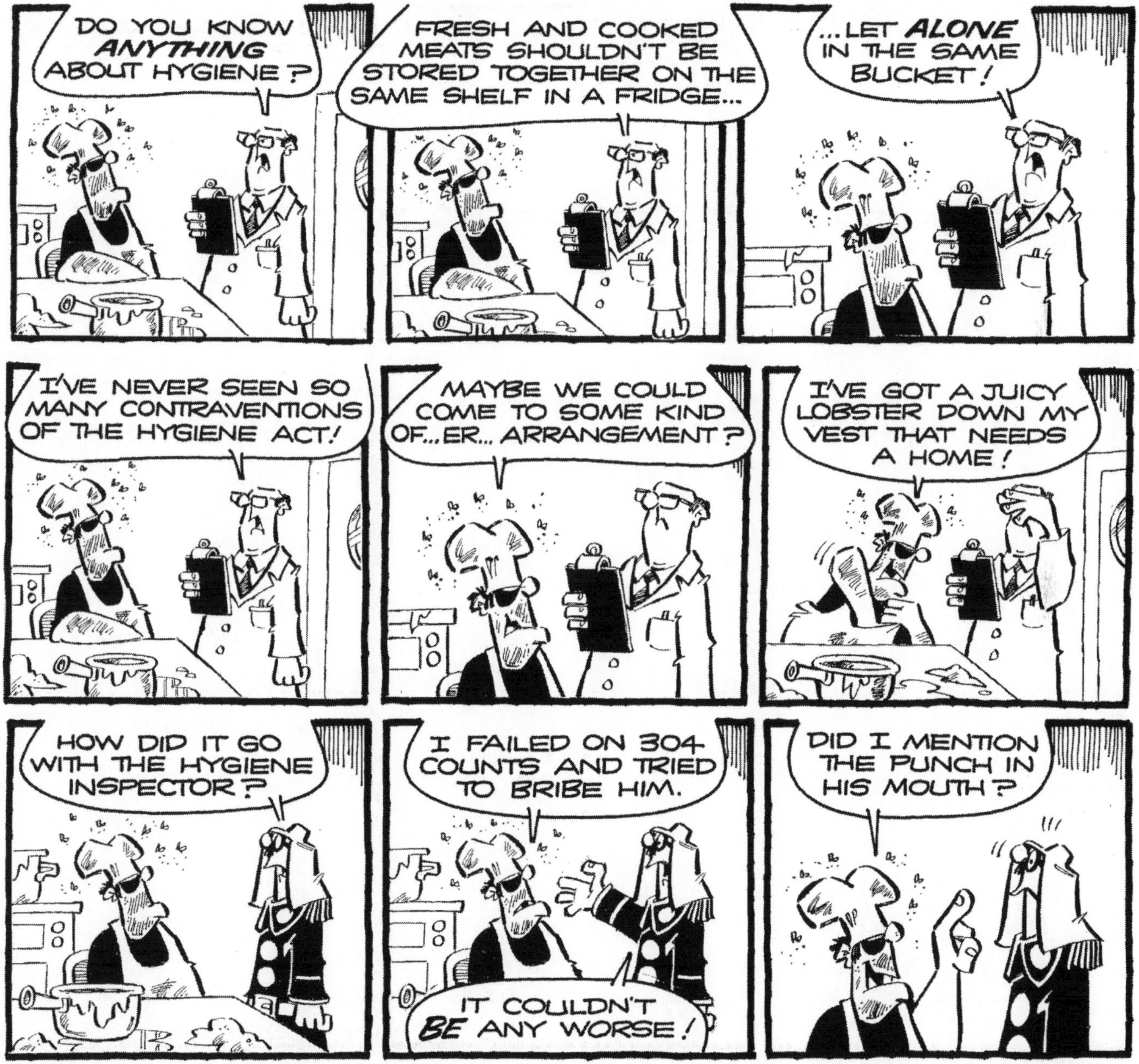
DO YOU KNOW ANYTHING ABOUT HYGIENE?
FRESH AND COOKED MEATS SHOULDN'T BE STORED TOGETHER ON THE SAME SHELF IN A FRIDGE...
...LET ALONE IN THE SAME BUCKET!
I'VE NEVER SEEN SO MANY CONTRAVENTIONS OF THE HYGIENE ACT!
MAYBE WE COULD COME TO SOME KIND OF...ER... ARRANGEMENT?
I'VE GOT A JUICY LOBSTER DOWN MY VEST THAT NEEDS A HOME!
HOW DID IT GO WITH THE HYGIENE INSPECTOR?
I FAILED ON 304 COUNTS AND TRIED TO BRIBE HIM.
IT COULDN'T BE ANY WORSE!
DID I MENTION THE PUNCH IN HIS MOUTH?

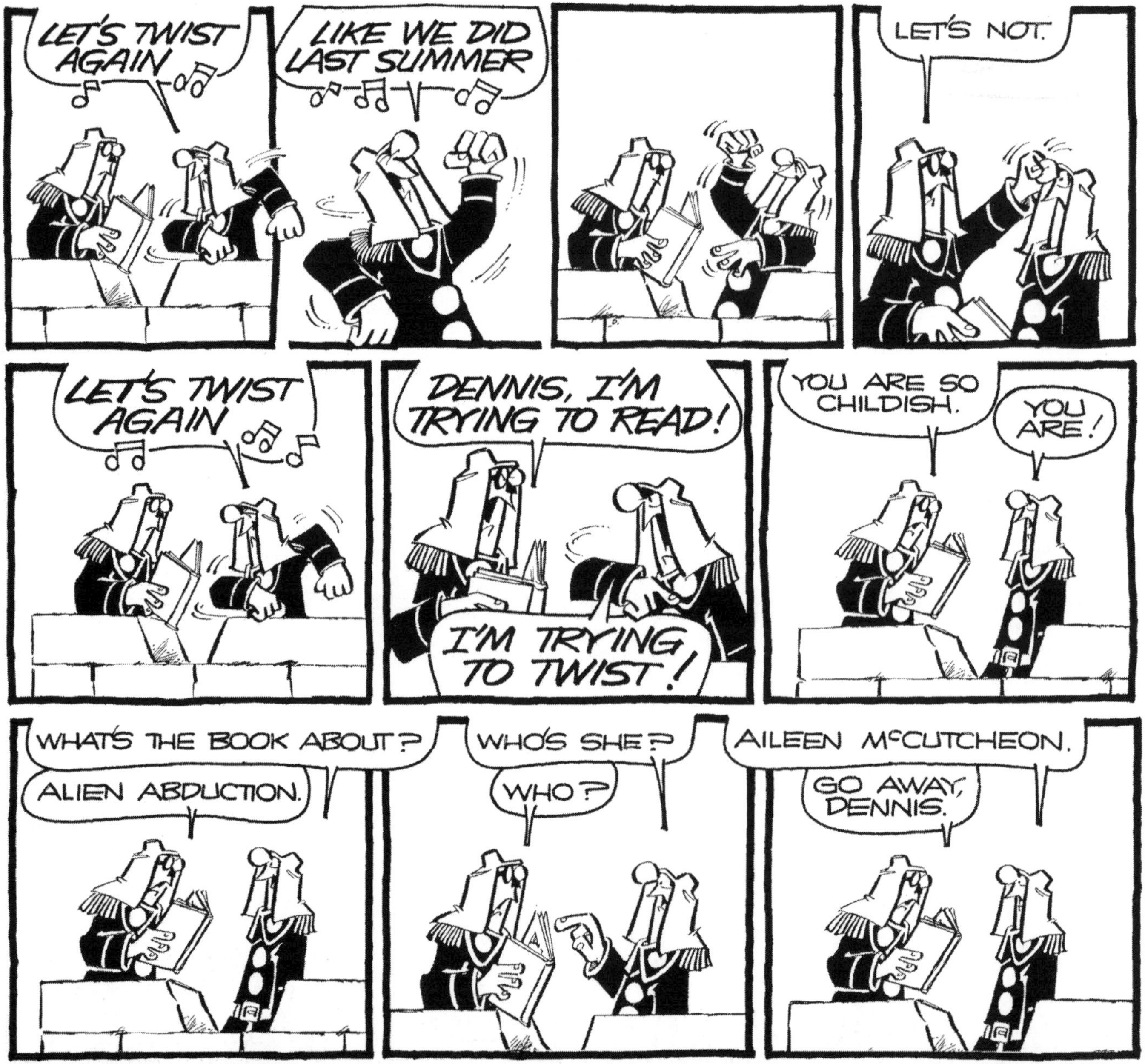
LET'S TWIST AGAIN
LIKE WE DID LAST SUMMER
LET'S NOT.
LET'S TWIST AGAIN
DENNIS, I'M TRYING TO READ!
I'M TRYING TO TWIST!
YOU ARE SO CHILDISH.
YOU ARE!
WHAT'S THE BOOK ABOUT?
ALIEN ABDUCTION.
WHO'S SHE?
WHO?
AILEEN McCUTCHEON.
GO AWAY, DENNIS.

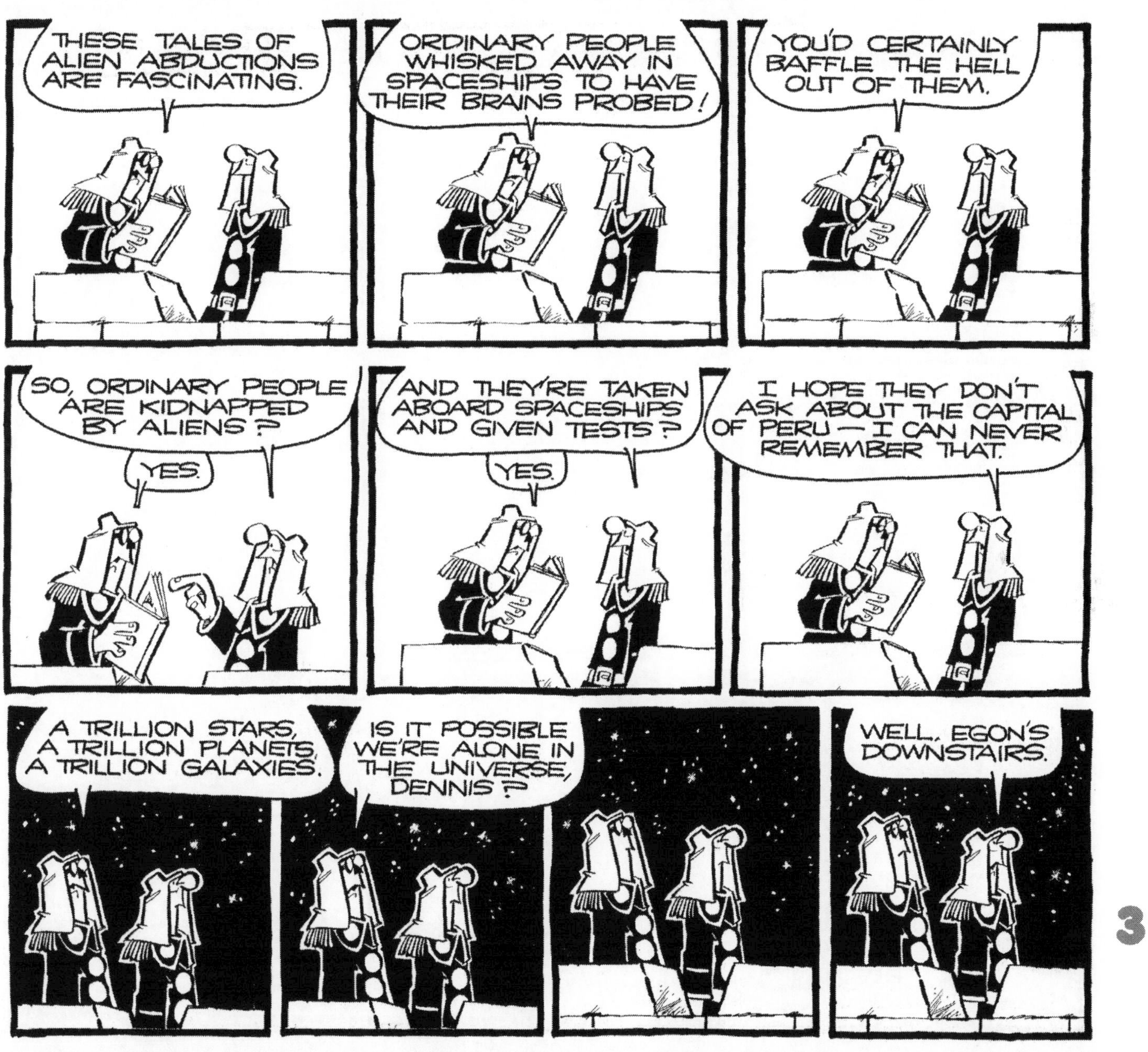
THESE TALES OF ALIEN ABDUCTIONS ARE FASCINATING.
ORDINARY PEOPLE WHISKED AWAY IN SPACESHIPS TO HAVE THEIR BRAINS PROBED!
YOU'D CERTAINLY BAFFLE THE HELL OUT OF THEM.
SO, ORDINARY PEOPLE ARE KIDNAPPED BY ALIENS?
YES.
AND THEY'RE TAKEN ABOARD SPACESHIPS AND GIVEN TESTS?
YES.
I HOPE THEY DON'T ASK ABOUT THE CAPITAL OF PERU — I CAN NEVER REMEMBER THAT.
A TRILLION STARS, A TRILLION PLANETS, A TRILLION GALAXIES.
IS IT POSSIBLE WE'RE ALONE IN THE UNIVERSE, DENNIS?
WELL, EGON'S DOWNSTAIRS.

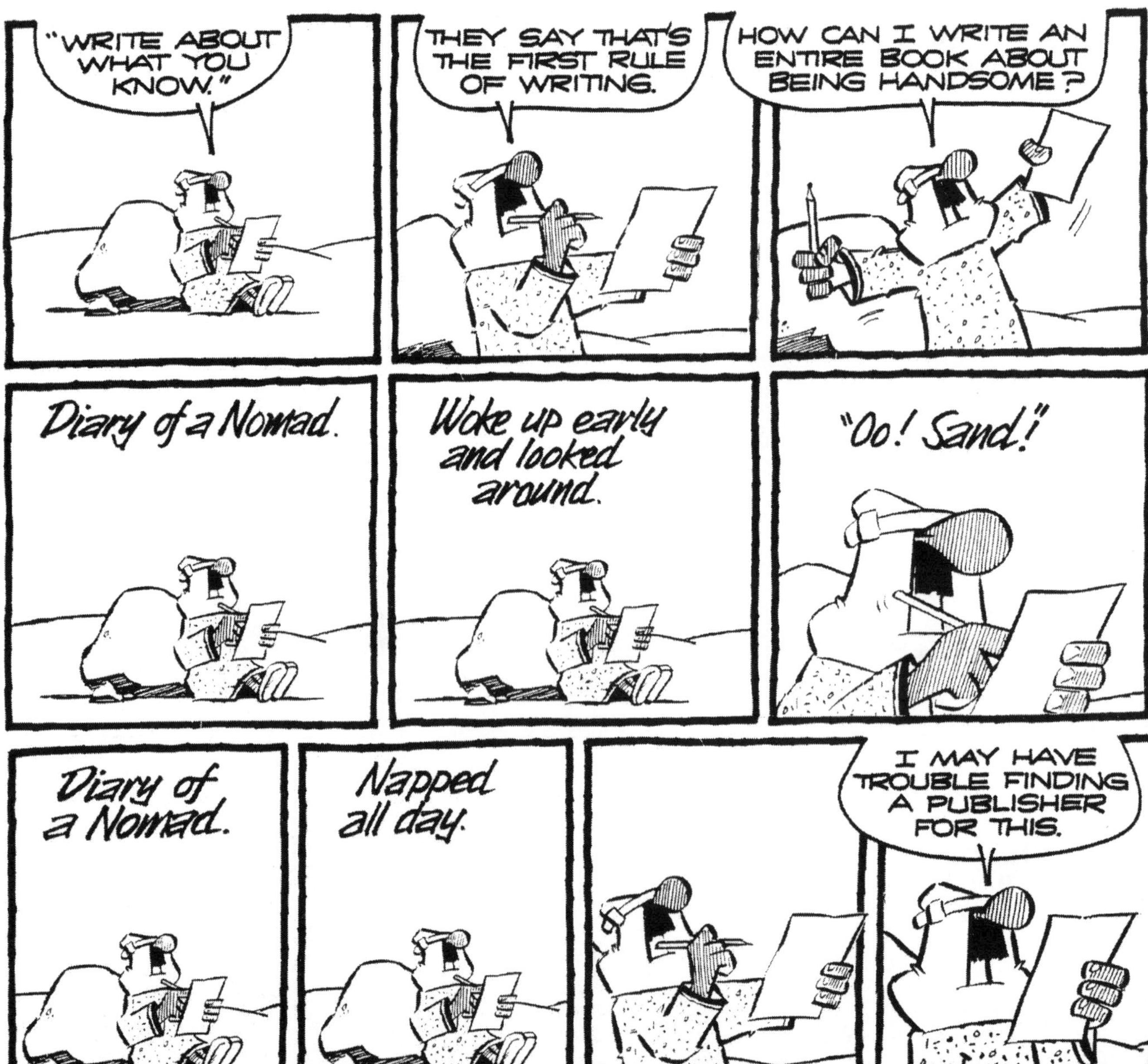
"WRITE ABOUT WHAT YOU KNOW."
THEY SAY THAT'S THE FIRST RULE OF WRITING.
HOW CAN I WRITE AN ENTIRE BOOK ABOUT BEING HANDSOME?
Diary of a Nomad.
Woke up early and looked around.
"Oo! Sand!"
Diary of a Nomad.
Napped all day.
I MAY HAVE TROUBLE FINDING A PUBLISHER FOR THIS.

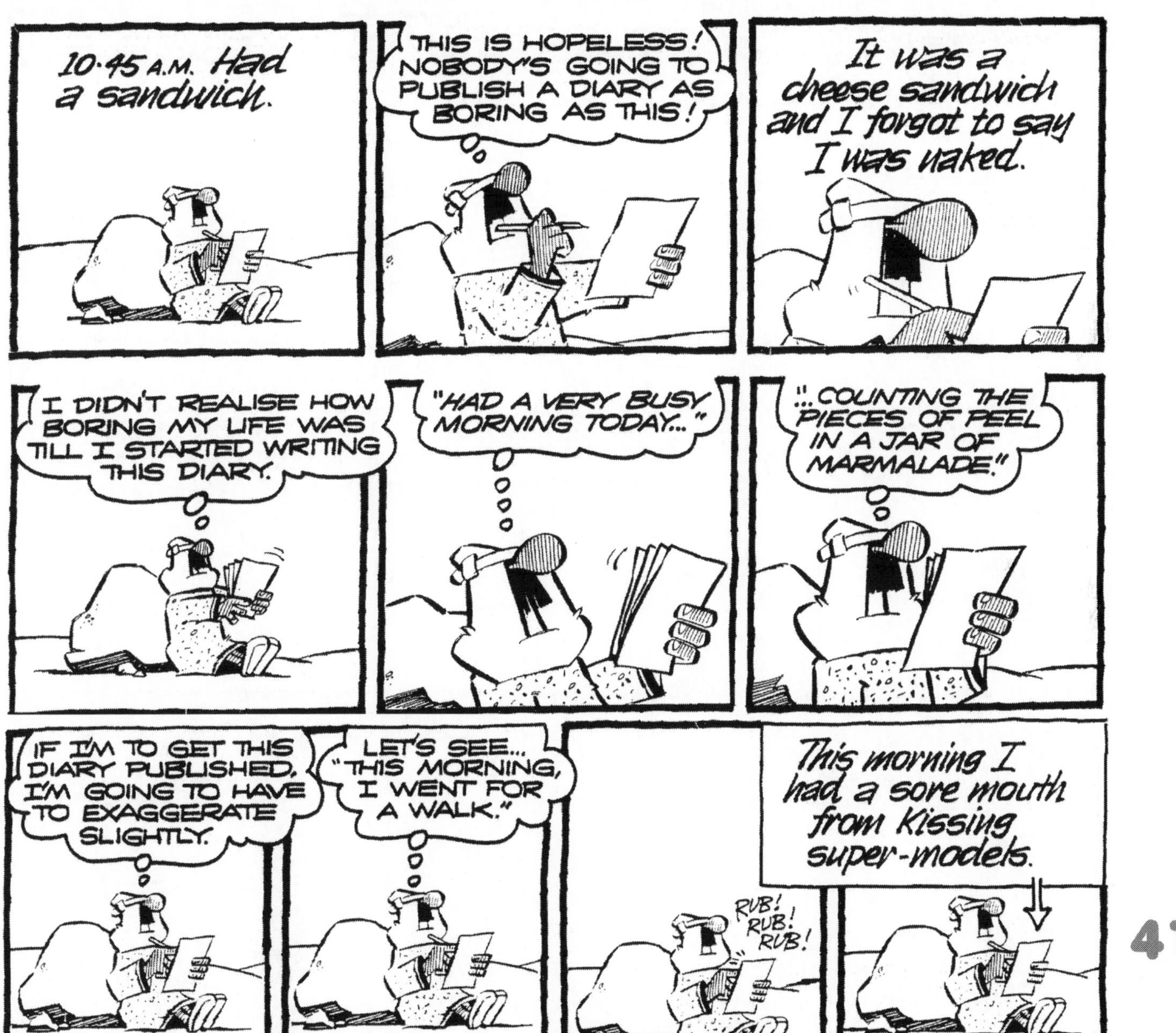
10·45 A.M. Had a sandwich.
THIS IS HOPELESS! NOBODY'S GOING TO PUBLISH A DIARY AS BORING AS THIS!
It was a cheese sandwich and I forgot to say I was naked.
I DIDN'T REALISE HOW BORING MY LIFE WAS TILL I STARTED WRITING THIS DIARY.
"HAD A VERY BUSY MORNING TODAY..."
"...COUNTING THE PIECES OF PEEL IN A JAR OF MARMALADE."
IF I'M TO GET THIS DIARY PUBLISHED, I'M GOING TO HAVE TO EXAGGERATE SLIGHTLY.
LET'S SEE... "THIS MORNING, I WENT FOR A WALK."
RUB! RUB! RUB!
This morning I had a sore mouth from kissing super-models.

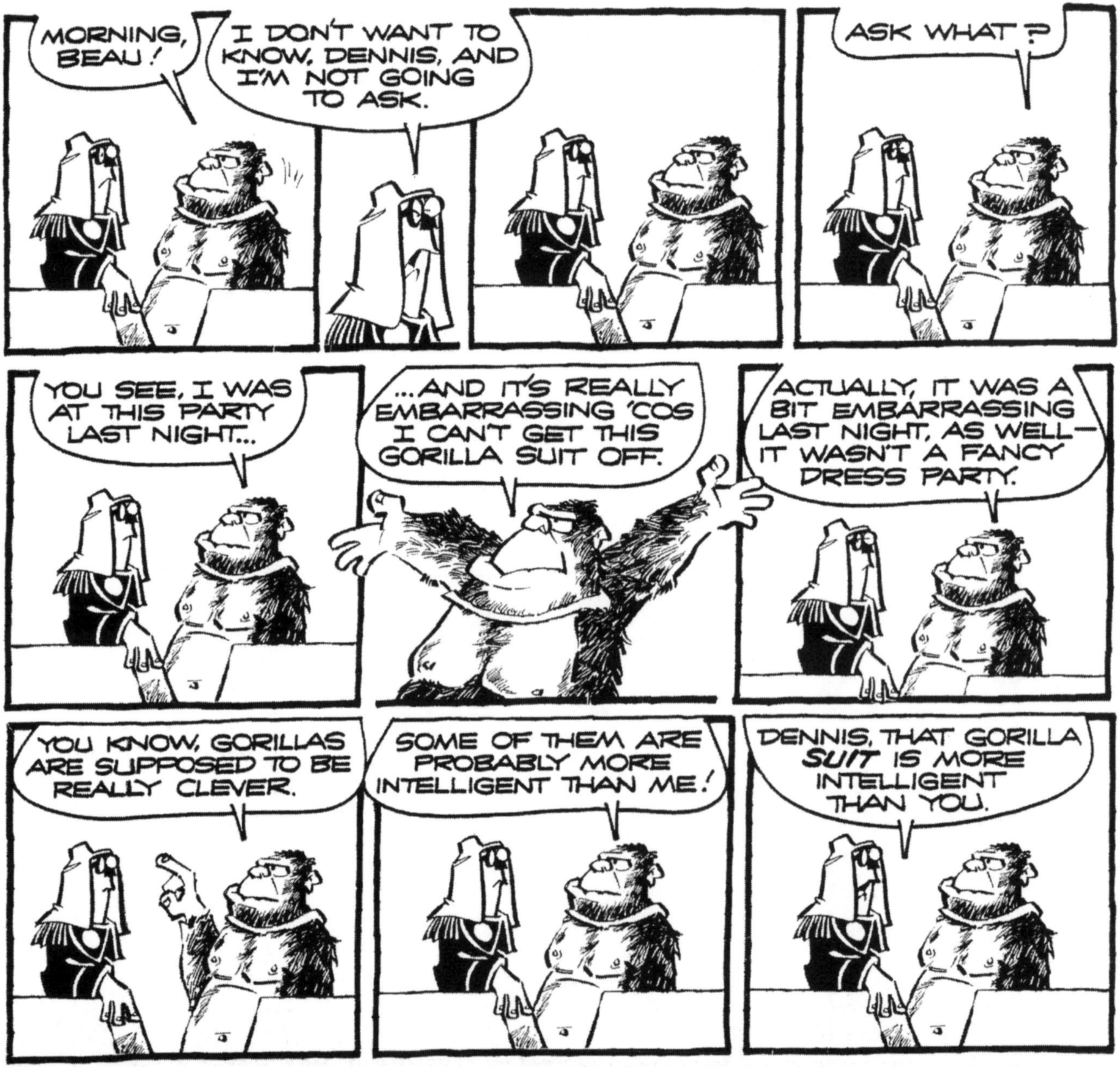
MORNING, BEAU!
I DON'T WANT TO KNOW, DENNIS, AND I'M NOT GOING TO ASK.
ASK WHAT?
YOU SEE, I WAS AT THIS PARTY LAST NIGHT...
...AND IT'S REALLY EMBARRASSING 'COS I CAN'T GET THIS GORILLA SUIT OFF.
ACTUALLY, IT WAS A BIT EMBARRASSING LAST NIGHT, AS WELL— IT WASN'T A FANCY DRESS PARTY.
YOU KNOW, GORILLAS ARE SUPPOSED TO BE REALLY CLEVER.
SOME OF THEM ARE PROBABLY MORE INTELLIGENT THAN ME!
DENNIS, THAT GORILLA *SUIT* IS MORE INTELLIGENT THAN YOU.

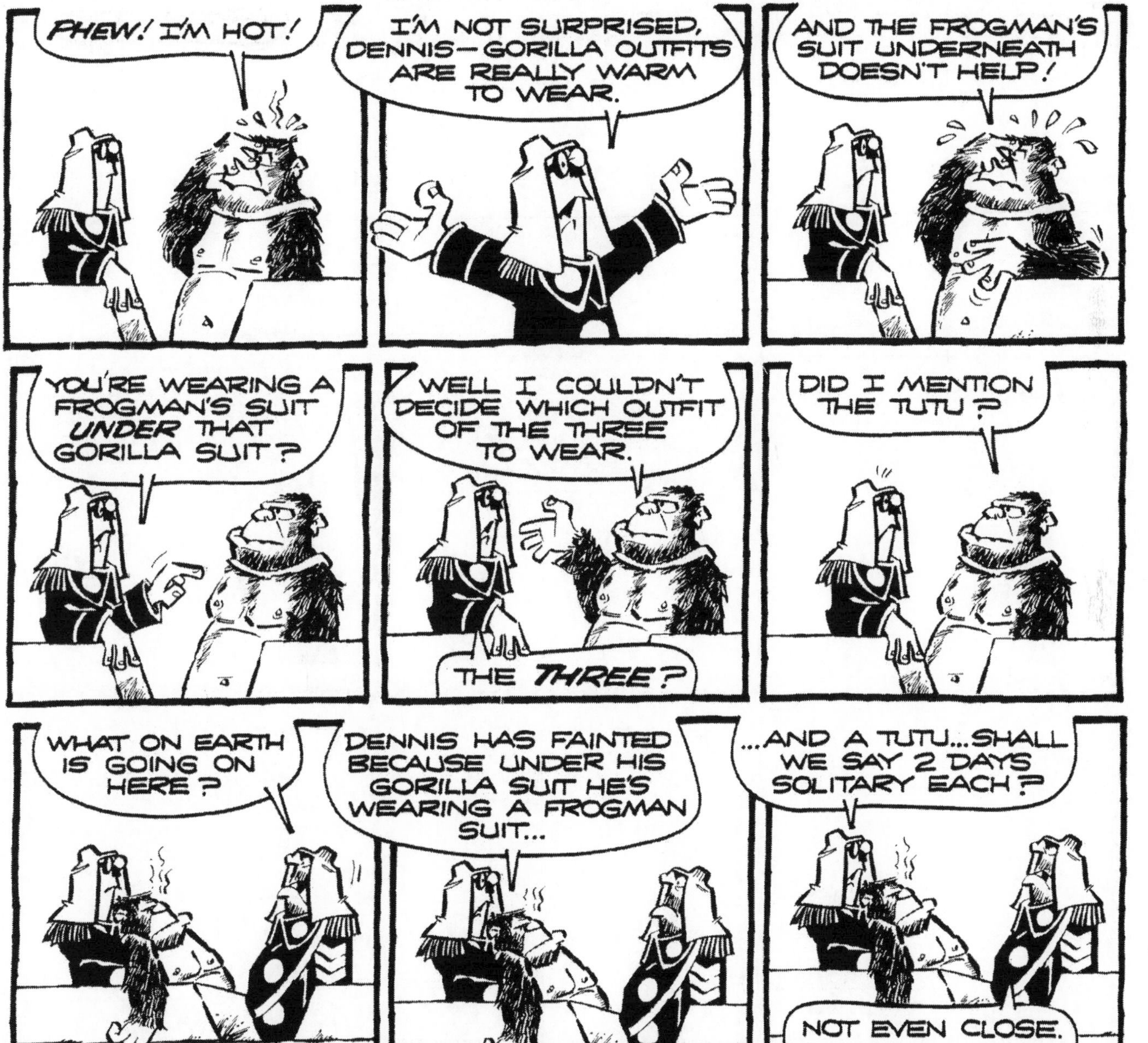
PHEW! I'M HOT!
I'M NOT SURPRISED, DENNIS—GORILLA OUTFITS ARE REALLY WARM TO WEAR.
AND THE FROGMAN'S SUIT UNDERNEATH DOESN'T HELP!
YOU'RE WEARING A FROGMAN'S SUIT UNDER THAT GORILLA SUIT?
WELL I COULDN'T DECIDE WHICH OUTFIT OF THE THREE TO WEAR.
THE THREE?
DID I MENTION THE TUTU?
WHAT ON EARTH IS GOING ON HERE?
DENNIS HAS FAINTED BECAUSE UNDER HIS GORILLA SUIT HE'S WEARING A FROGMAN SUIT...
...AND A TUTU...SHALL WE SAY 2 DAYS SOLITARY EACH?
NOT EVEN CLOSE.

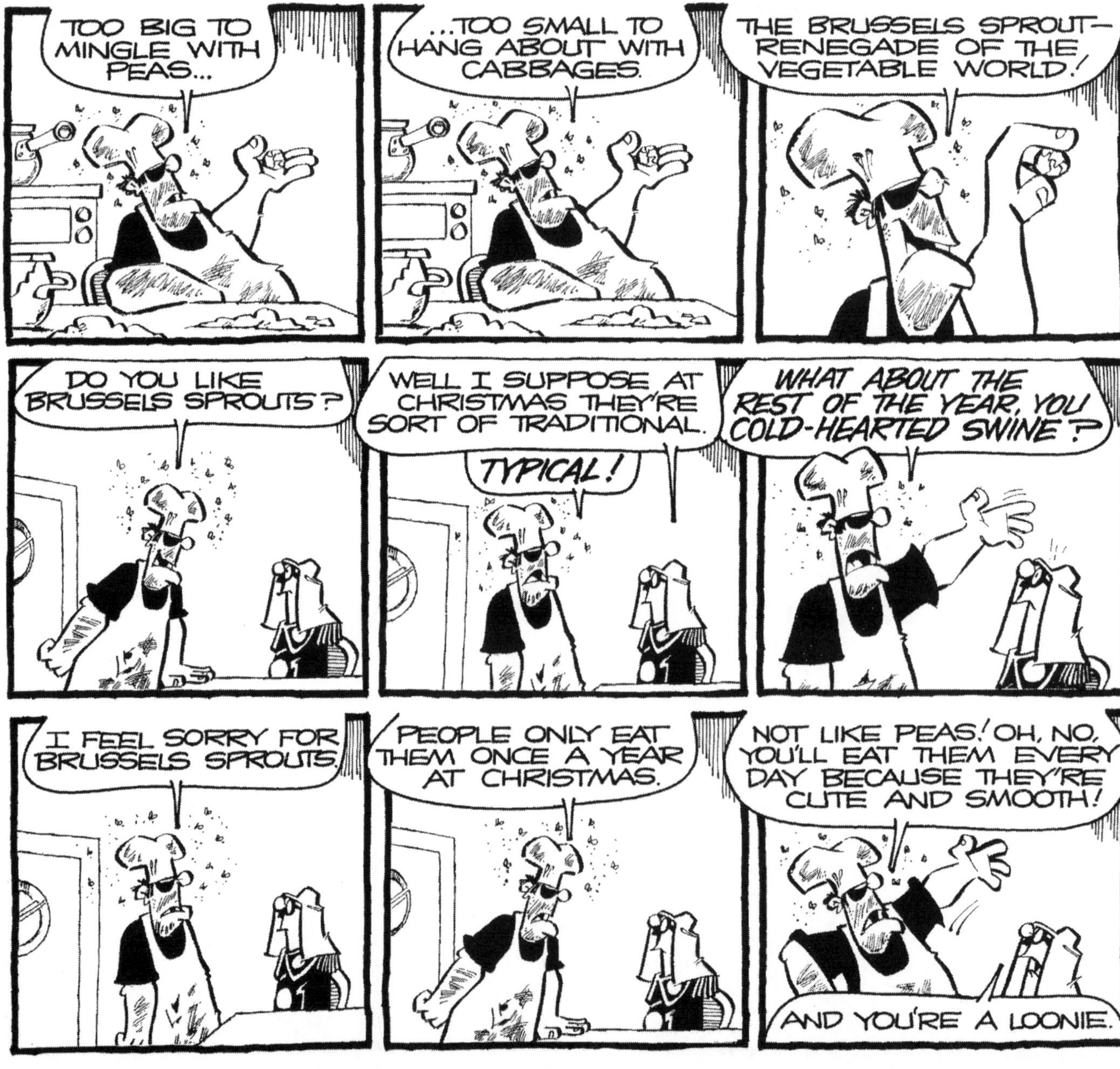
TOO BIG TO MINGLE WITH PEAS...
...TOO SMALL TO HANG ABOUT WITH CABBAGES.
THE BRUSSELS SPROUT—RENEGADE OF THE VEGETABLE WORLD!
DO YOU LIKE BRUSSELS SPROUTS?
WELL I SUPPOSE AT CHRISTMAS THEY'RE SORT OF TRADITIONAL.
TYPICAL!
WHAT ABOUT THE REST OF THE YEAR, YOU COLD-HEARTED SWINE?
I FEEL SORRY FOR BRUSSELS SPROUTS.
PEOPLE ONLY EAT THEM ONCE A YEAR AT CHRISTMAS.
NOT LIKE PEAS! OH, NO, YOU'LL EAT THEM EVERY DAY BECAUSE THEY'RE CUTE AND SMOOTH!
AND YOU'RE A LOONIE.

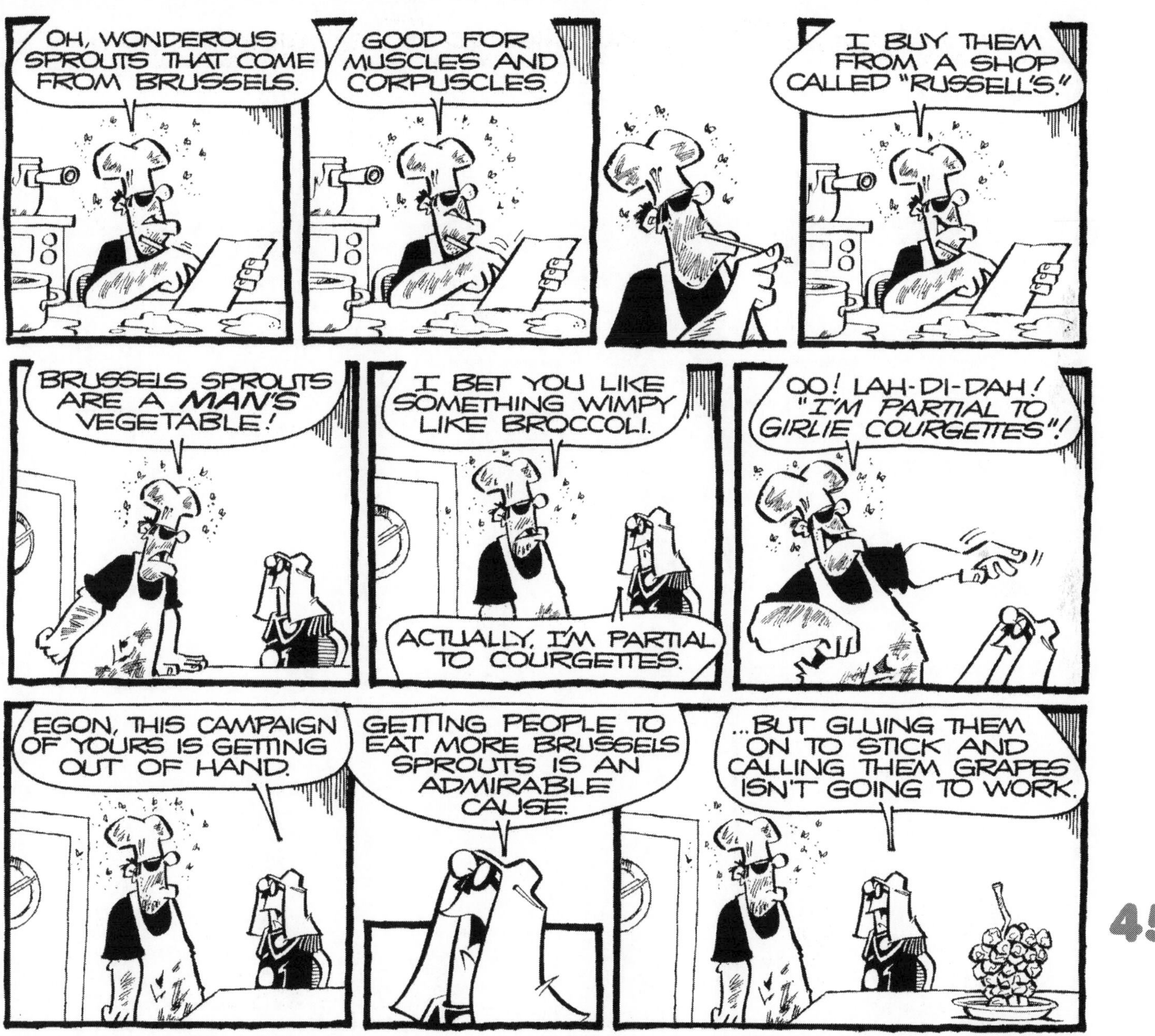
OH, WONDEROUS SPROUTS THAT COME FROM BRUSSELS.
GOOD FOR MUSCLES AND CORPUSCLES.
I BUY THEM FROM A SHOP CALLED "RUSSELL'S."
BRUSSELS SPROUTS ARE A MAN'S VEGETABLE!
I BET YOU LIKE SOMETHING WIMPY LIKE BROCCOLI.
ACTUALLY, I'M PARTIAL TO COURGETTES.
OO! LAH-DI-DAH! "I'M PARTIAL TO GIRLIE COURGETTES"!
EGON, THIS CAMPAIGN OF YOURS IS GETTING OUT OF HAND.
GETTING PEOPLE TO EAT MORE BRUSSELS SPROUTS IS AN ADMIRABLE CAUSE.
...BUT GLUING THEM ON TO STICK AND CALLING THEM GRAPES ISN'T GOING TO WORK.

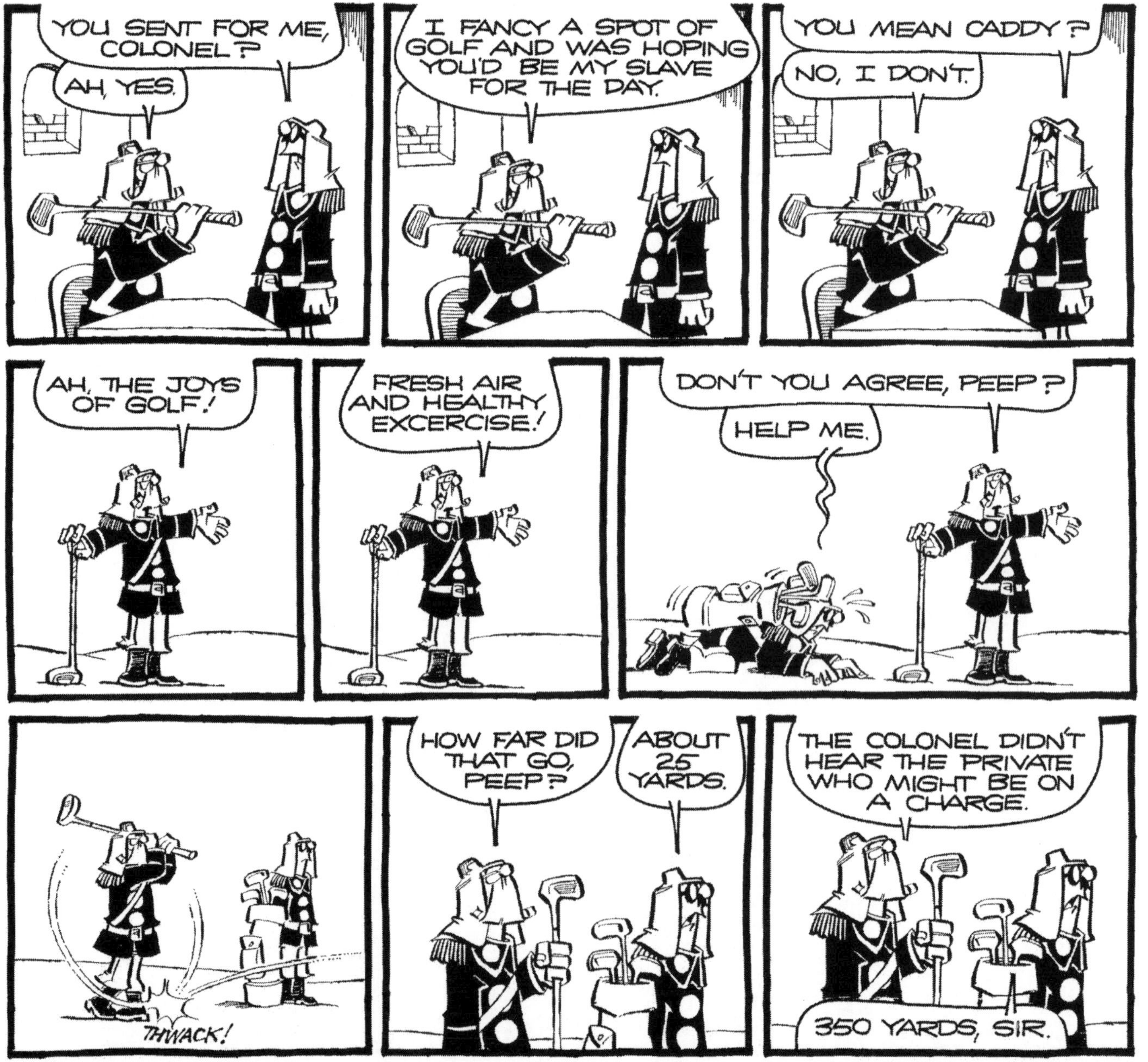
YOU SENT FOR ME, COLONEL?
AH, YES.
I FANCY A SPOT OF GOLF AND WAS HOPING YOU'D BE MY SLAVE FOR THE DAY.
YOU MEAN CADDY?
NO, I DON'T.
AH, THE JOYS OF GOLF!
FRESH AIR AND HEALTHY EXCERCISE!
DON'T YOU AGREE, PEEP?
HELP ME.
THWACK!
HOW FAR DID THAT GO, PEEP?
ABOUT 25 YARDS.
THE COLONEL DIDN'T HEAR THE PRIVATE WHO MIGHT BE ON A CHARGE.
350 YARDS, SIR.

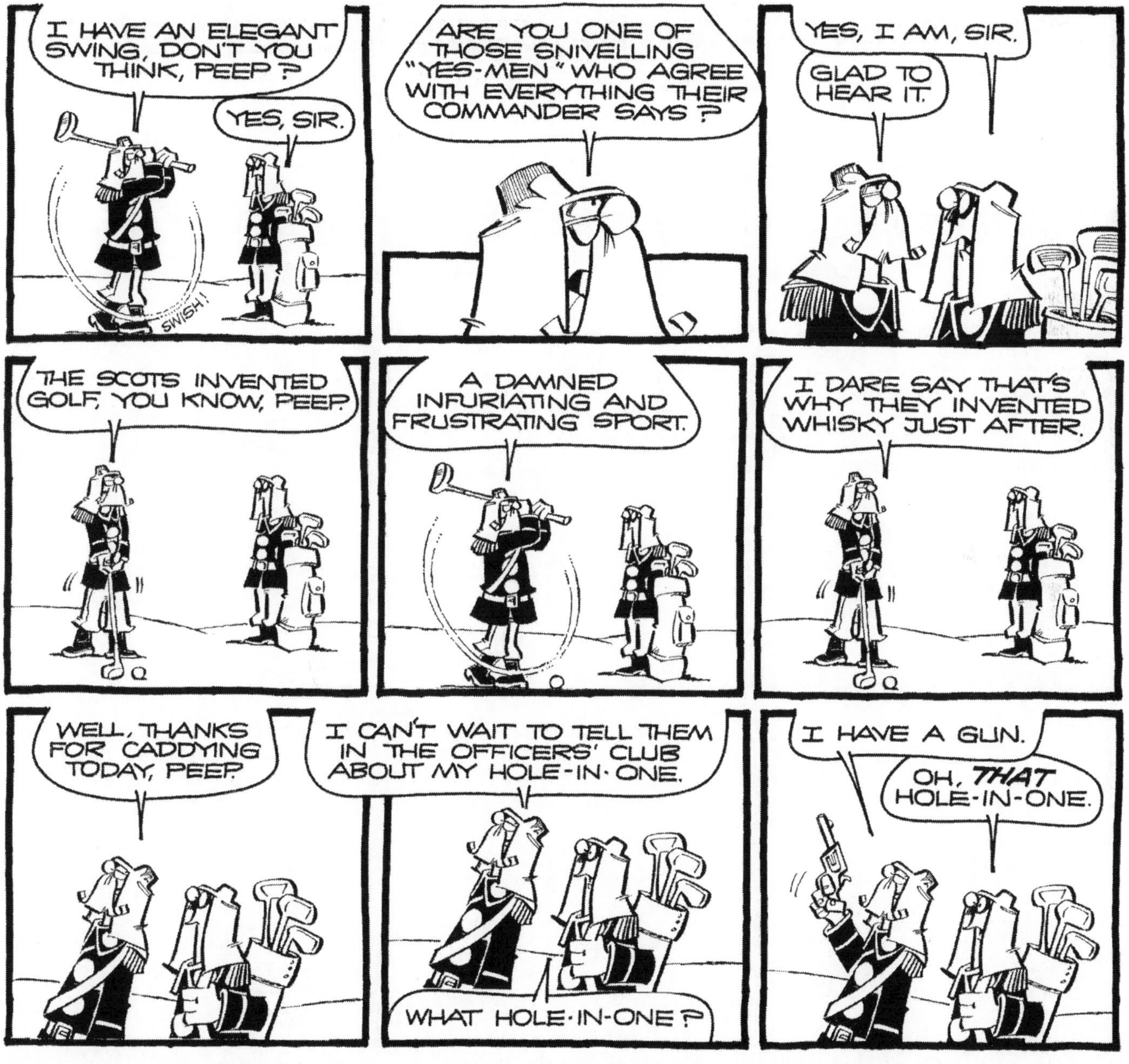

I HAVE AN ELEGANT SWING, DON'T YOU THINK, PEEP?
SWISH!
YES, SIR.
ARE YOU ONE OF THOSE SNIVELLING "YES-MEN" WHO AGREE WITH EVERYTHING THEIR COMMANDER SAYS?
YES, I AM, SIR.
GLAD TO HEAR IT.
THE SCOTS INVENTED GOLF, YOU KNOW, PEEP.
A DAMNED INFURIATING AND FRUSTRATING SPORT.
I DARE SAY THAT'S WHY THEY INVENTED WHISKY JUST AFTER.
WELL, THANKS FOR CADDYING TODAY, PEEP.
I CAN'T WAIT TO TELL THEM IN THE OFFICERS' CLUB ABOUT MY HOLE-IN-ONE.
WHAT HOLE-IN-ONE?
I HAVE A GUN.
OH, *THAT* HOLE-IN-ONE.

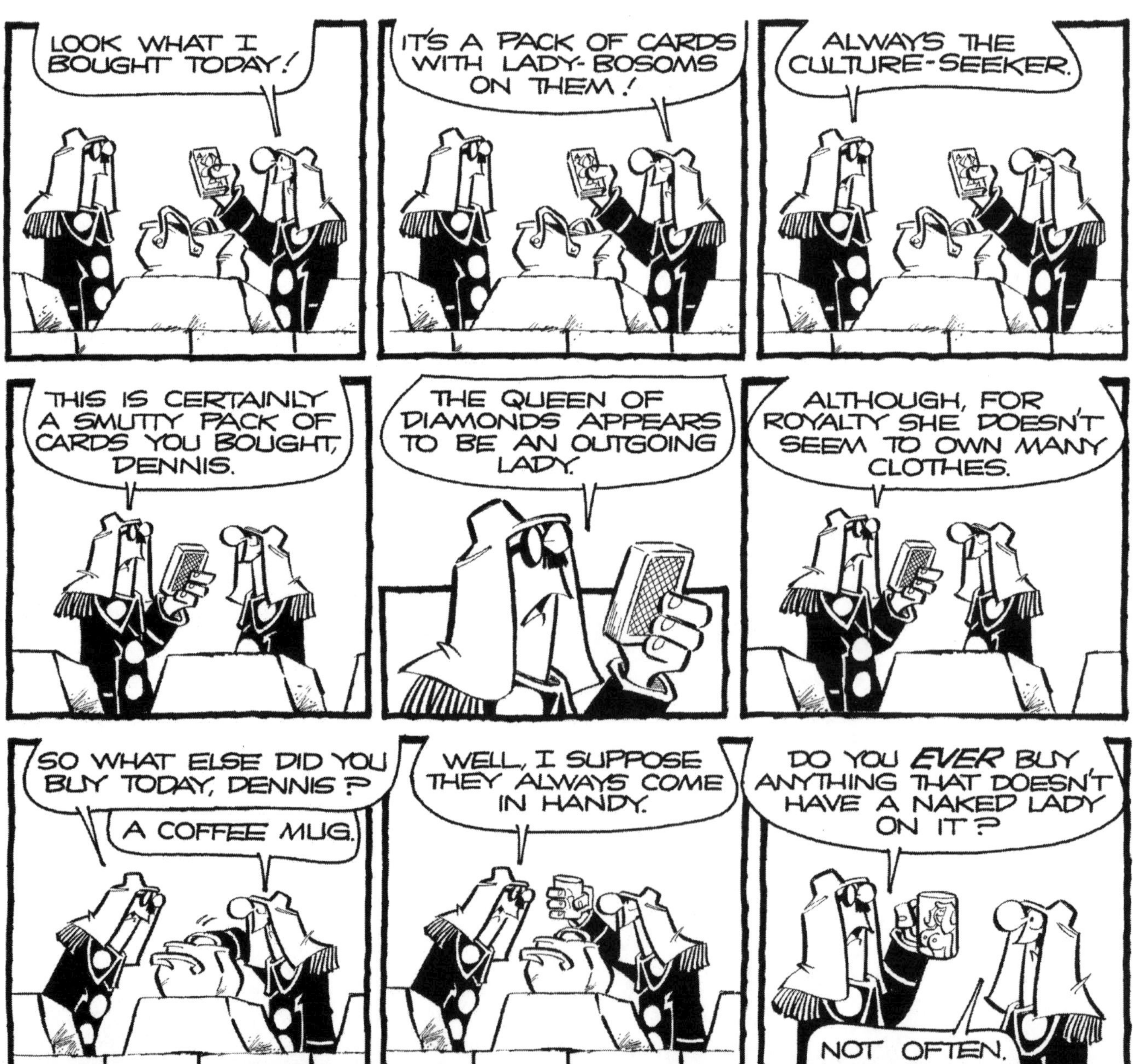
LOOK WHAT I BOUGHT TODAY!
IT'S A PACK OF CARDS WITH LADY-BOSOMS ON THEM!
ALWAYS THE CULTURE-SEEKER.
THIS IS CERTAINLY A SMUTTY PACK OF CARDS YOU BOUGHT, DENNIS.
THE QUEEN OF DIAMONDS APPEARS TO BE AN OUTGOING LADY.
ALTHOUGH, FOR ROYALTY SHE DOESN'T SEEM TO OWN MANY CLOTHES.
SO WHAT ELSE DID YOU BUY TODAY, DENNIS?
A COFFEE MUG.
WELL, I SUPPOSE THEY ALWAYS COME IN HANDY.
DO YOU EVER BUY ANYTHING THAT DOESN'T HAVE A NAKED LADY ON IT?
NOT OFTEN.

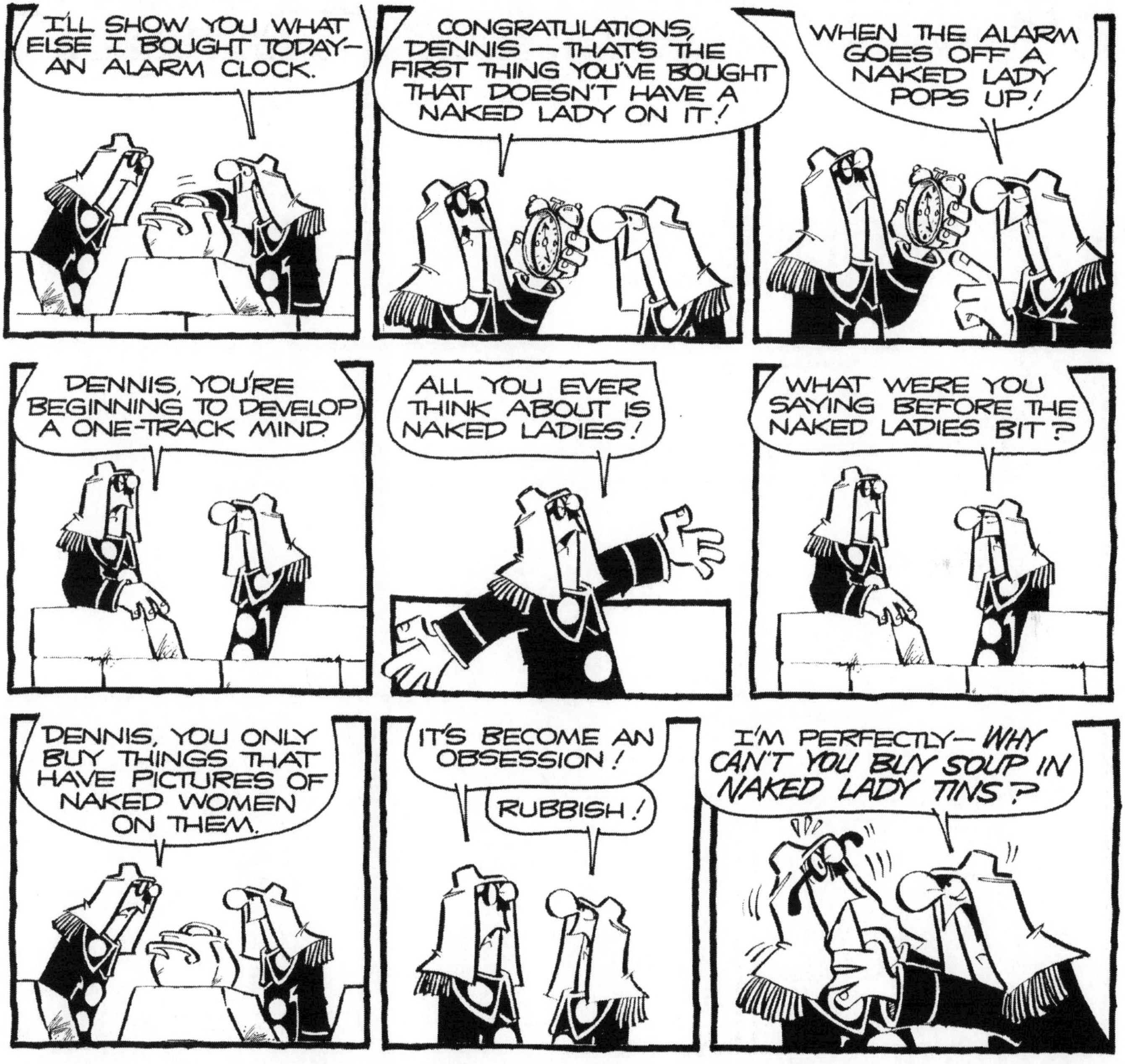

I'LL SHOW YOU WHAT ELSE I BOUGHT TODAY— AN ALARM CLOCK.
CONGRATULATIONS, DENNIS — THAT'S THE FIRST THING YOU'VE BOUGHT THAT DOESN'T HAVE A NAKED LADY ON IT!
WHEN THE ALARM GOES OFF A NAKED LADY POPS UP!
DENNIS, YOU'RE BEGINNING TO DEVELOP A ONE-TRACK MIND.
ALL YOU EVER THINK ABOUT IS NAKED LADIES!
WHAT WERE YOU SAYING BEFORE THE NAKED LADIES BIT?
DENNIS, YOU ONLY BUY THINGS THAT HAVE PICTURES OF NAKED WOMEN ON THEM.
IT'S BECOME AN OBSESSION!
RUBBISH!
I'M PERFECTLY— *WHY CAN'T YOU BUY SOUP IN NAKED LADY TINS?*

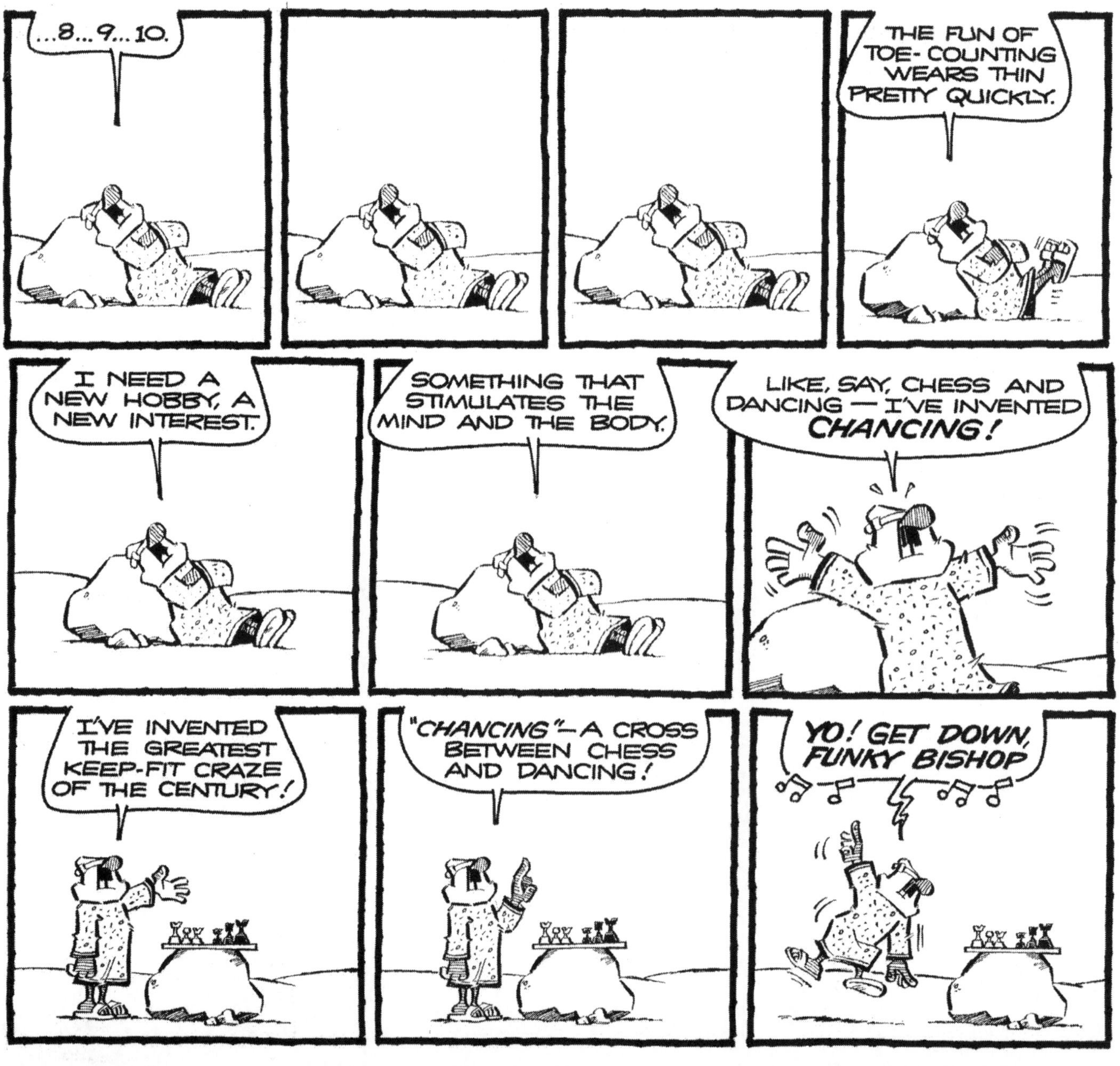
...8...9...10.
THE FUN OF TOE-COUNTING WEARS THIN PRETTY QUICKLY.
I NEED A NEW HOBBY, A NEW INTEREST.
SOMETHING THAT STIMULATES THE MIND AND THE BODY.
LIKE, SAY, CHESS AND DANCING — I'VE INVENTED *CHANCING!*
I'VE INVENTED THE GREATEST KEEP-FIT CRAZE OF THE CENTURY!
"*CHANCING*"— A CROSS BETWEEN CHESS AND DANCING!
YO! GET DOWN, FUNKY BISHOP

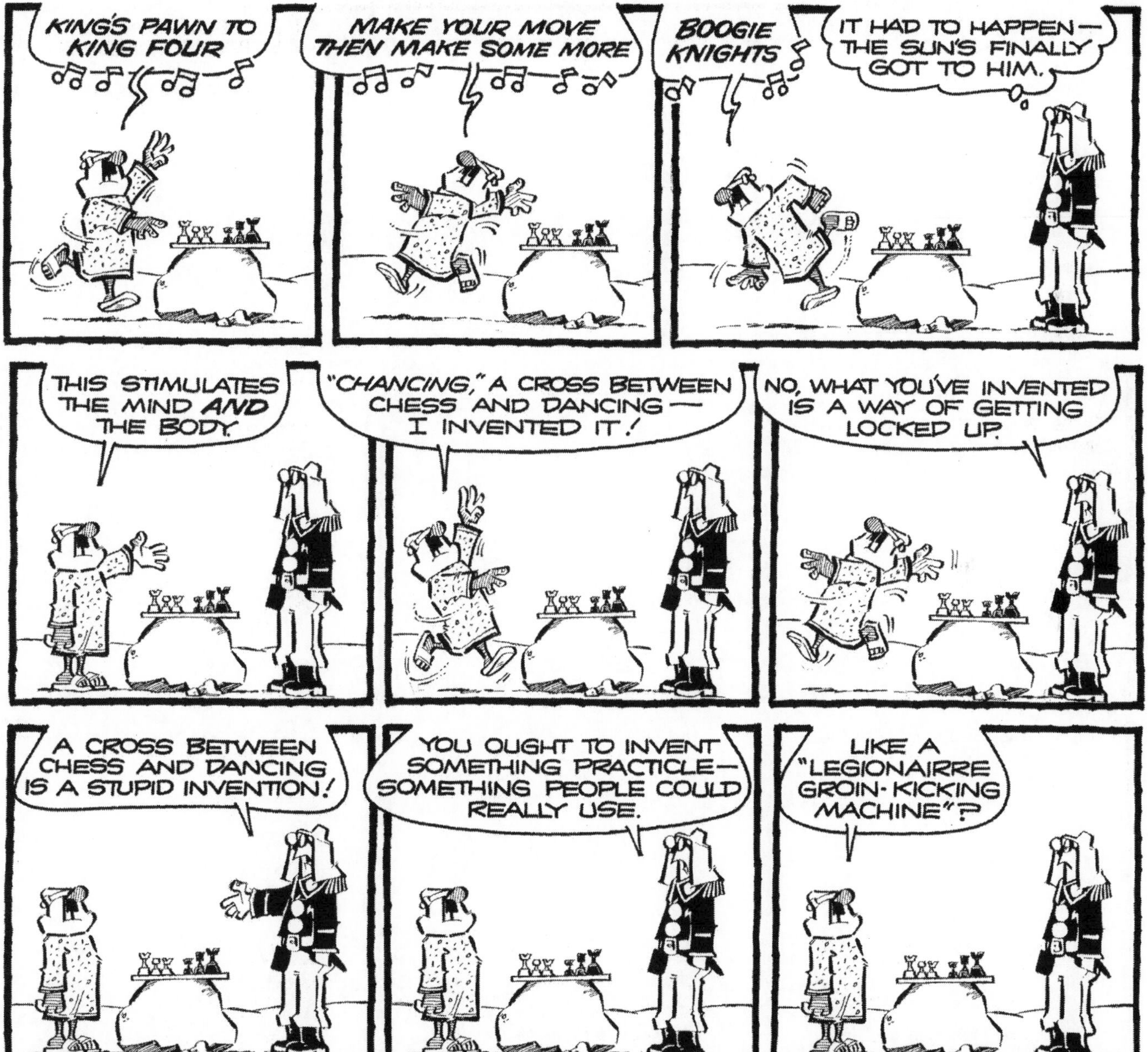

KING'S PAWN TO KING FOUR
MAKE YOUR MOVE THEN MAKE SOME MORE
BOOGIE KNIGHTS
IT HAD TO HAPPEN— THE SUN'S FINALLY GOT TO HIM.
THIS STIMULATES THE MIND AND THE BODY.
"CHANCING," A CROSS BETWEEN CHESS AND DANCING— I INVENTED IT!
NO, WHAT YOU'VE INVENTED IS A WAY OF GETTING LOCKED UP.
A CROSS BETWEEN CHESS AND DANCING IS A STUPID INVENTION!
YOU OUGHT TO INVENT SOMETHING PRACTICLE— SOMETHING PEOPLE COULD REALLY USE.
LIKE A "LEGIONAIRRE GROIN-KICKING MACHINE"?

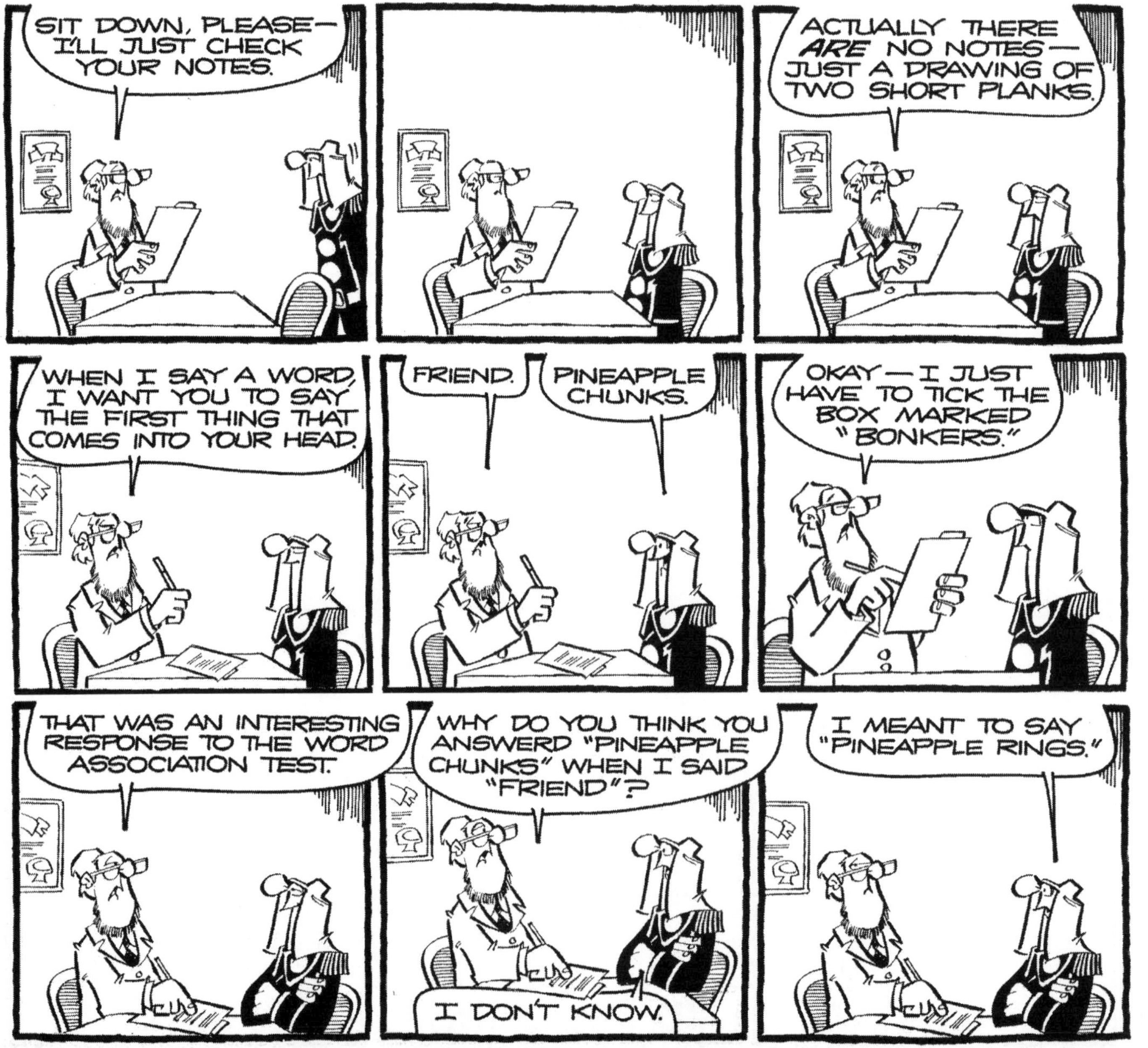
SIT DOWN, PLEASE— I'LL JUST CHECK YOUR NOTES.
ACTUALLY THERE *ARE* NO NOTES— JUST A DRAWING OF TWO SHORT PLANKS.
WHEN I SAY A WORD, I WANT YOU TO SAY THE FIRST THING THAT COMES INTO YOUR HEAD.
FRIEND.
PINEAPPLE CHUNKS.
OKAY — I JUST HAVE TO TICK THE BOX MARKED "BONKERS."
THAT WAS AN INTERESTING RESPONSE TO THE WORD ASSOCIATION TEST.
WHY DO YOU THINK YOU ANSWERED "PINEAPPLE CHUNKS" WHEN I SAID "FRIEND"?
I DON'T KNOW.
I MEANT TO SAY "PINEAPPLE RINGS."

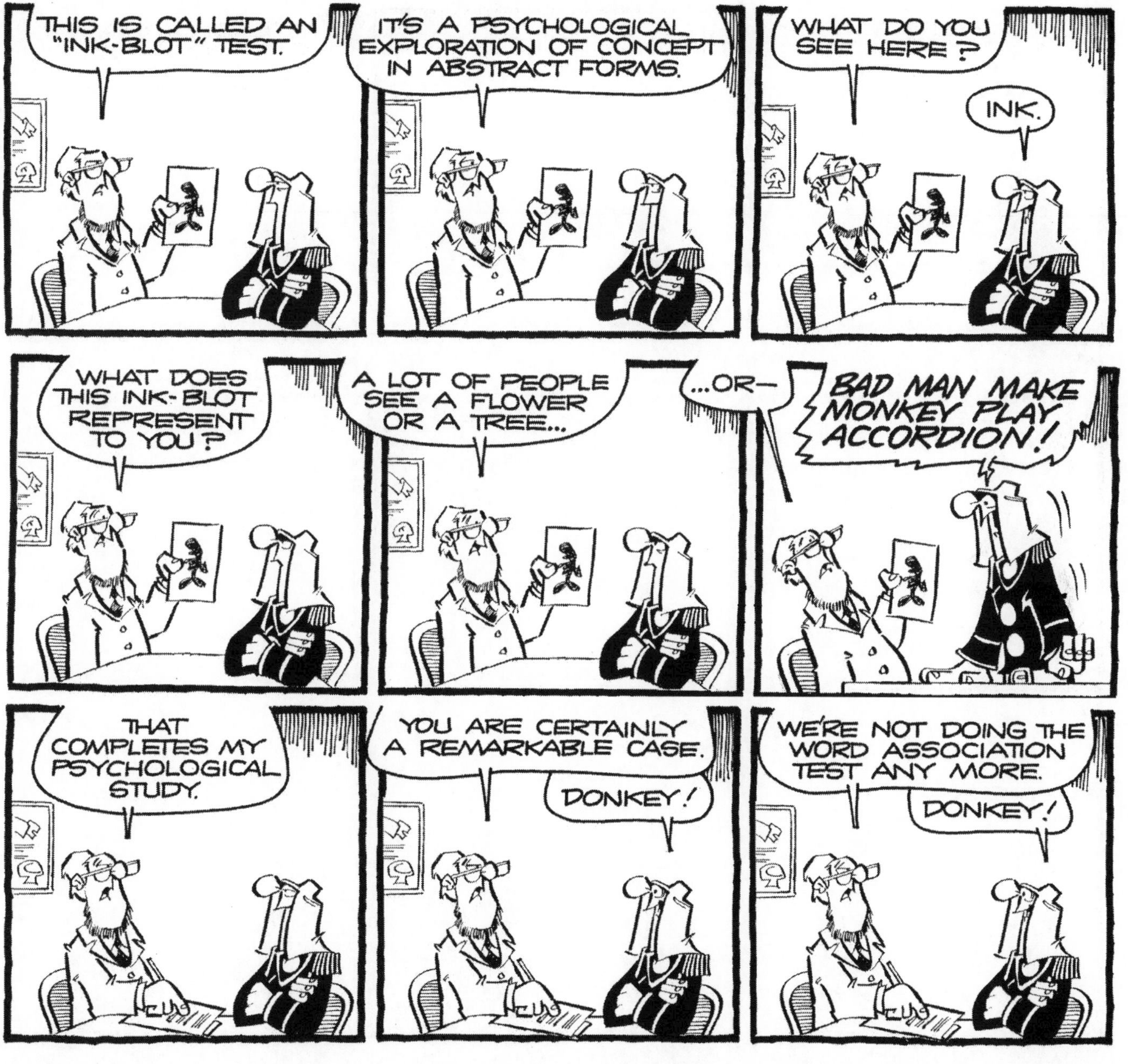
THIS IS CALLED AN "INK-BLOT" TEST.
IT'S A PSYCHOLOGICAL EXPLORATION OF CONCEPT IN ABSTRACT FORMS.
WHAT DO YOU SEE HERE ?
INK.
WHAT DOES THIS INK-BLOT REPRESENT TO YOU ?
A LOT OF PEOPLE SEE A FLOWER OR A TREE...
...OR—
BAD MAN MAKE MONKEY PLAY ACCORDION !
THAT COMPLETES MY PSYCHOLOGICAL STUDY.
YOU ARE CERTAINLY A REMARKABLE CASE.
DONKEY !
WE'RE NOT DOING THE WORD ASSOCIATION TEST ANY MORE.
DONKEY !

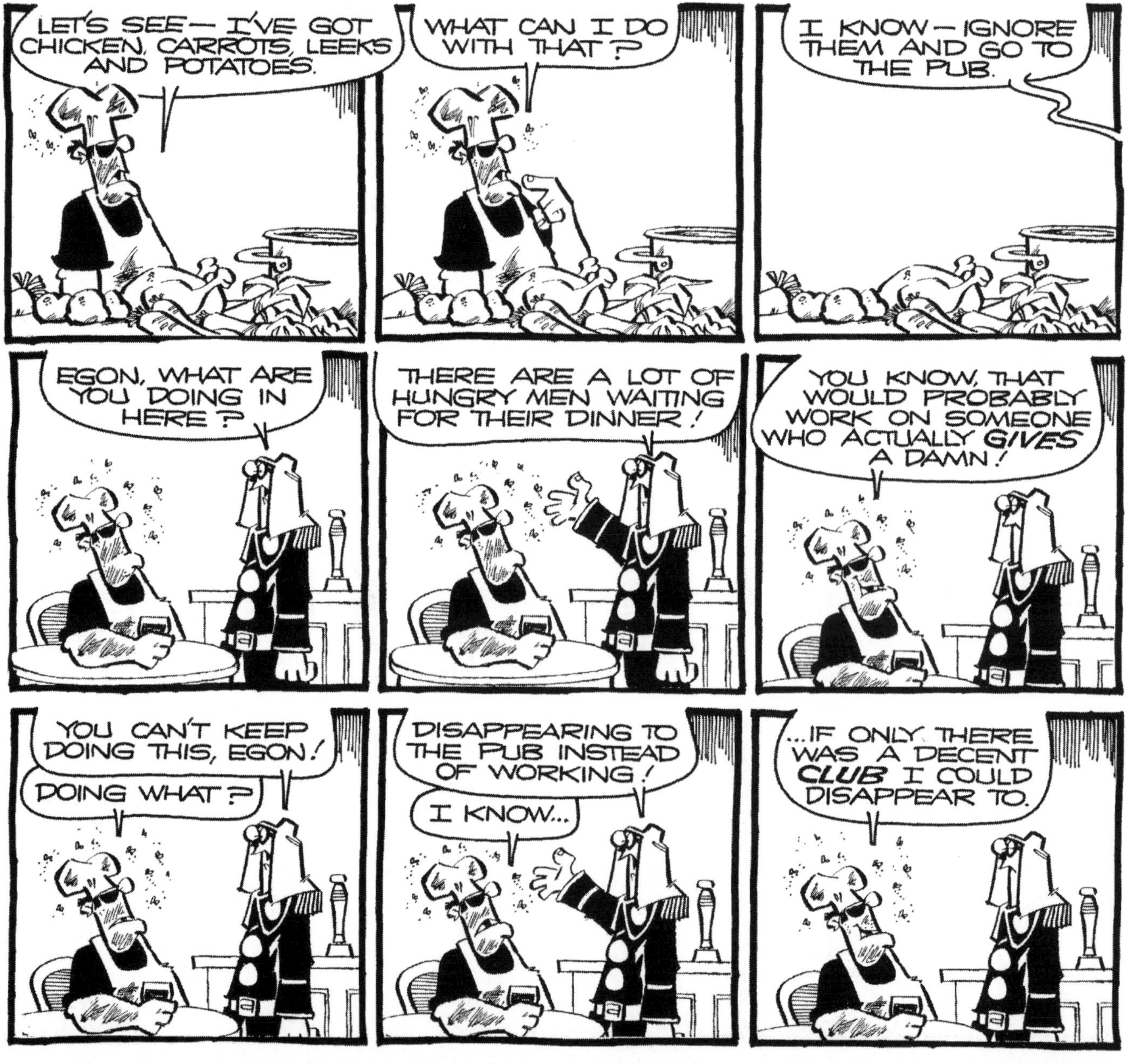
LET'S SEE— I'VE GOT CHICKEN, CARROTS, LEEKS AND POTATOES.
WHAT CAN I DO WITH THAT?
I KNOW— IGNORE THEM AND GO TO THE PUB.
EGON, WHAT ARE YOU DOING IN HERE?
THERE ARE A LOT OF HUNGRY MEN WAITING FOR THEIR DINNER!
YOU KNOW, THAT WOULD PROBABLY WORK ON SOMEONE WHO ACTUALLY GIVES A DAMN!
YOU CAN'T KEEP DOING THIS, EGON!
DOING WHAT?
DISAPPEARING TO THE PUB INSTEAD OF WORKING!
I KNOW...
...IF ONLY THERE WAS A DECENT CLUB I COULD DISAPPEAR TO.

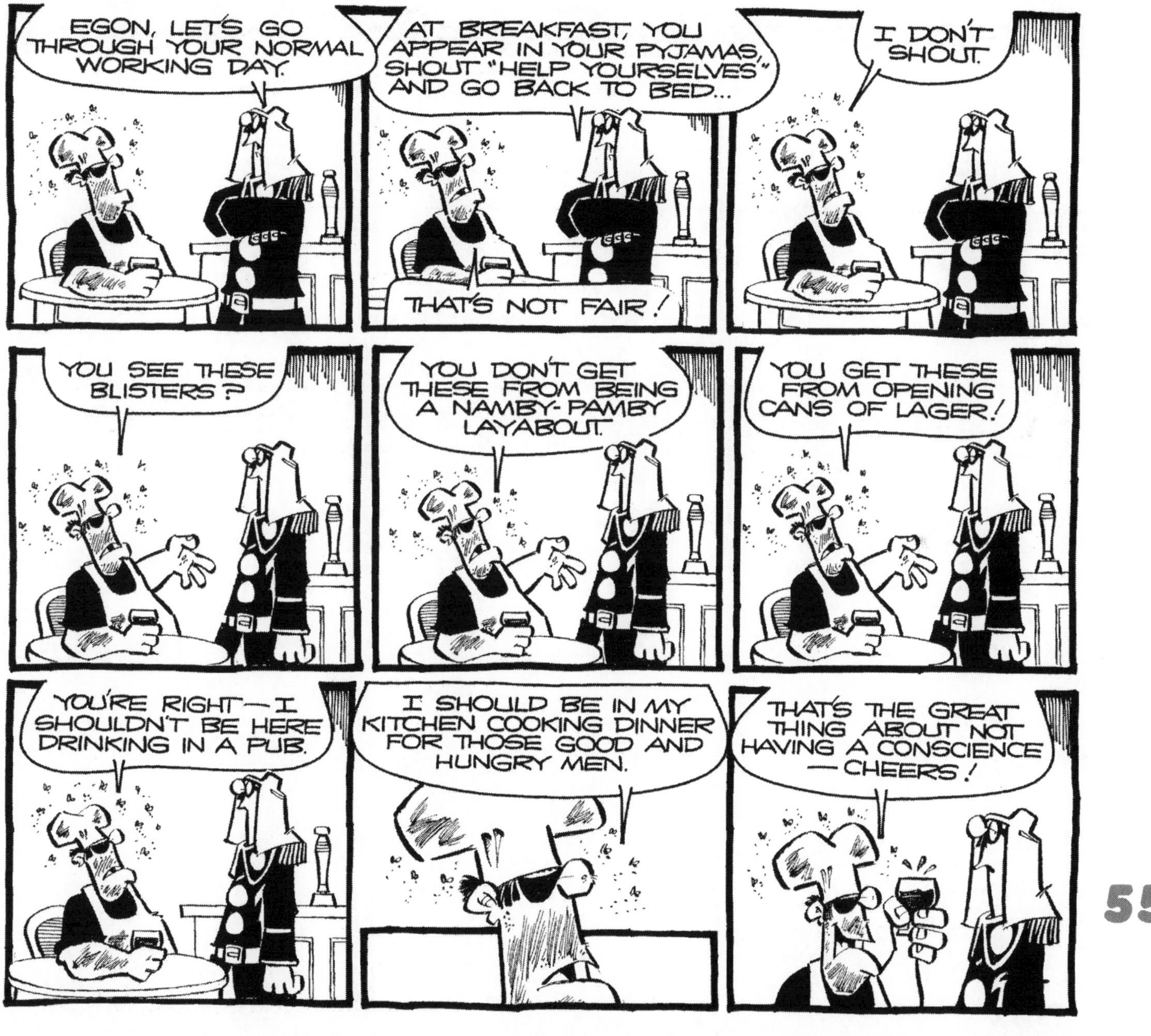
EGON, LET'S GO THROUGH YOUR NORMAL WORKING DAY.
AT BREAKFAST, YOU APPEAR IN YOUR PYJAMAS, SHOUT "HELP YOURSELVES" AND GO BACK TO BED...
THAT'S NOT FAIR!
I DON'T SHOUT.
YOU SEE THESE BLISTERS?
YOU DON'T GET THESE FROM BEING A NAMBY-PAMBY LAYABOUT.
YOU GET THESE FROM OPENING CANS OF LAGER!
YOU'RE RIGHT — I SHOULDN'T BE HERE DRINKING IN A PUB.
I SHOULD BE IN MY KITCHEN COOKING DINNER FOR THOSE GOOD AND HUNGRY MEN.
THAT'S THE GREAT THING ABOUT NOT HAVING A CONSCIENCE — CHEERS!

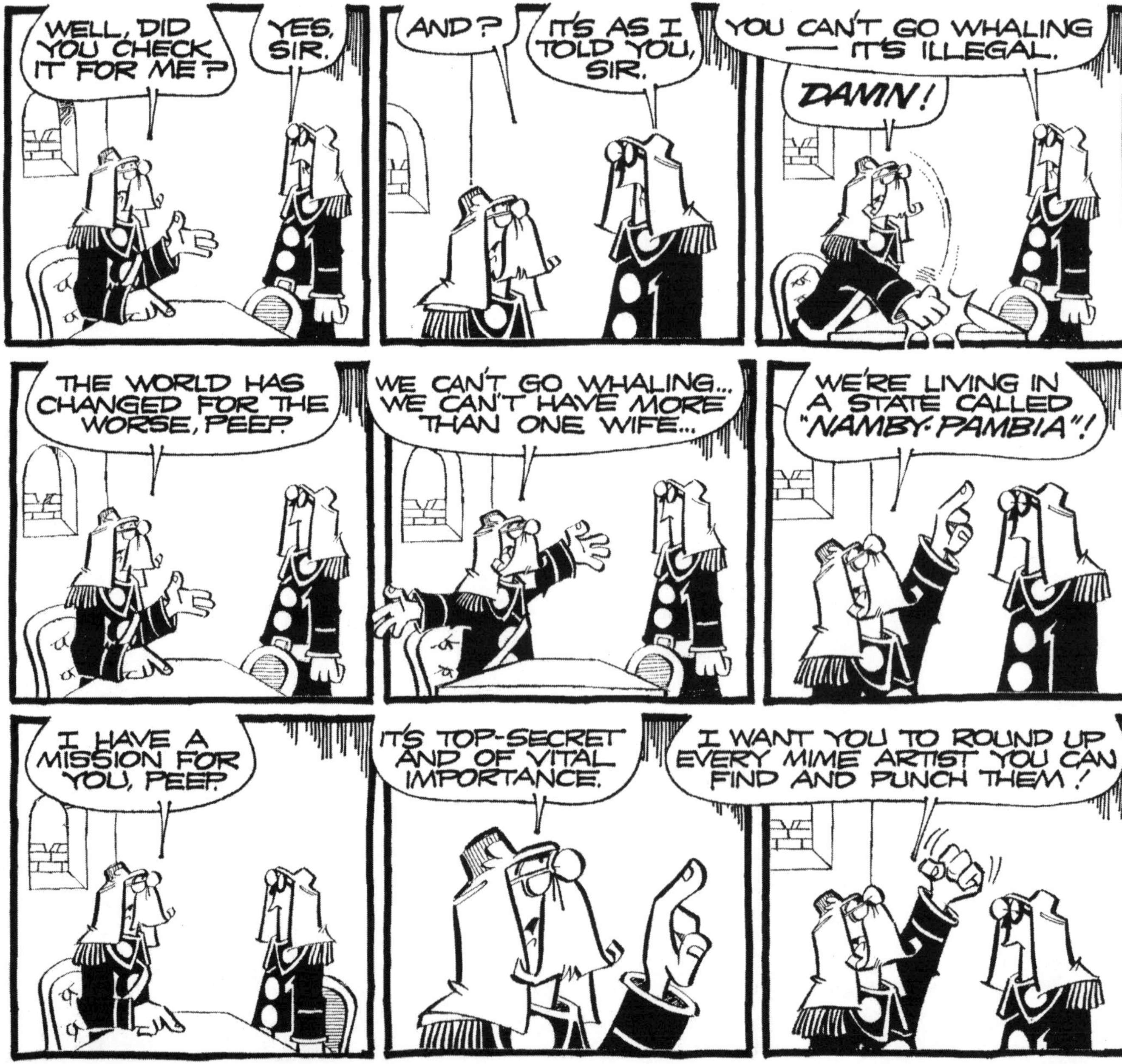
WELL, DID YOU CHECK IT FOR ME?
YES, SIR.
AND?
IT'S AS I TOLD YOU, SIR.
YOU CAN'T GO WHALING — IT'S ILLEGAL.
DAMN!
THE WORLD HAS CHANGED FOR THE WORSE, PEEP.
WE CAN'T GO WHALING... WE CAN'T HAVE MORE THAN ONE WIFE...
WE'RE LIVING IN A STATE CALLED "NAMBY-PAMBIA"!
I HAVE A MISSION FOR YOU, PEEP.
IT'S TOP-SECRET AND OF VITAL IMPORTANCE.
I WANT YOU TO ROUND UP EVERY MIME ARTIST YOU CAN FIND AND PUNCH THEM!

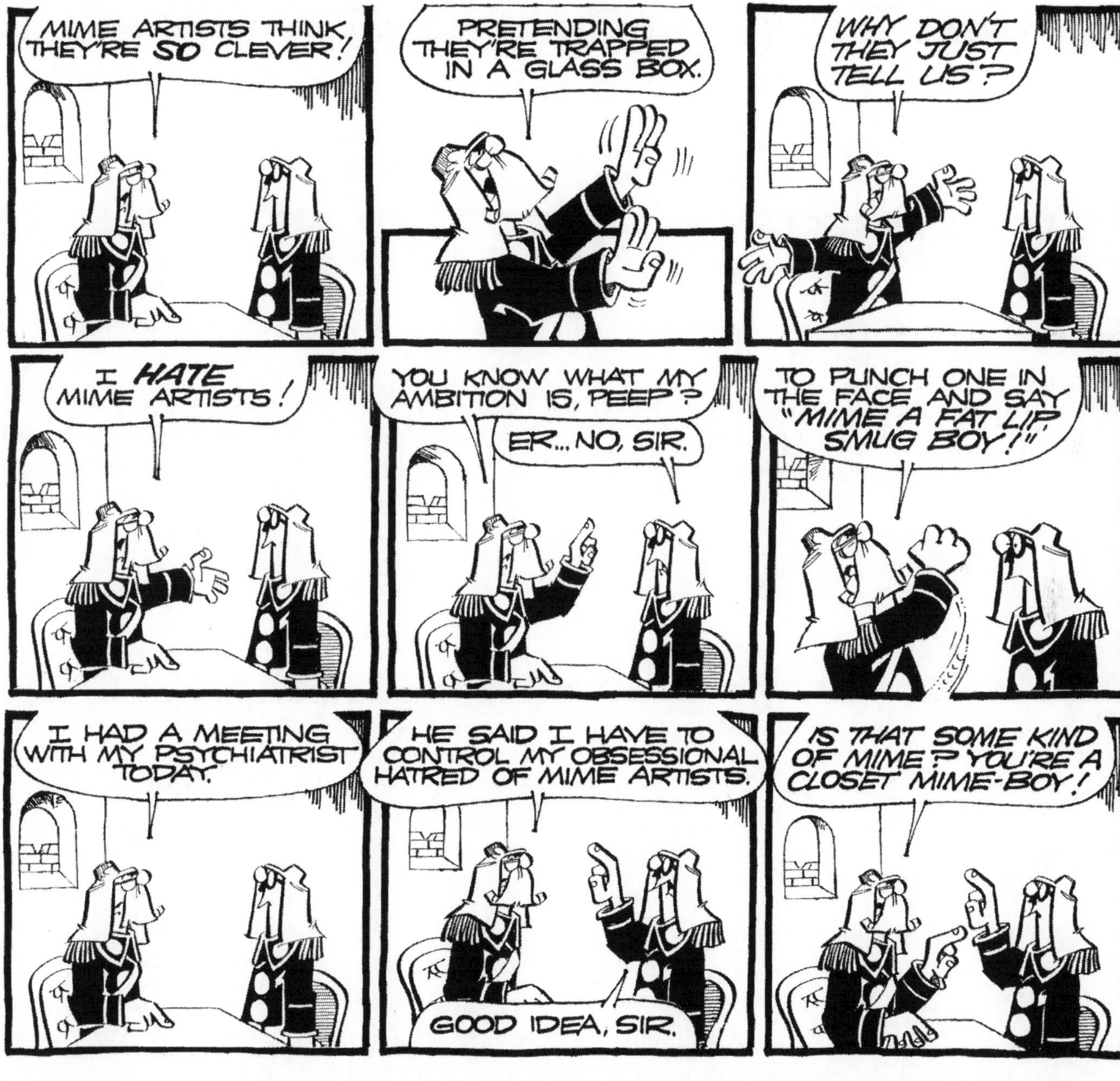
MIME ARTISTS THINK THEY'RE SO CLEVER!
PRETENDING THEY'RE TRAPPED IN A GLASS BOX.
WHY DON'T THEY JUST TELL US?
I HATE MIME ARTISTS!
YOU KNOW WHAT MY AMBITION IS, PEEP?
ER... NO, SIR.
TO PUNCH ONE IN THE FACE AND SAY "MIME A FAT LIP, SMUG BOY!"
I HAD A MEETING WITH MY PSYCHIATRIST TODAY.
HE SAID I HAVE TO CONTROL MY OBSESSIONAL HATRED OF MIME ARTISTS.
GOOD IDEA, SIR.
IS THAT SOME KIND OF MIME? YOU'RE A CLOSET MIME-BOY!

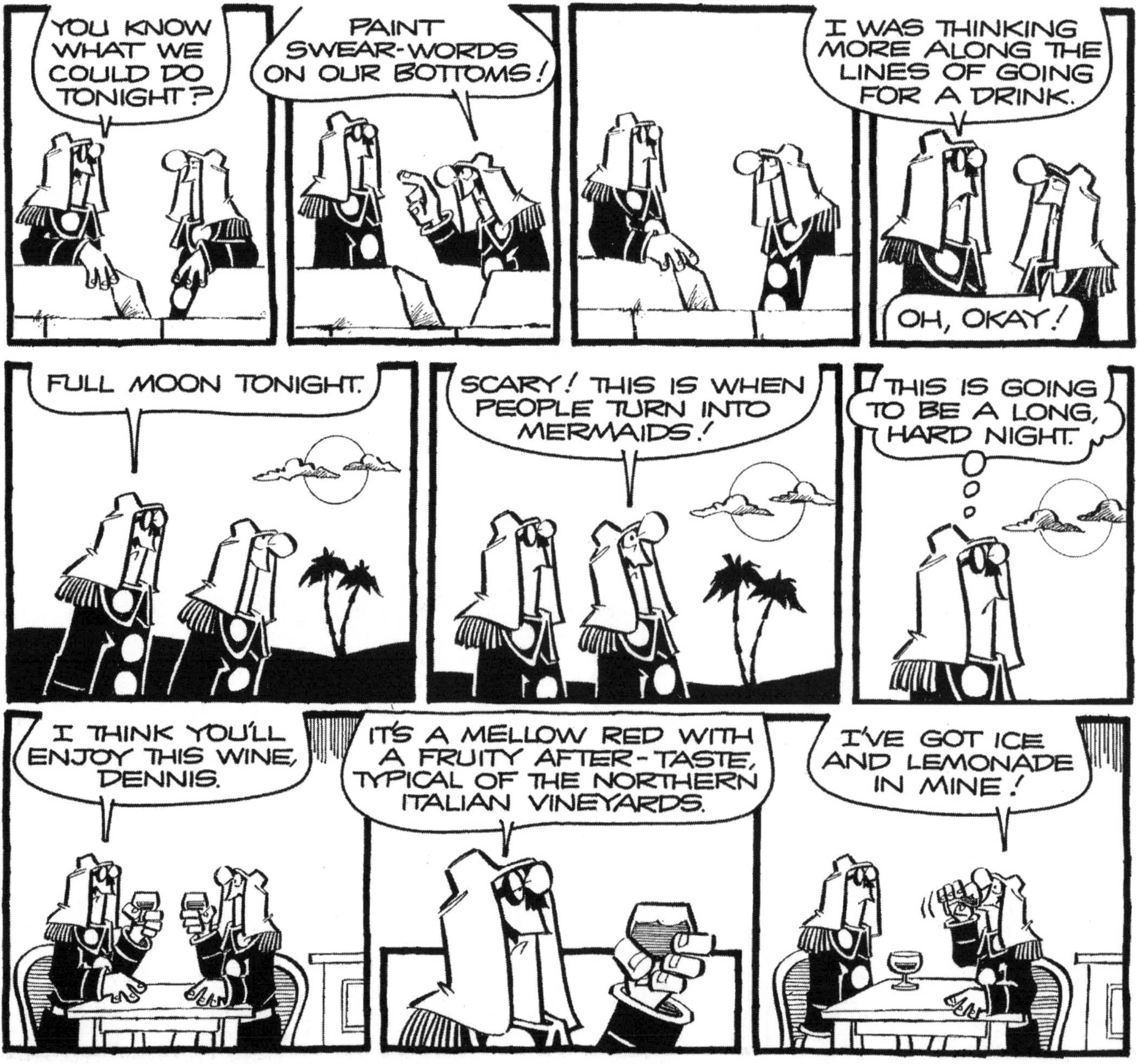
YOU KNOW WHAT WE COULD DO TONIGHT?
PAINT SWEAR-WORDS ON OUR BOTTOMS!
I WAS THINKING MORE ALONG THE LINES OF GOING FOR A DRINK.
OH, OKAY!
FULL MOON TONIGHT.
SCARY! THIS IS WHEN PEOPLE TURN INTO MERMAIDS!
THIS IS GOING TO BE A LONG, HARD NIGHT.
I THINK YOU'LL ENJOY THIS WINE, DENNIS.
IT'S A MELLOW RED WITH A FRUITY AFTER-TASTE, TYPICAL OF THE NORTHERN ITALIAN VINEYARDS.
I'VE GOT ICE AND LEMONADE IN MINE!

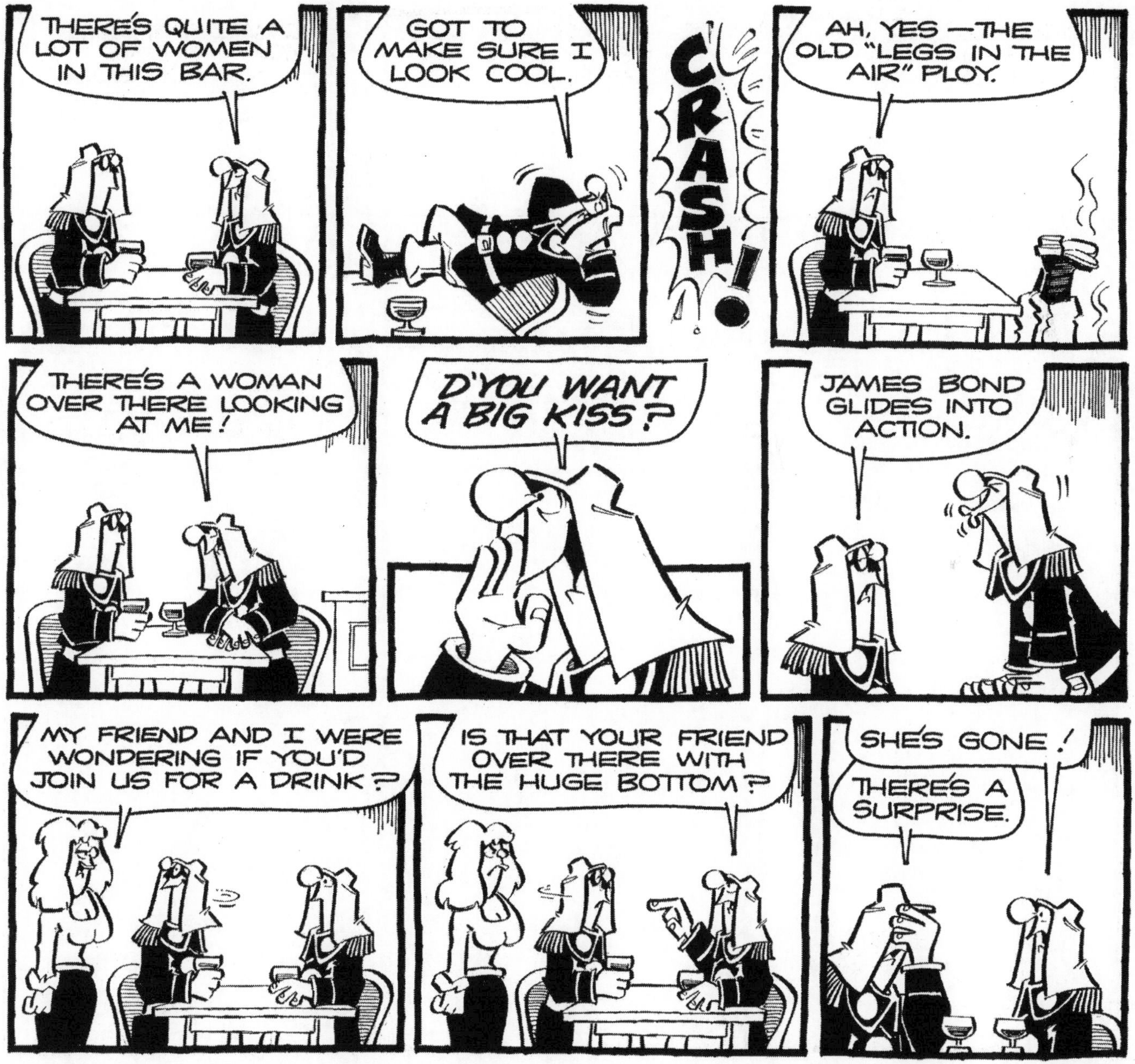
THERE'S QUITE A LOT OF WOMEN IN THIS BAR.
GOT TO MAKE SURE I LOOK COOL.
CRASH!
AH, YES—THE OLD "LEGS IN THE AIR" PLOY.
THERE'S A WOMAN OVER THERE LOOKING AT ME!
D'YOU WANT A BIG KISS?
JAMES BOND GLIDES INTO ACTION.
MY FRIEND AND I WERE WONDERING IF YOU'D JOIN US FOR A DRINK?
IS THAT YOUR FRIEND OVER THERE WITH THE HUGE BOTTOM?
SHE'S GONE!
THERE'S A SURPRISE.

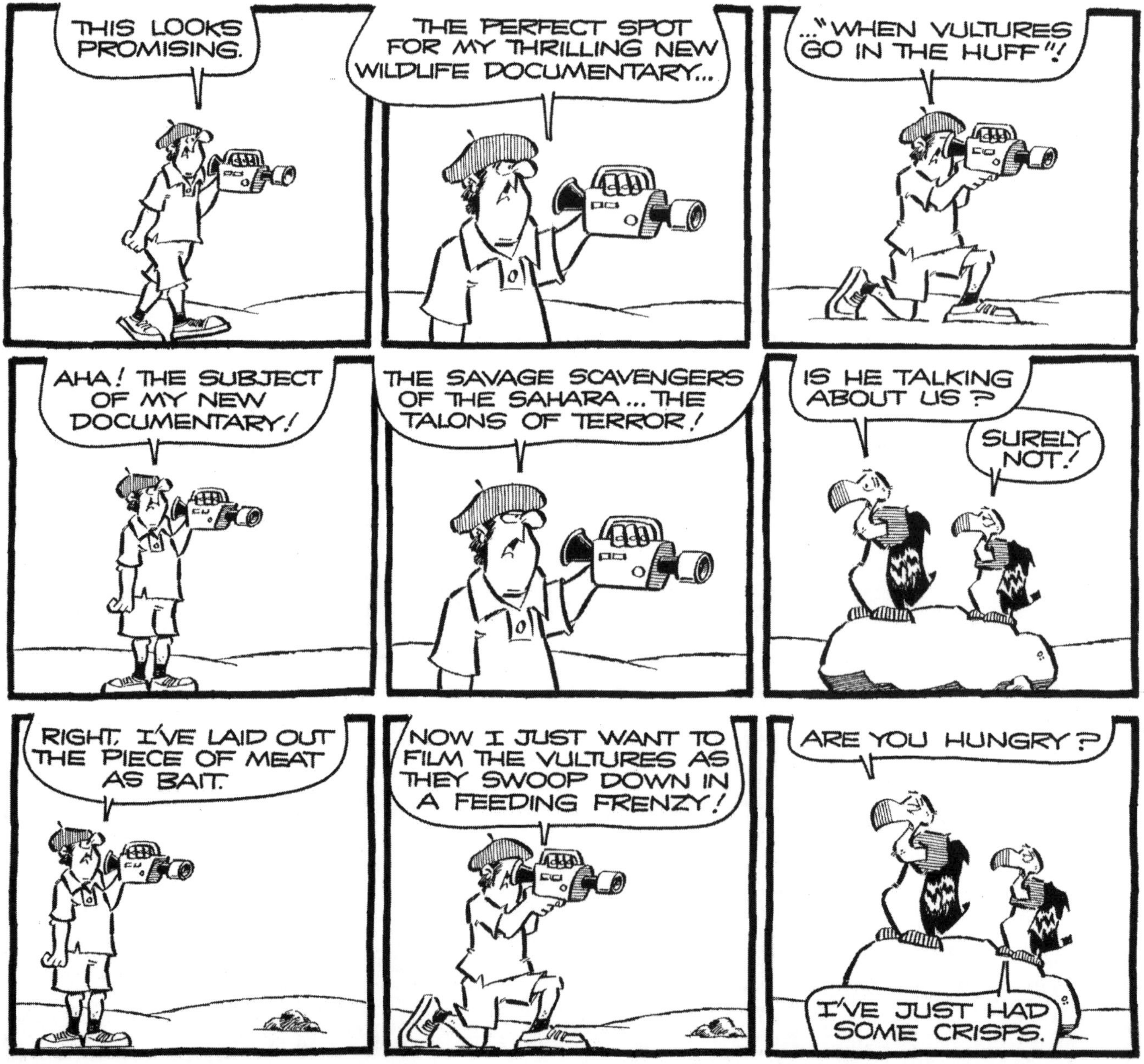

THIS LOOKS PROMISING.
THE PERFECT SPOT FOR MY THRILLING NEW WILDLIFE DOCUMENTARY...
..."WHEN VULTURES GO IN THE HUFF"!
AHA! THE SUBJECT OF MY NEW DOCUMENTARY!
THE SAVAGE SCAVENGERS OF THE SAHARA... THE TALONS OF TERROR!
IS HE TALKING ABOUT US?
SURELY NOT!
RIGHT, I'VE LAID OUT THE PIECE OF MEAT AS BAIT.
NOW I JUST WANT TO FILM THE VULTURES AS THEY SWOOP DOWN IN A FEEDING FRENZY!
ARE YOU HUNGRY?
I'VE JUST HAD SOME CRISPS.

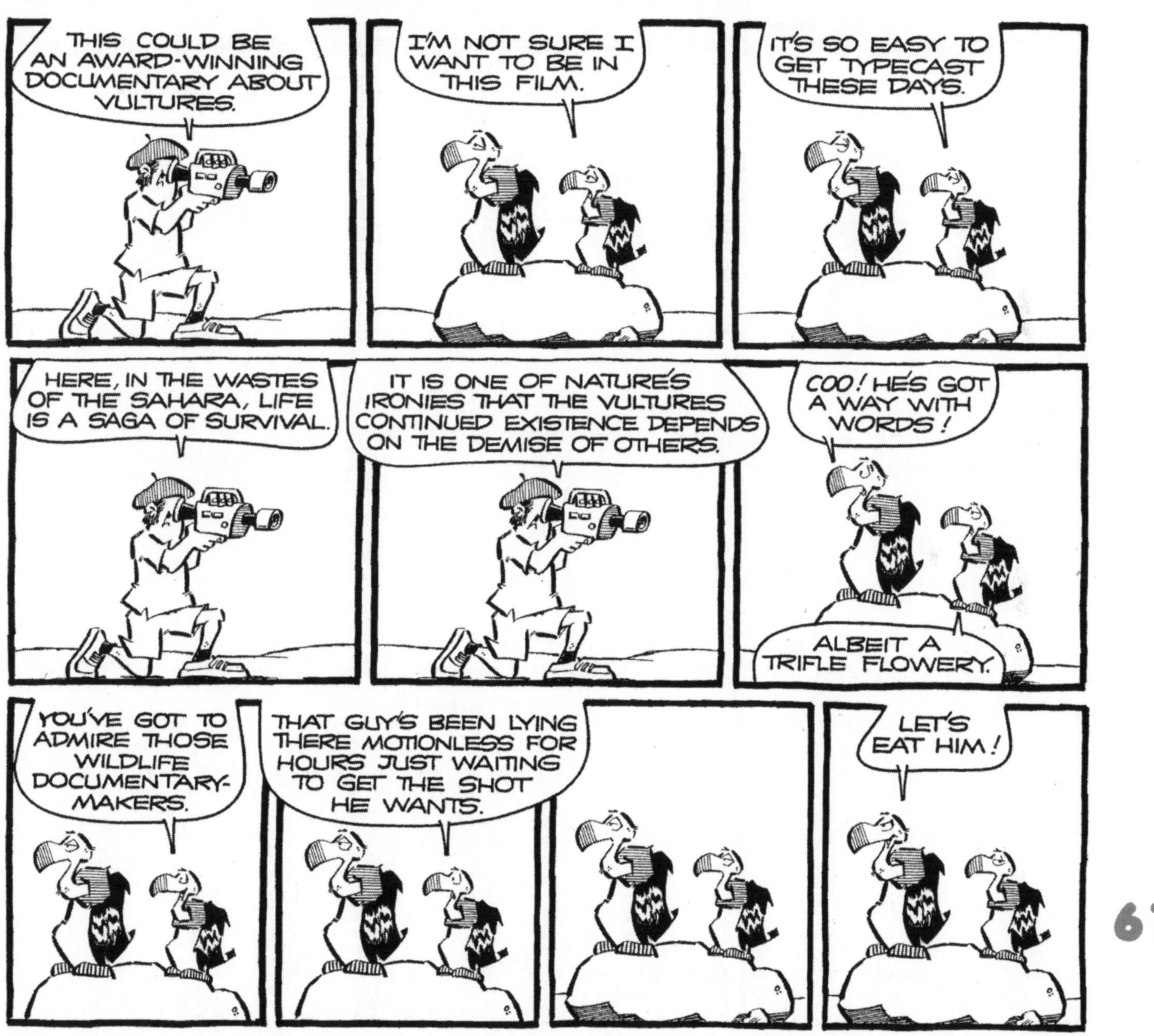
THIS COULD BE AN AWARD-WINNING DOCUMENTARY ABOUT VULTURES.
I'M NOT SURE I WANT TO BE IN THIS FILM.
IT'S SO EASY TO GET TYPECAST THESE DAYS.
HERE, IN THE WASTES OF THE SAHARA, LIFE IS A SAGA OF SURVIVAL.
IT IS ONE OF NATURE'S IRONIES THAT THE VULTURES CONTINUED EXISTENCE DEPENDS ON THE DEMISE OF OTHERS.
COO! HE'S GOT A WAY WITH WORDS!
ALBEIT A TRIFLE FLOWERY.
YOU'VE GOT TO ADMIRE THOSE WILDLIFE DOCUMENTARY-MAKERS.
THAT GUY'S BEEN LYING THERE MOTIONLESS FOR HOURS JUST WAITING TO GET THE SHOT HE WANTS.
LET'S EAT HIM!

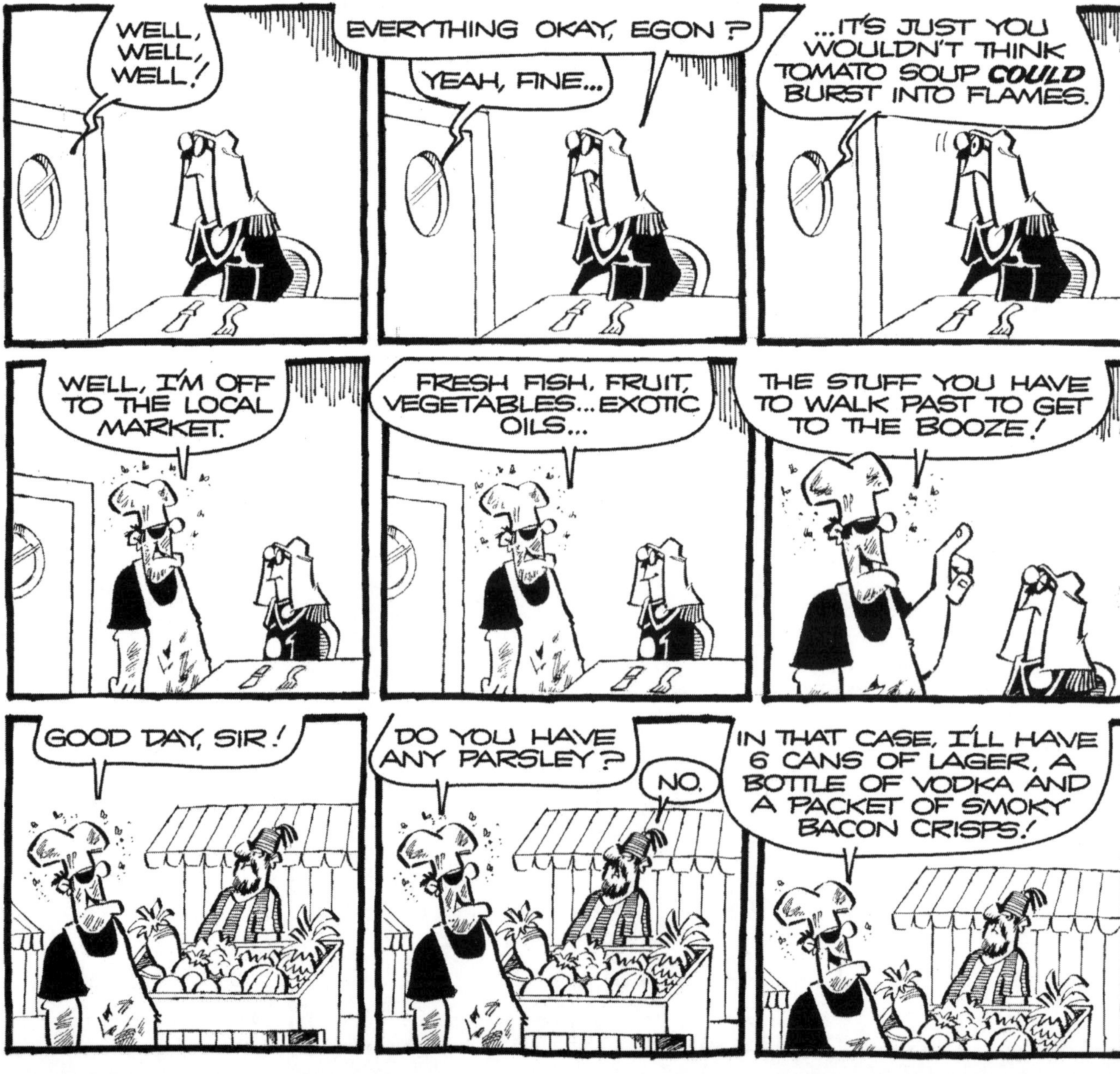
WELL, WELL, WELL!
EVERYTHING OKAY, EGON?
YEAH, FINE...
...IT'S JUST YOU WOULDN'T THINK TOMATO SOUP **COULD** BURST INTO FLAMES.
WELL, I'M OFF TO THE LOCAL MARKET.
FRESH FISH, FRUIT, VEGETABLES... EXOTIC OILS...
THE STUFF YOU HAVE TO WALK PAST TO GET TO THE BOOZE!
GOOD DAY, SIR!
DO YOU HAVE ANY PARSLEY?
NO.
IN THAT CASE, I'LL HAVE 6 CANS OF LAGER, A BOTTLE OF VODKA AND A PACKET OF SMOKY BACON CRISPS!

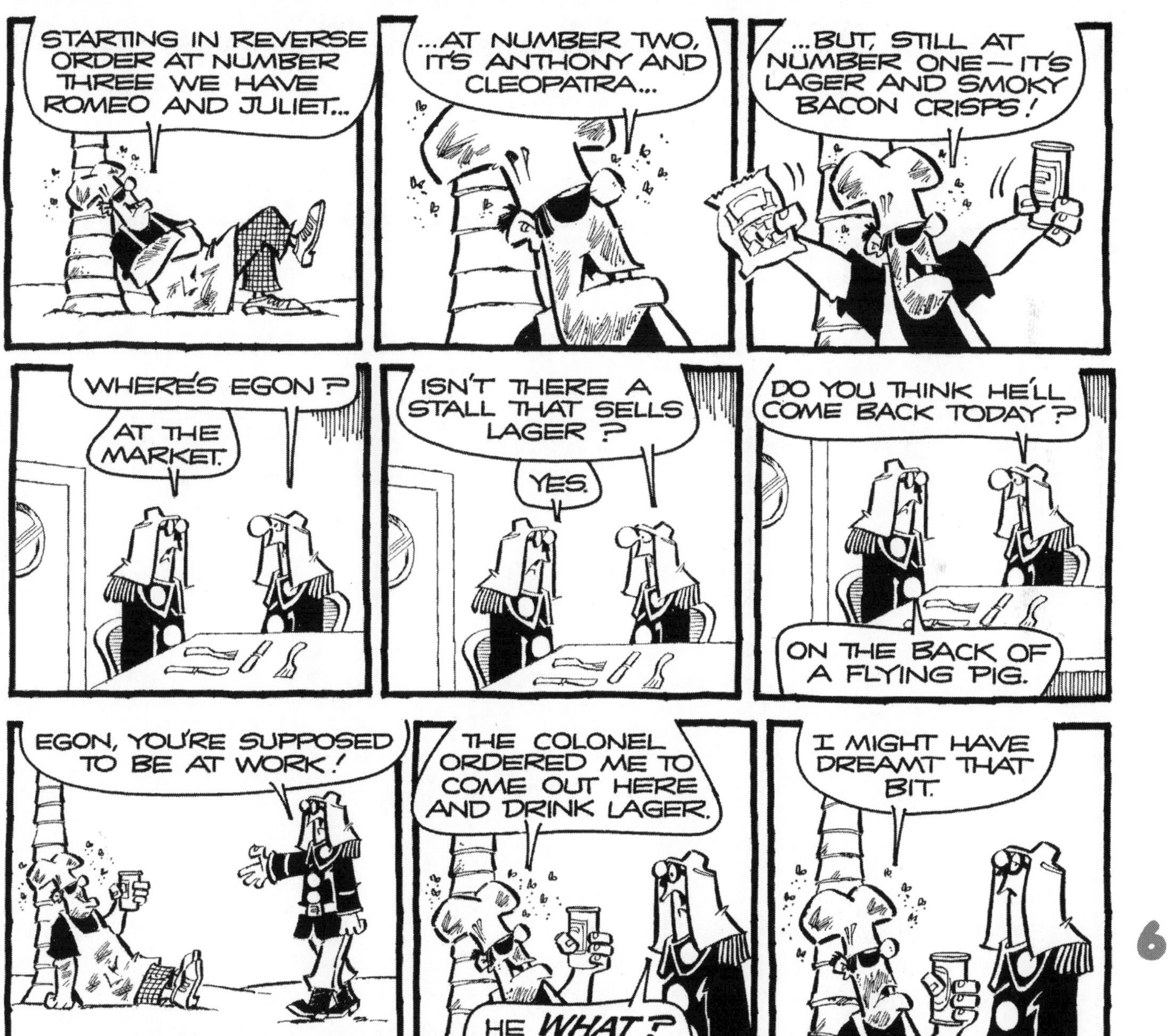
STARTING IN REVERSE ORDER AT NUMBER THREE WE HAVE ROMEO AND JULIET...
...AT NUMBER TWO, IT'S ANTHONY AND CLEOPATRA...
...BUT, STILL AT NUMBER ONE—IT'S LAGER AND SMOKY BACON CRISPS!
WHERE'S EGON?
AT THE MARKET.
ISN'T THERE A STALL THAT SELLS LAGER?
YES.
DO YOU THINK HE'LL COME BACK TODAY?
ON THE BACK OF A FLYING PIG.
EGON, YOU'RE SUPPOSED TO BE AT WORK!
THE COLONEL ORDERED ME TO COME OUT HERE AND DRINK LAGER.
HE *WHAT*?
I MIGHT HAVE DREAMT THAT BIT.

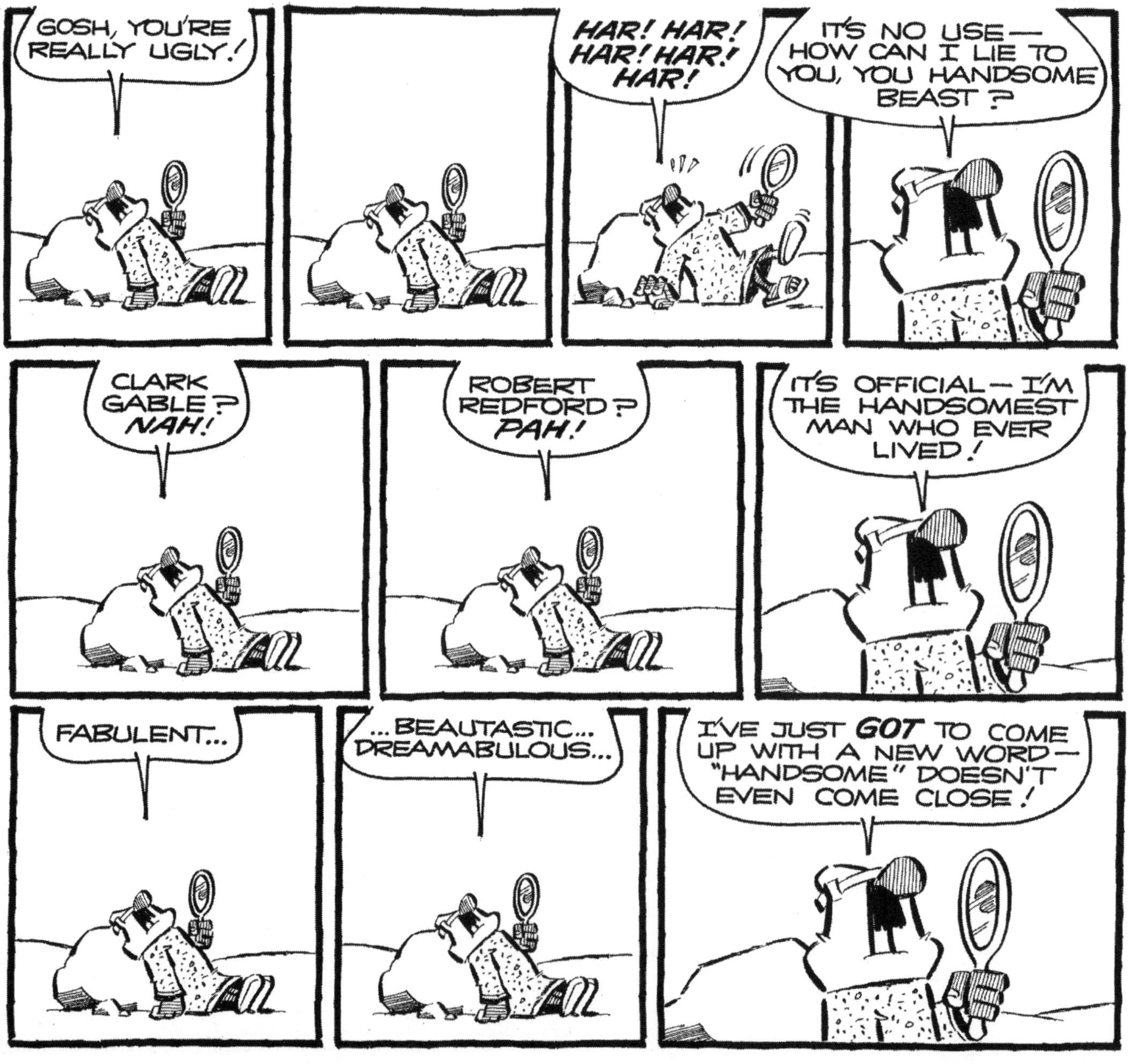
GOSH, YOU'RE REALLY UGLY!
HAR! HAR! HAR! HAR! HAR!
IT'S NO USE— HOW CAN I LIE TO YOU, YOU HANDSOME BEAST?
CLARK GABLE? NAH!
ROBERT REDFORD? PAH!
IT'S OFFICIAL—I'M THE HANDSOMEST MAN WHO EVER LIVED!
FABULENT...
...BEAUTASTIC... DREAMABULOUS...
I'VE JUST GOT TO COME UP WITH A NEW WORD— "HANDSOME" DOESN'T EVEN COME CLOSE!

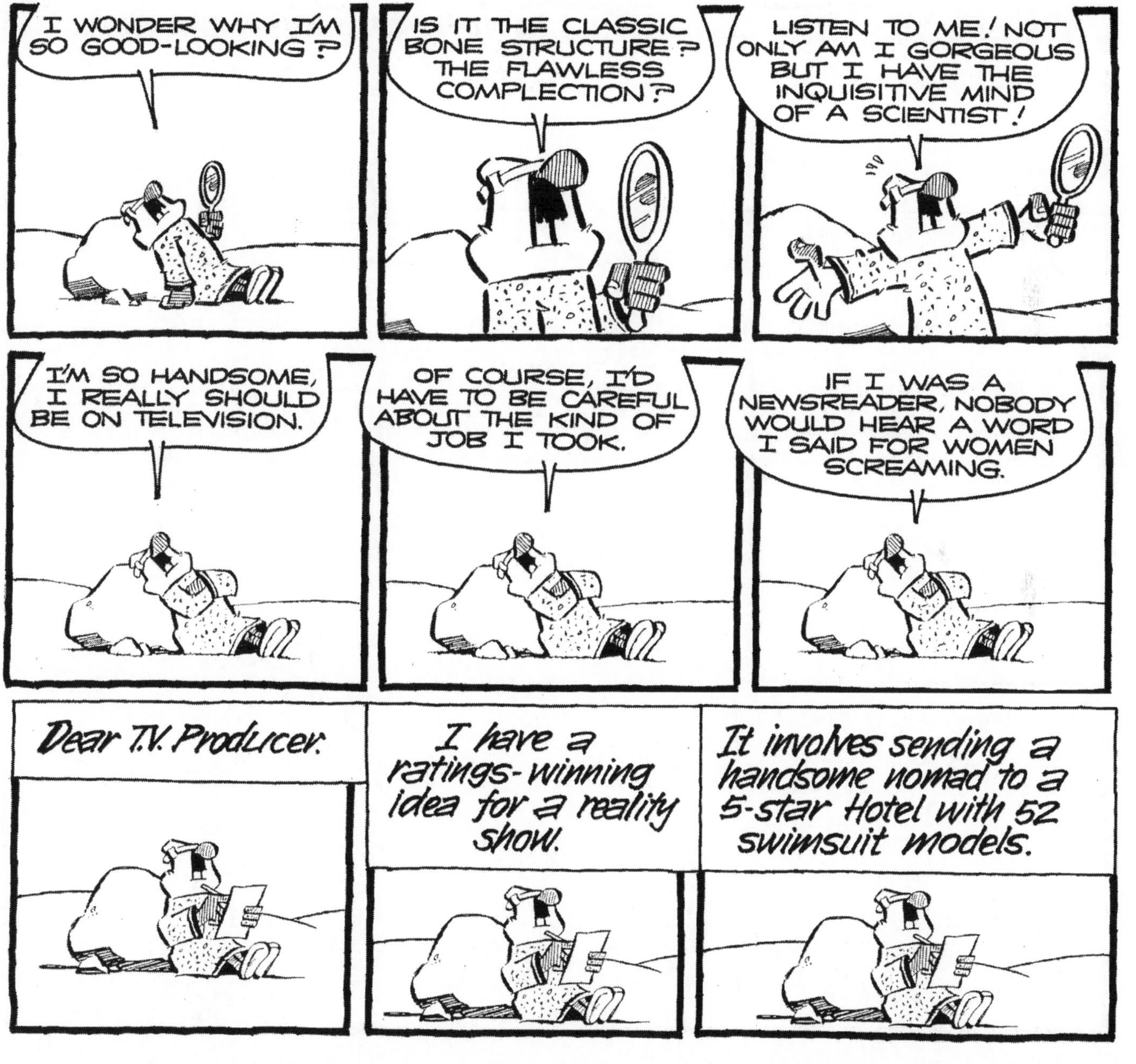
I WONDER WHY I'M SO GOOD-LOOKING?
IS IT THE CLASSIC BONE STRUCTURE? THE FLAWLESS COMPLECTION?
LISTEN TO ME! NOT ONLY AM I GORGEOUS BUT I HAVE THE INQUISITIVE MIND OF A SCIENTIST!
I'M SO HANDSOME, I REALLY SHOULD BE ON TELEVISION.
OF COURSE, I'D HAVE TO BE CAREFUL ABOUT THE KIND OF JOB I TOOK.
IF I WAS A NEWSREADER, NOBODY WOULD HEAR A WORD I SAID FOR WOMEN SCREAMING.
Dear T.V. Producer:
I have a ratings-winning idea for a reality show.
It involves sending a handsome nomad to a 5-star Hotel with 52 swimsuit models.

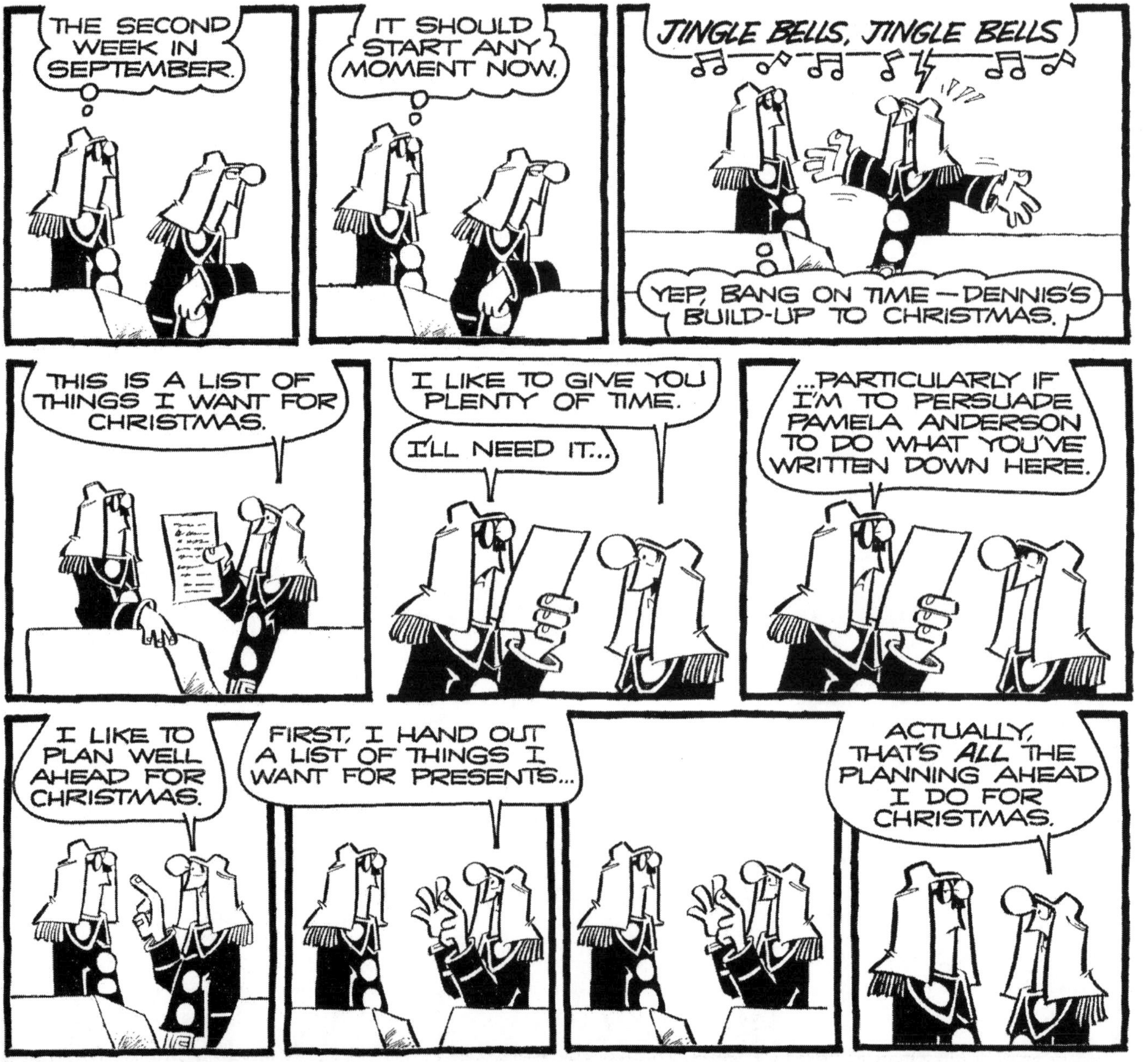
THE SECOND WEEK IN SEPTEMBER.
IT SHOULD START ANY MOMENT NOW.
JINGLE BELLS, JINGLE BELLS
YEP, BANG ON TIME — DENNIS'S BUILD-UP TO CHRISTMAS.
THIS IS A LIST OF THINGS I WANT FOR CHRISTMAS.
I LIKE TO GIVE YOU PLENTY OF TIME.
I'LL NEED IT...
...PARTICULARLY IF I'M TO PERSUADE PAMELA ANDERSON TO DO WHAT YOU'VE WRITTEN DOWN HERE.
I LIKE TO PLAN WELL AHEAD FOR CHRISTMAS.
FIRST, I HAND OUT A LIST OF THINGS I WANT FOR PRESENTS...
ACTUALLY, THAT'S *ALL* THE PLANNING AHEAD I DO FOR CHRISTMAS.

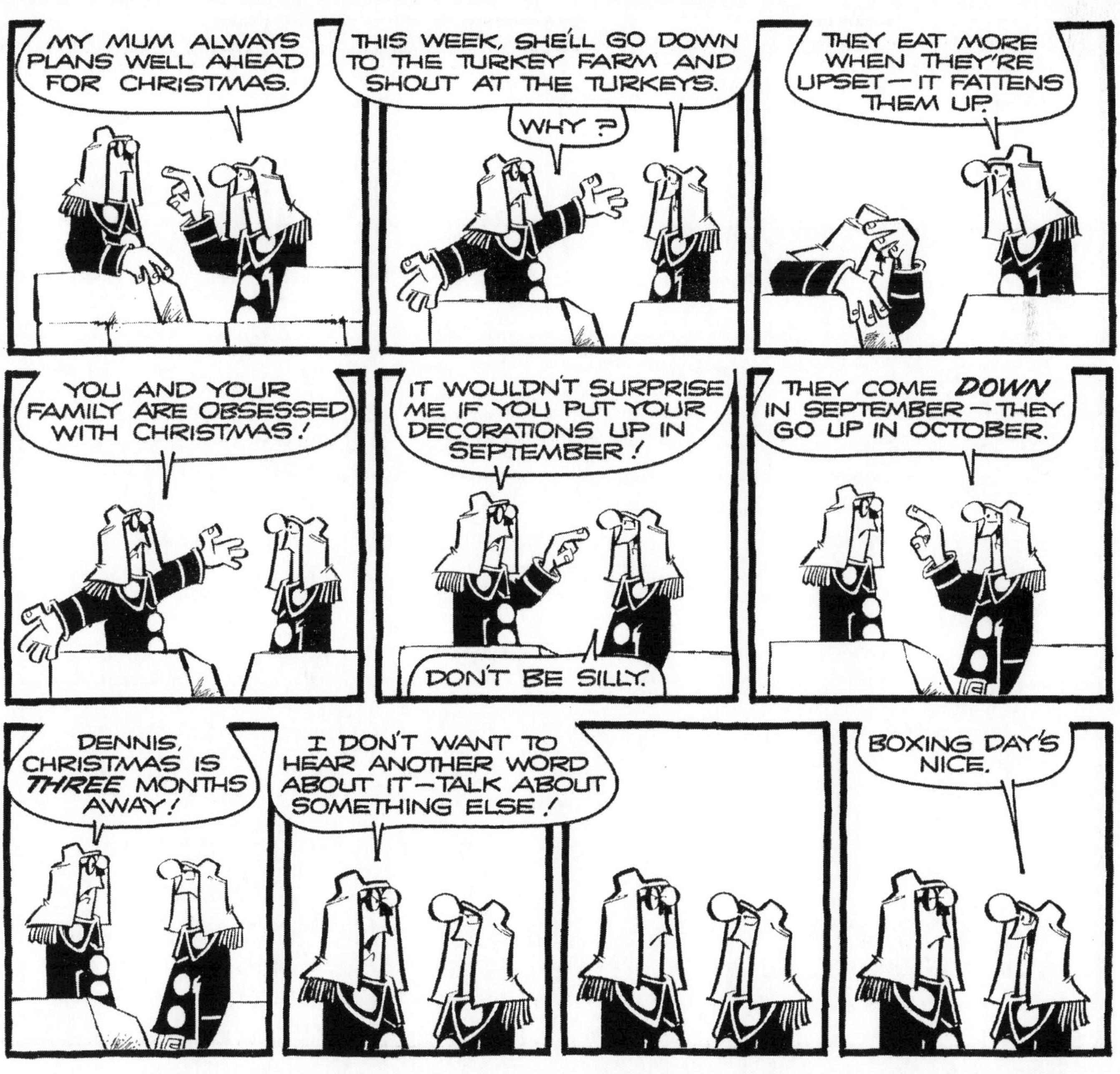
MY MUM ALWAYS PLANS WELL AHEAD FOR CHRISTMAS.
THIS WEEK, SHE'LL GO DOWN TO THE TURKEY FARM AND SHOUT AT THE TURKEYS.
WHY ?
THEY EAT MORE WHEN THEY'RE UPSET — IT FATTENS THEM UP.
YOU AND YOUR FAMILY ARE OBSESSED WITH CHRISTMAS !
IT WOULDN'T SURPRISE ME IF YOU PUT YOUR DECORATIONS UP IN SEPTEMBER !
DON'T BE SILLY.
THEY COME *DOWN* IN SEPTEMBER — THEY GO UP IN OCTOBER.
DENNIS, CHRISTMAS IS *THREE* MONTHS AWAY !
I DON'T WANT TO HEAR ANOTHER WORD ABOUT IT — TALK ABOUT SOMETHING ELSE !
BOXING DAY'S NICE.

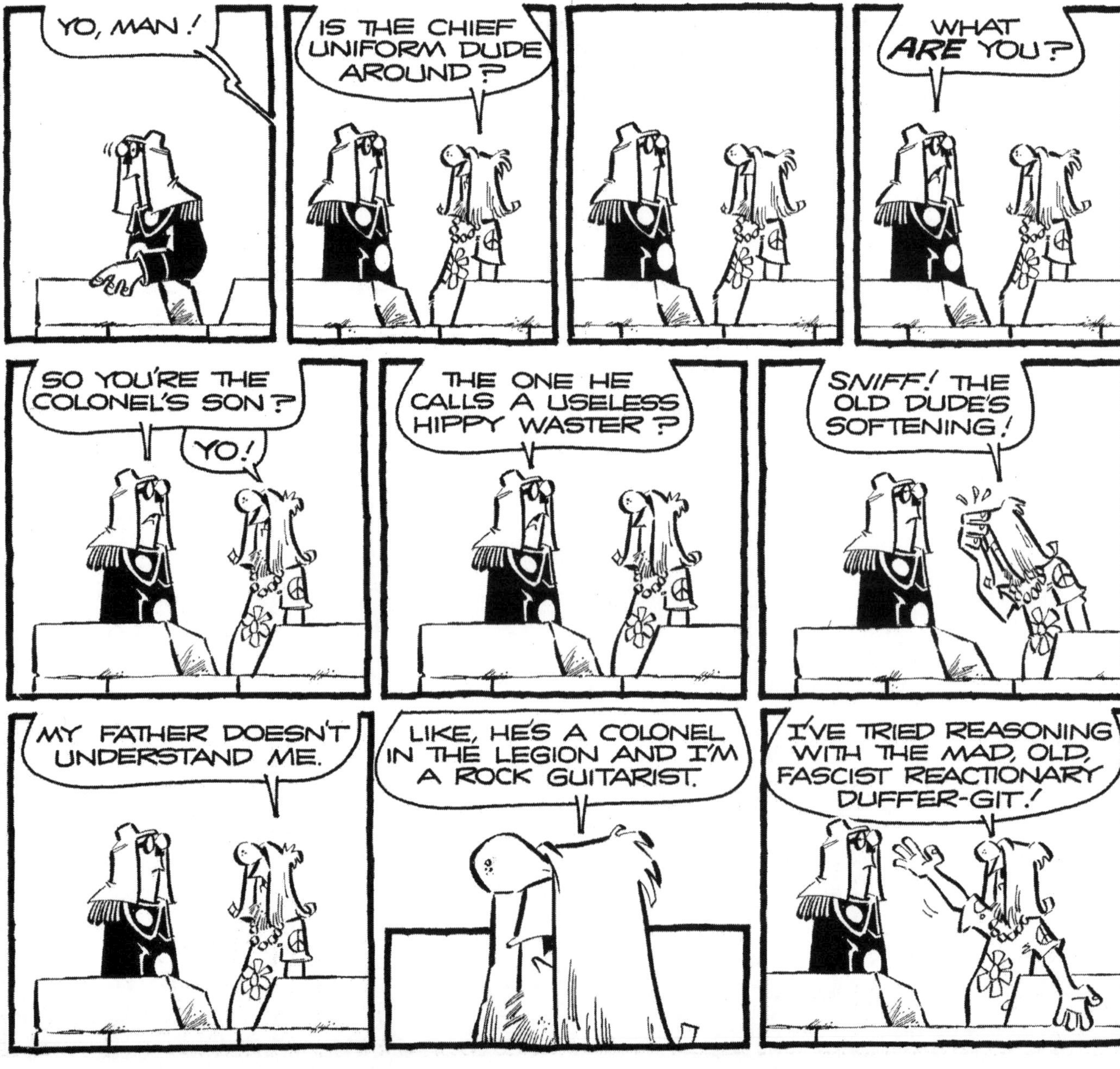
YO, MAN!
IS THE CHIEF UNIFORM DUDE AROUND?
WHAT ARE YOU?
SO YOU'RE THE COLONEL'S SON?
YO!
THE ONE HE CALLS A USELESS HIPPY WASTER?
SNIFF! THE OLD DUDE'S SOFTENING!
MY FATHER DOESN'T UNDERSTAND ME.
LIKE, HE'S A COLONEL IN THE LEGION AND I'M A ROCK GUITARIST.
I'VE TRIED REASONING WITH THE MAD, OLD, FASCIST REACTIONARY DUFFER-GIT!

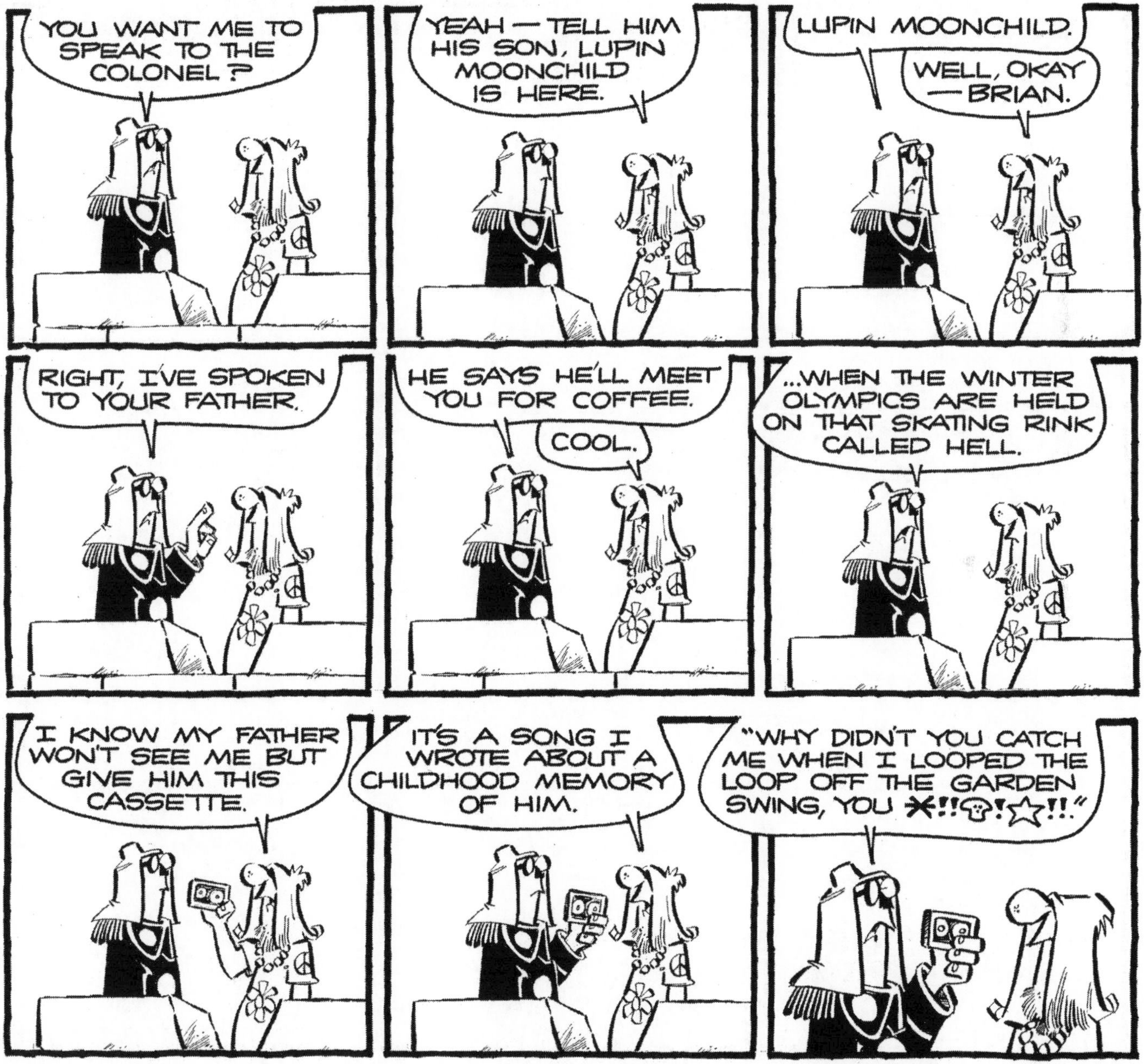
YOU WANT ME TO SPEAK TO THE COLONEL?
YEAH — TELL HIM HIS SON, LUPIN MOONCHILD IS HERE.
LUPIN MOONCHILD.
WELL, OKAY — BRIAN.
RIGHT, I'VE SPOKEN TO YOUR FATHER.
HE SAYS HE'LL MEET YOU FOR COFFEE.
COOL.
...WHEN THE WINTER OLYMPICS ARE HELD ON THAT SKATING RINK CALLED HELL.
I KNOW MY FATHER WON'T SEE ME BUT GIVE HIM THIS CASSETTE.
IT'S A SONG I WROTE ABOUT A CHILDHOOD MEMORY OF HIM.
"WHY DIDN'T YOU CATCH ME WHEN I LOOPED THE LOOP OFF THE GARDEN SWING, YOU *!!?!☆!!."

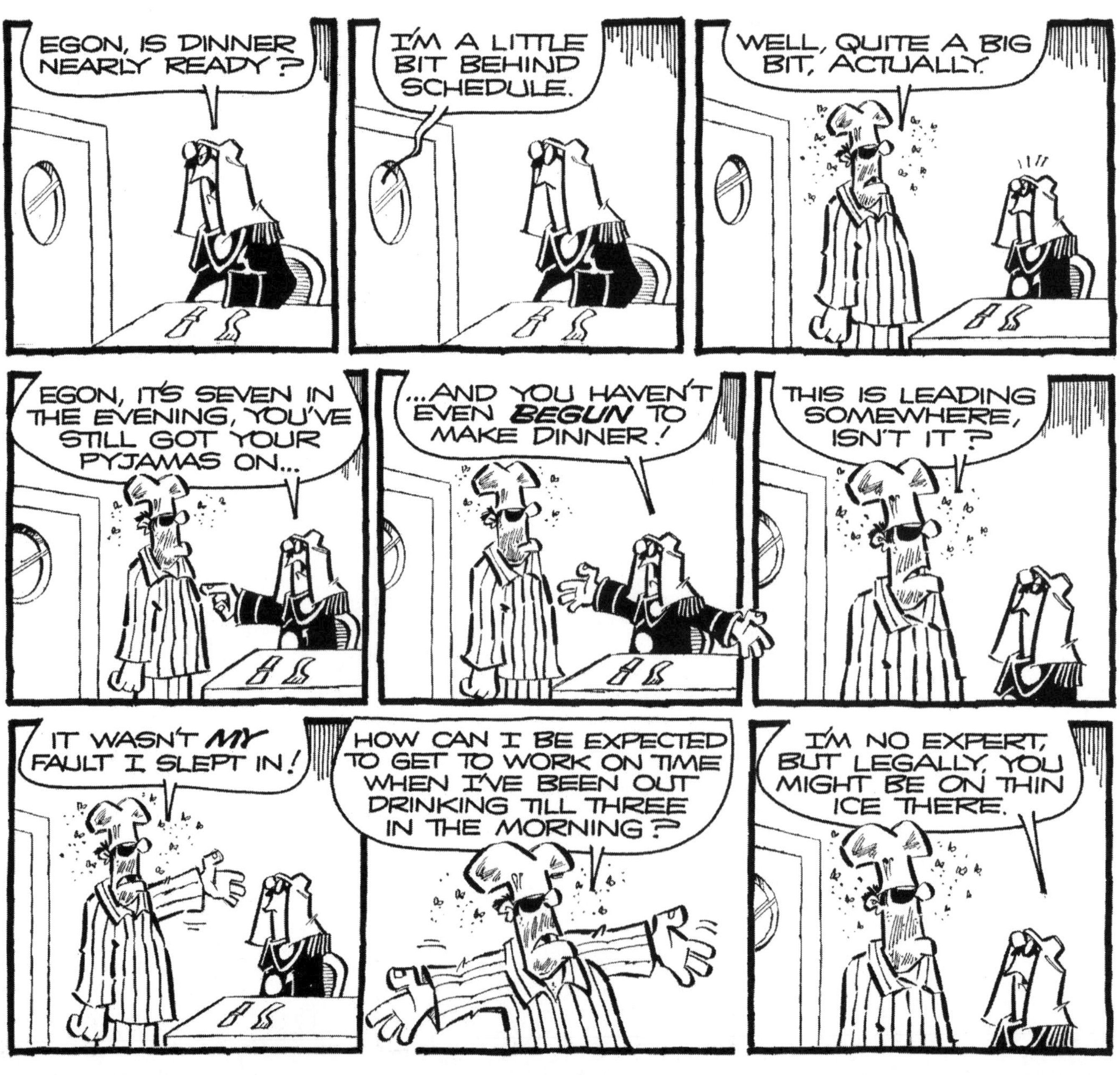
EGON, IS DINNER NEARLY READY?
I'M A LITTLE BIT BEHIND SCHEDULE.
WELL, QUITE A BIG BIT, ACTUALLY.
EGON, IT'S SEVEN IN THE EVENING, YOU'VE STILL GOT YOUR PYJAMAS ON...
...AND YOU HAVEN'T EVEN BEGUN TO MAKE DINNER!
THIS IS LEADING SOMEWHERE, ISN'T IT?
IT WASN'T MY FAULT I SLEPT IN!
HOW CAN I BE EXPECTED TO GET TO WORK ON TIME WHEN I'VE BEEN OUT DRINKING TILL THREE IN THE MORNING?
I'M NO EXPERT, BUT LEGALLY, YOU MIGHT BE ON THIN ICE THERE.

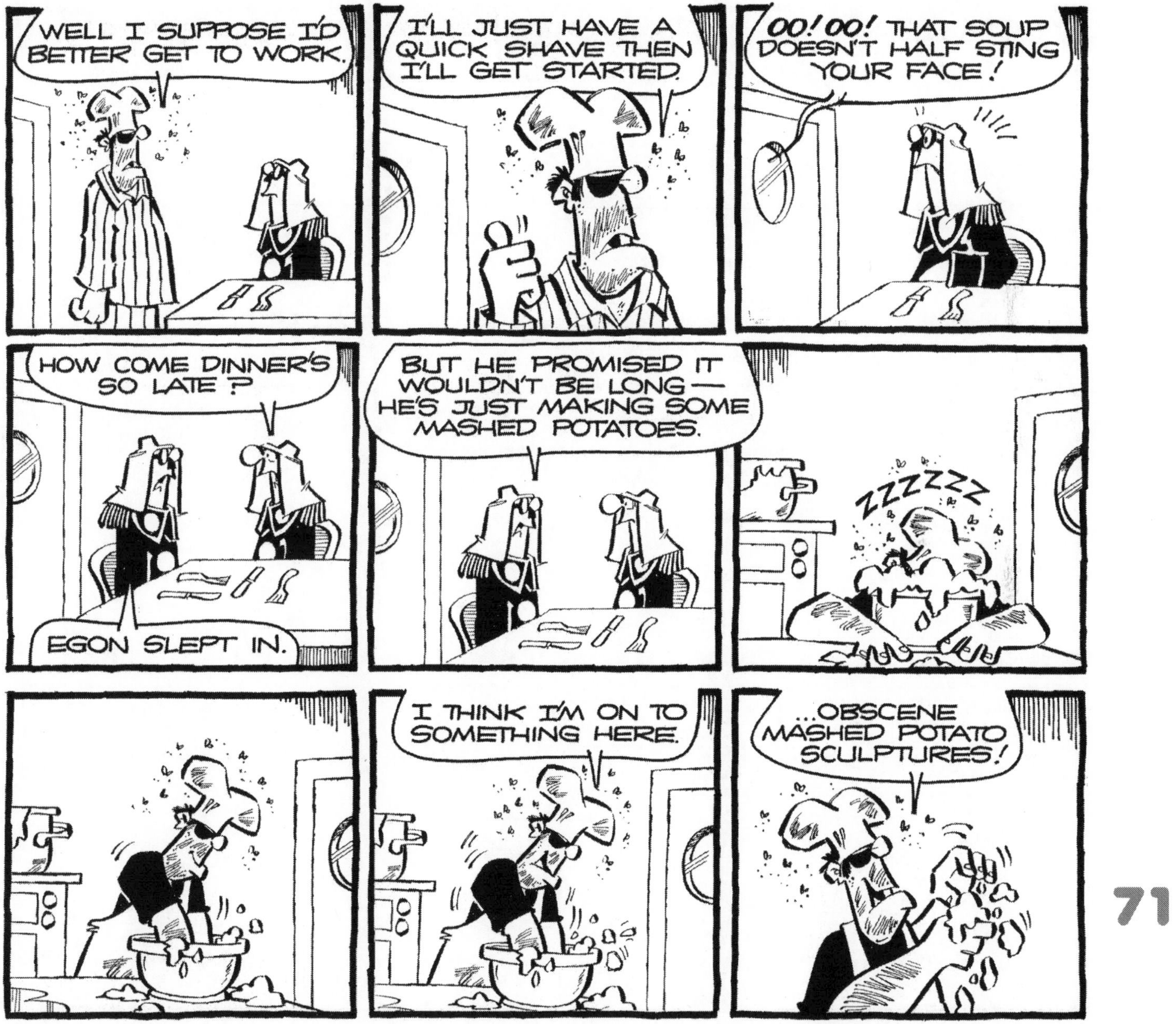
WELL I SUPPOSE I'D BETTER GET TO WORK.
I'LL JUST HAVE A QUICK SHAVE THEN I'LL GET STARTED.
OO! OO! THAT SOUP DOESN'T HALF STING YOUR FACE!
HOW COME DINNER'S SO LATE?
EGON SLEPT IN.
BUT HE PROMISED IT WOULDN'T BE LONG— HE'S JUST MAKING SOME MASHED POTATOES.
ZZZZZZ
I THINK I'M ON TO SOMETHING HERE.
...OBSCENE MASHED POTATO SCULPTURES!

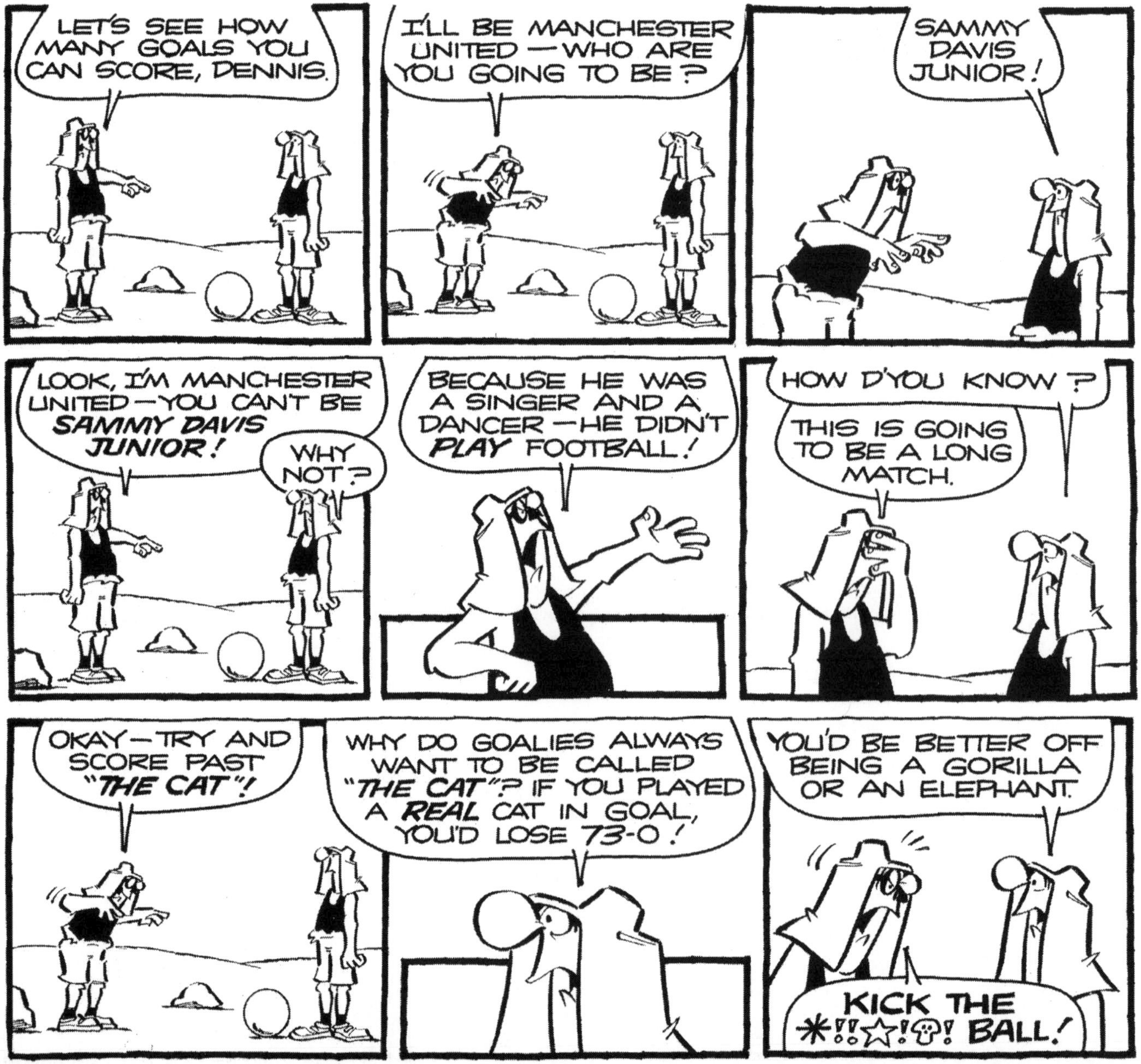
LET'S SEE HOW MANY GOALS YOU CAN SCORE, DENNIS.
I'LL BE MANCHESTER UNITED — WHO ARE YOU GOING TO BE ?
SAMMY DAVIS JUNIOR !
LOOK, I'M MANCHESTER UNITED — YOU CAN'T BE *SAMMY DAVIS JUNIOR* !
WHY NOT ?
BECAUSE HE WAS A SINGER AND A DANCER — HE DIDN'T *PLAY* FOOTBALL !
HOW D'YOU KNOW ?
THIS IS GOING TO BE A LONG MATCH.
OKAY — TRY AND SCORE PAST "*THE CAT*" !
WHY DO GOALIES ALWAYS WANT TO BE CALLED "*THE CAT*" ? IF YOU PLAYED A *REAL* CAT IN GOAL, YOU'D LOSE 73-0 !
YOU'D BE BETTER OFF BEING A GORILLA OR AN ELEPHANT.
KICK THE *!!☆!☠! BALL !

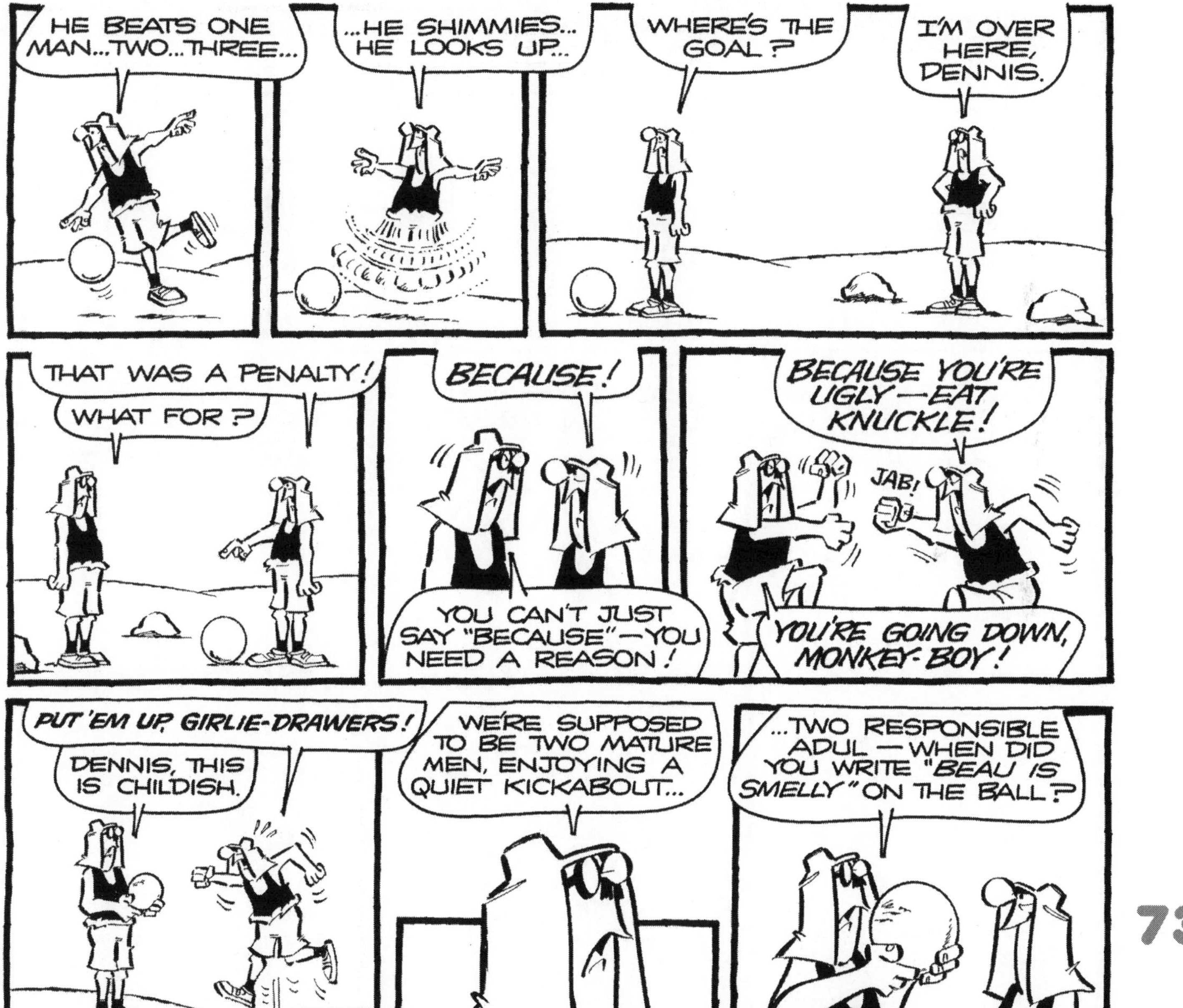
HE BEATS ONE MAN...TWO...THREE...
...HE SHIMMIES... HE LOOKS UP...
WHERE'S THE GOAL?
I'M OVER HERE, DENNIS.
THAT WAS A PENALTY!
WHAT FOR?
BECAUSE!
YOU CAN'T JUST SAY "BECAUSE"—YOU NEED A REASON!
BECAUSE YOU'RE UGLY—EAT KNUCKLE!
JAB!
YOU'RE GOING DOWN, MONKEY-BOY!
PUT 'EM UP, GIRLIE-DRAWERS!
DENNIS, THIS IS CHILDISH.
WE'RE SUPPOSED TO BE TWO MATURE MEN, ENJOYING A QUIET KICKABOUT...
...TWO RESPONSIBLE ADUL—WHEN DID YOU WRITE "BEAU IS SMELLY" ON THE BALL?

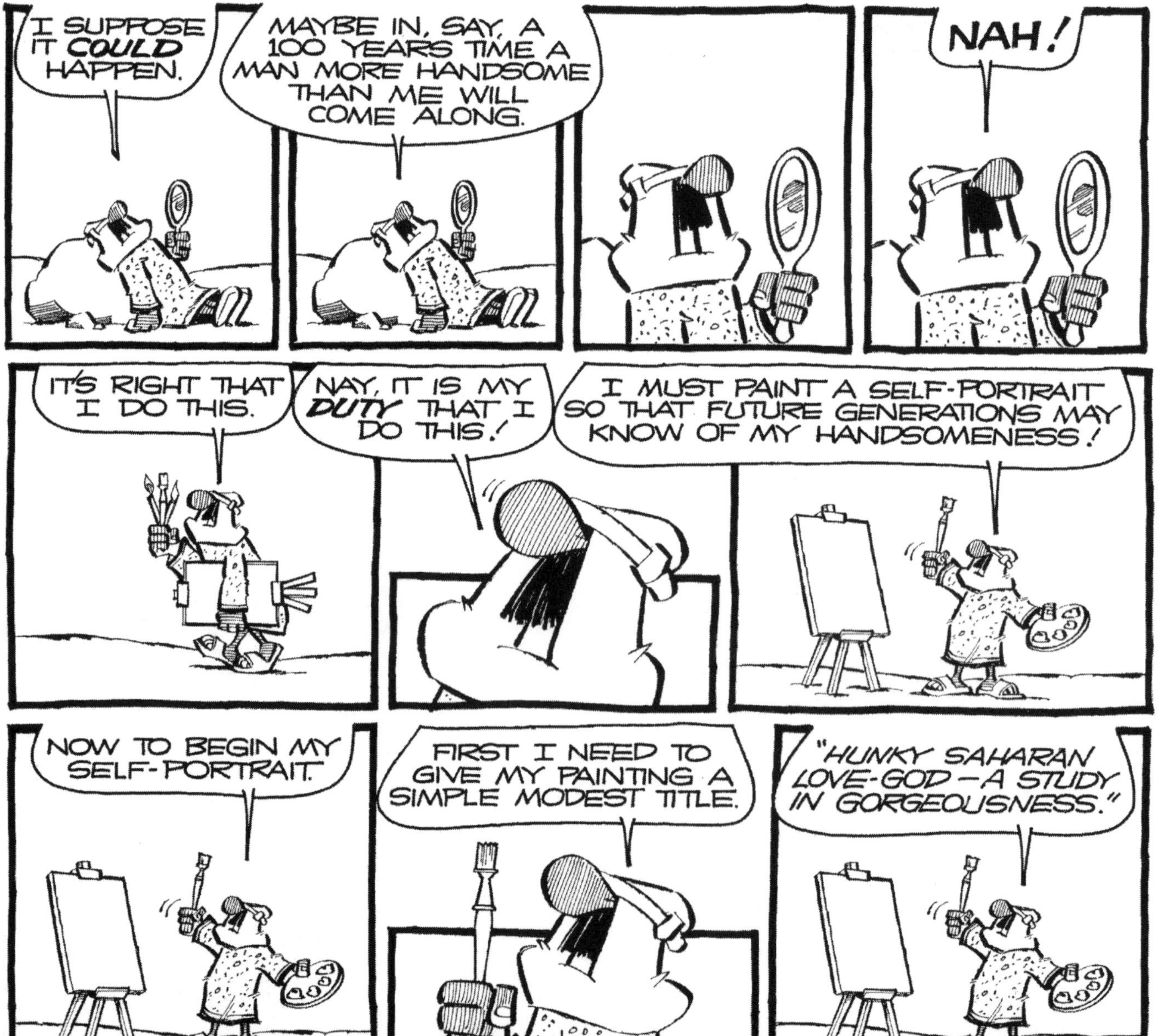
I SUPPOSE IT **COULD** HAPPEN.
MAYBE IN, SAY, A 100 YEARS TIME A MAN MORE HANDSOME THAN ME WILL COME ALONG.
NAH!
IT'S RIGHT THAT I DO THIS.
NAY, IT IS MY ***DUTY*** THAT I DO THIS!
I MUST PAINT A SELF-PORTRAIT SO THAT FUTURE GENERATIONS MAY KNOW OF MY HANDSOMENESS!
NOW TO BEGIN MY SELF-PORTRAIT.
FIRST I NEED TO GIVE MY PAINTING A SIMPLE MODEST TITLE.
"HUNKY SAHARAN LOVE-GOD—A STUDY IN GORGEOUSNESS."

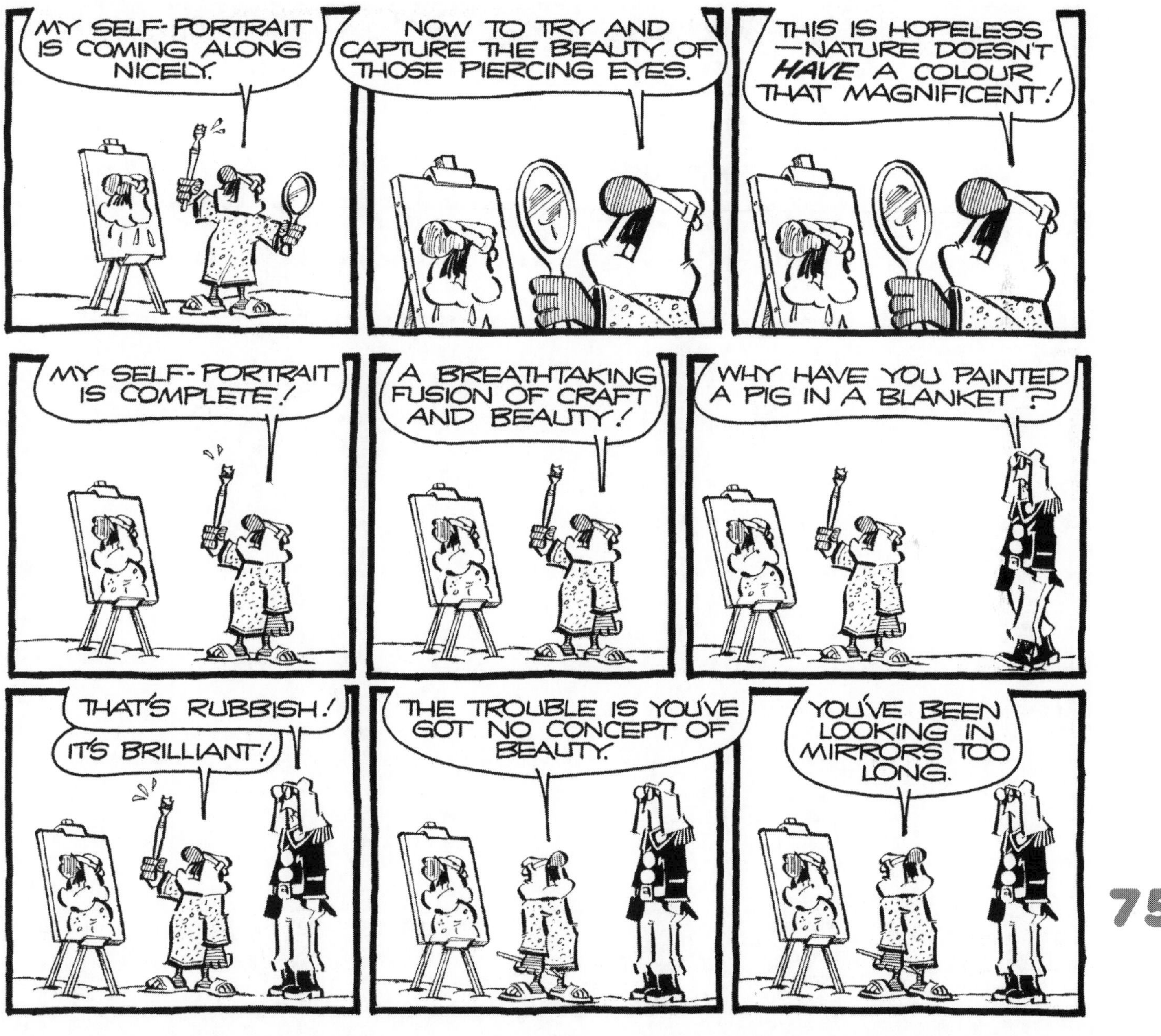
MY SELF-PORTRAIT IS COMING ALONG NICELY.
NOW TO TRY AND CAPTURE THE BEAUTY OF THOSE PIERCING EYES.
THIS IS HOPELESS —NATURE DOESN'T *HAVE* A COLOUR THAT MAGNIFICENT!
MY SELF-PORTRAIT IS COMPLETE!
A BREATHTAKING FUSION OF CRAFT AND BEAUTY!
WHY HAVE YOU PAINTED A PIG IN A BLANKET?
THAT'S RUBBISH!
IT'S BRILLIANT!
THE TROUBLE IS YOU'VE GOT NO CONCEPT OF BEAUTY.
YOU'VE BEEN LOOKING IN MIRRORS TOO LONG.

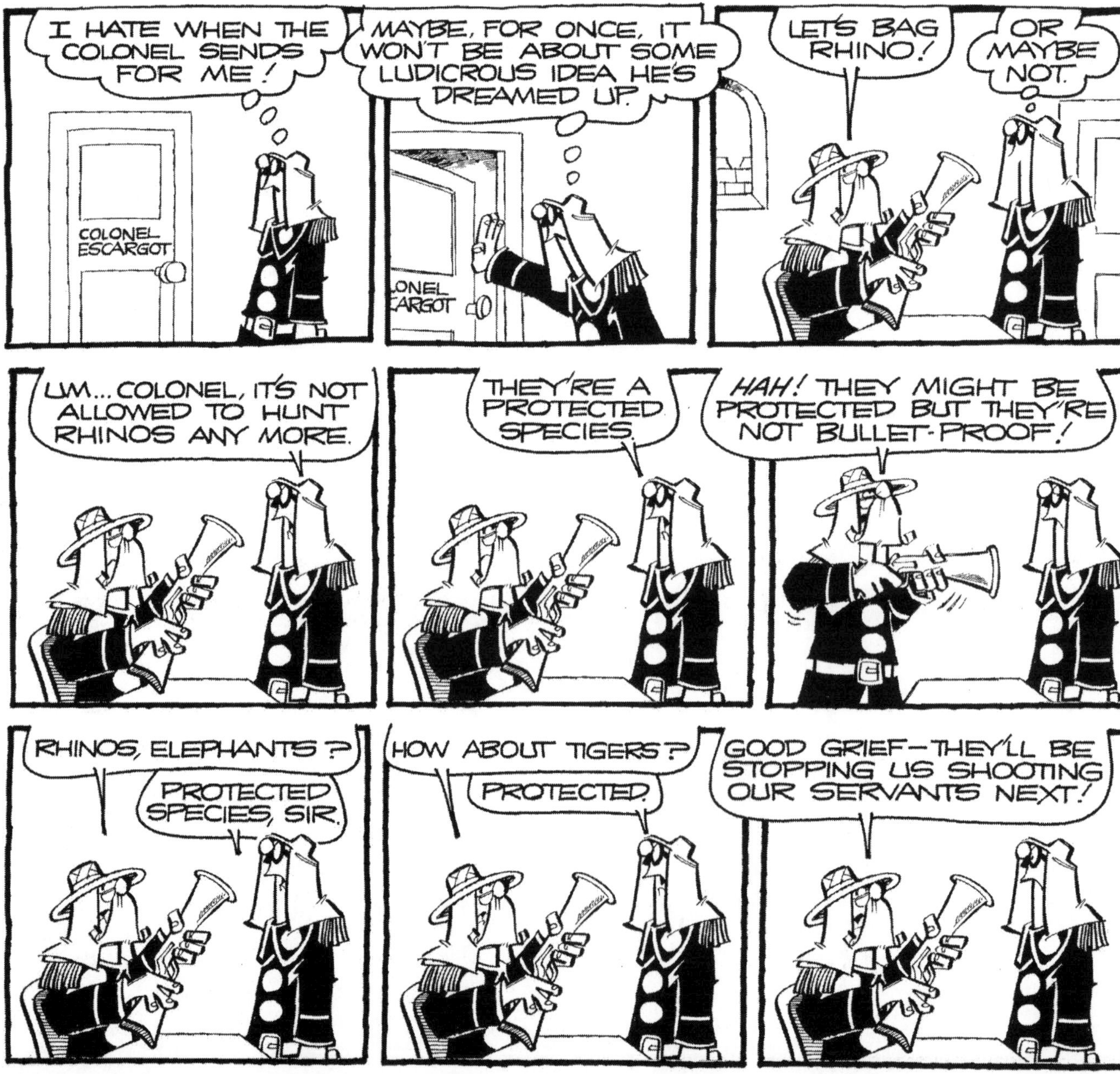
I HATE WHEN THE COLONEL SENDS FOR ME!
COLONEL ESCARGOT
MAYBE, FOR ONCE, IT WON'T BE ABOUT SOME LUDICROUS IDEA HE'S DREAMED UP.
LET'S BAG RHINO!
OR MAYBE NOT.
UM... COLONEL, IT'S NOT ALLOWED TO HUNT RHINOS ANY MORE.
THEY'RE A PROTECTED SPECIES.
HAH! THEY MIGHT BE PROTECTED BUT THEY'RE NOT BULLET-PROOF!
RHINOS, ELEPHANTS?
PROTECTED SPECIES, SIR.
HOW ABOUT TIGERS?
PROTECTED.
GOOD GRIEF—THEY'LL BE STOPPING US SHOOTING OUR SERVANTS NEXT!

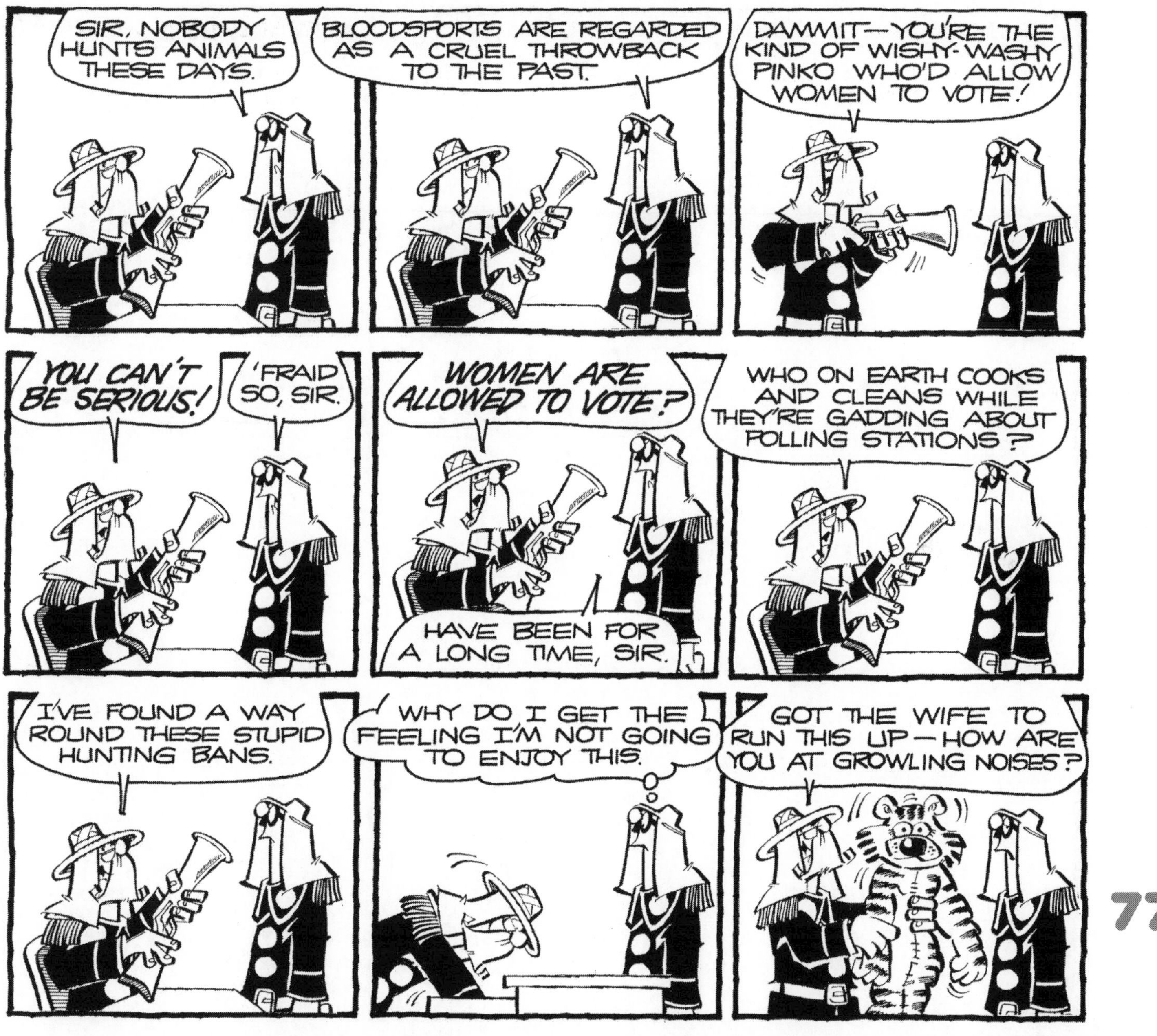
SIR, NOBODY HUNTS ANIMALS THESE DAYS.
BLOODSPORTS ARE REGARDED AS A CRUEL THROWBACK TO THE PAST.
DAMMIT—YOU'RE THE KIND OF WISHY-WASHY PINKO WHO'D ALLOW WOMEN TO VOTE!
YOU CAN'T BE SERIOUS!
'FRAID SO, SIR.
WOMEN ARE ALLOWED TO VOTE?
HAVE BEEN FOR A LONG TIME, SIR.
WHO ON EARTH COOKS AND CLEANS WHILE THEY'RE GADDING ABOUT POLLING STATIONS?
I'VE FOUND A WAY ROUND THESE STUPID HUNTING BANS.
WHY DO I GET THE FEELING I'M NOT GOING TO ENJOY THIS.
GOT THE WIFE TO RUN THIS UP—HOW ARE YOU AT GROWLING NOISES?

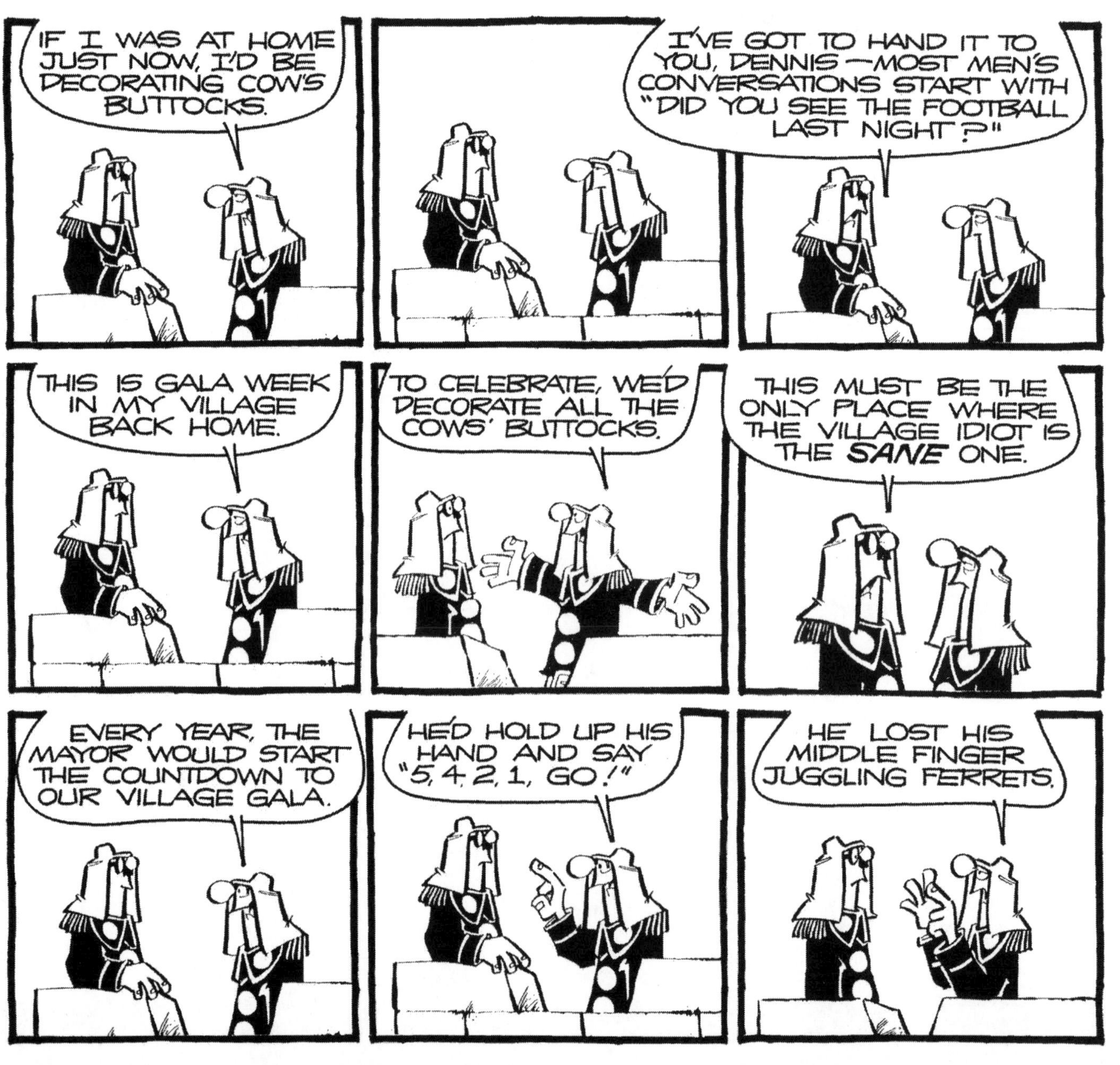
IF I WAS AT HOME JUST NOW, I'D BE DECORATING COW'S BUTTOCKS.
I'VE GOT TO HAND IT TO YOU, DENNIS—MOST MEN'S CONVERSATIONS START WITH "DID YOU SEE THE FOOTBALL LAST NIGHT?"
THIS IS GALA WEEK IN MY VILLAGE BACK HOME.
TO CELEBRATE, WE'D DECORATE ALL THE COWS' BUTTOCKS.
THIS MUST BE THE ONLY PLACE WHERE THE VILLAGE IDIOT IS THE SANE ONE.
EVERY YEAR, THE MAYOR WOULD START THE COUNTDOWN TO OUR VILLAGE GALA.
HE'D HOLD UP HIS HAND AND SAY "5, 4, 2, 1, GO!"
HE LOST HIS MIDDLE FINGER JUGGLING FERRETS.

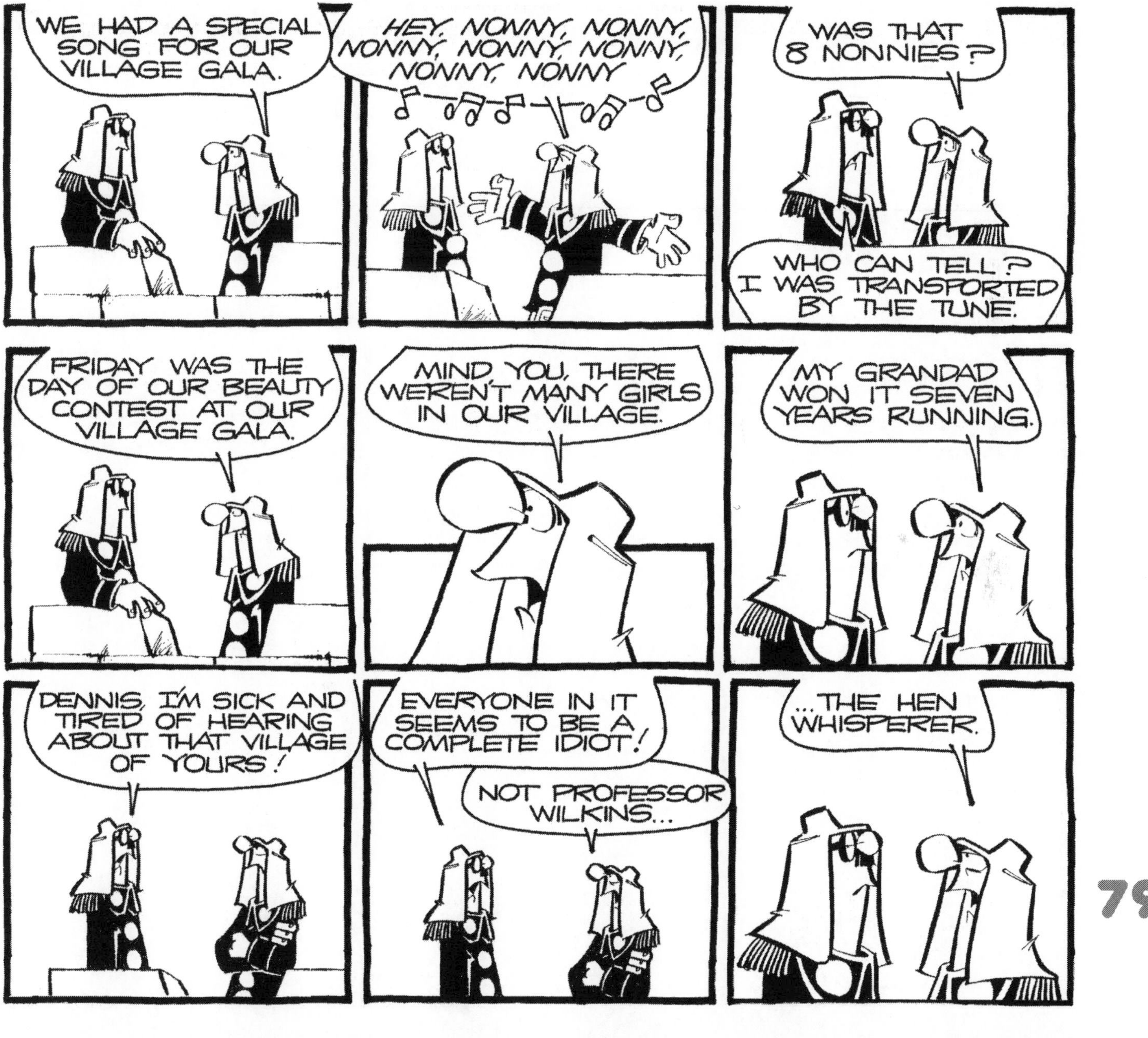
WE HAD A SPECIAL SONG FOR OUR VILLAGE GALA.
HEY, NONNY, NONNY, NONNY, NONNY, NONNY, NONNY, NONNY, NONNY
WAS THAT 8 NONNIES?
WHO CAN TELL? I WAS TRANSPORTED BY THE TUNE.
FRIDAY WAS THE DAY OF OUR BEAUTY CONTEST AT OUR VILLAGE GALA.
MIND YOU, THERE WEREN'T MANY GIRLS IN OUR VILLAGE.
MY GRANDAD WON IT SEVEN YEARS RUNNING.
DENNIS, I'M SICK AND TIRED OF HEARING ABOUT THAT VILLAGE OF YOURS!
EVERYONE IN IT SEEMS TO BE A COMPLETE IDIOT!
NOT PROFESSOR WILKINS...
...THE HEN WHISPERER.

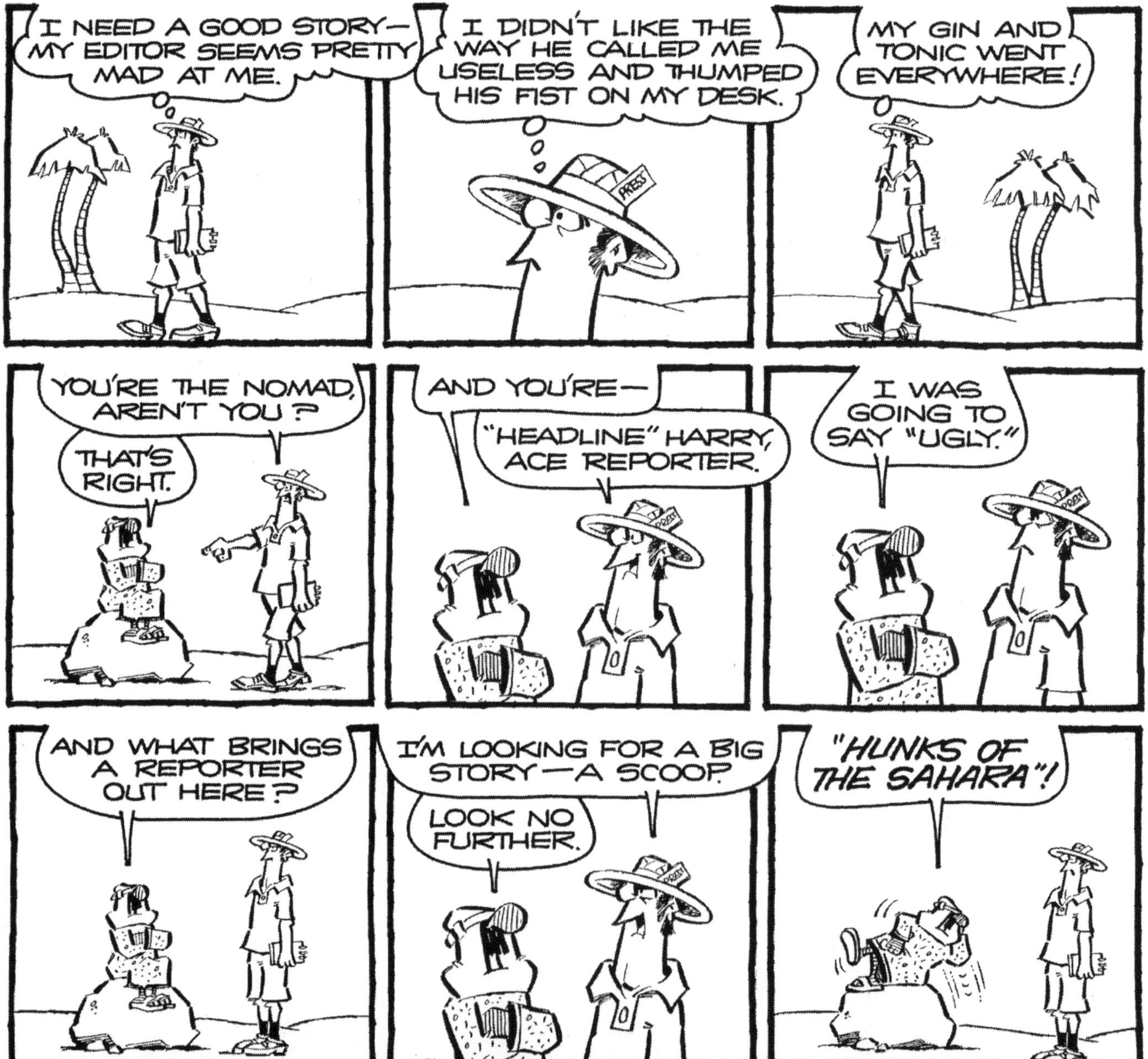
I NEED A GOOD STORY— MY EDITOR SEEMS PRETTY MAD AT ME.
I DIDN'T LIKE THE WAY HE CALLED ME USELESS AND THUMPED HIS FIST ON MY DESK.
PRESS
MY GIN AND TONIC WENT EVERYWHERE!
YOU'RE THE NOMAD, AREN'T YOU?
THAT'S RIGHT.
AND YOU'RE—
"HEADLINE" HARRY, ACE REPORTER.
I WAS GOING TO SAY "UGLY."
AND WHAT BRINGS A REPORTER OUT HERE?
I'M LOOKING FOR A BIG STORY—A SCOOP.
LOOK NO FURTHER.
"HUNKS OF THE SAHARA"!

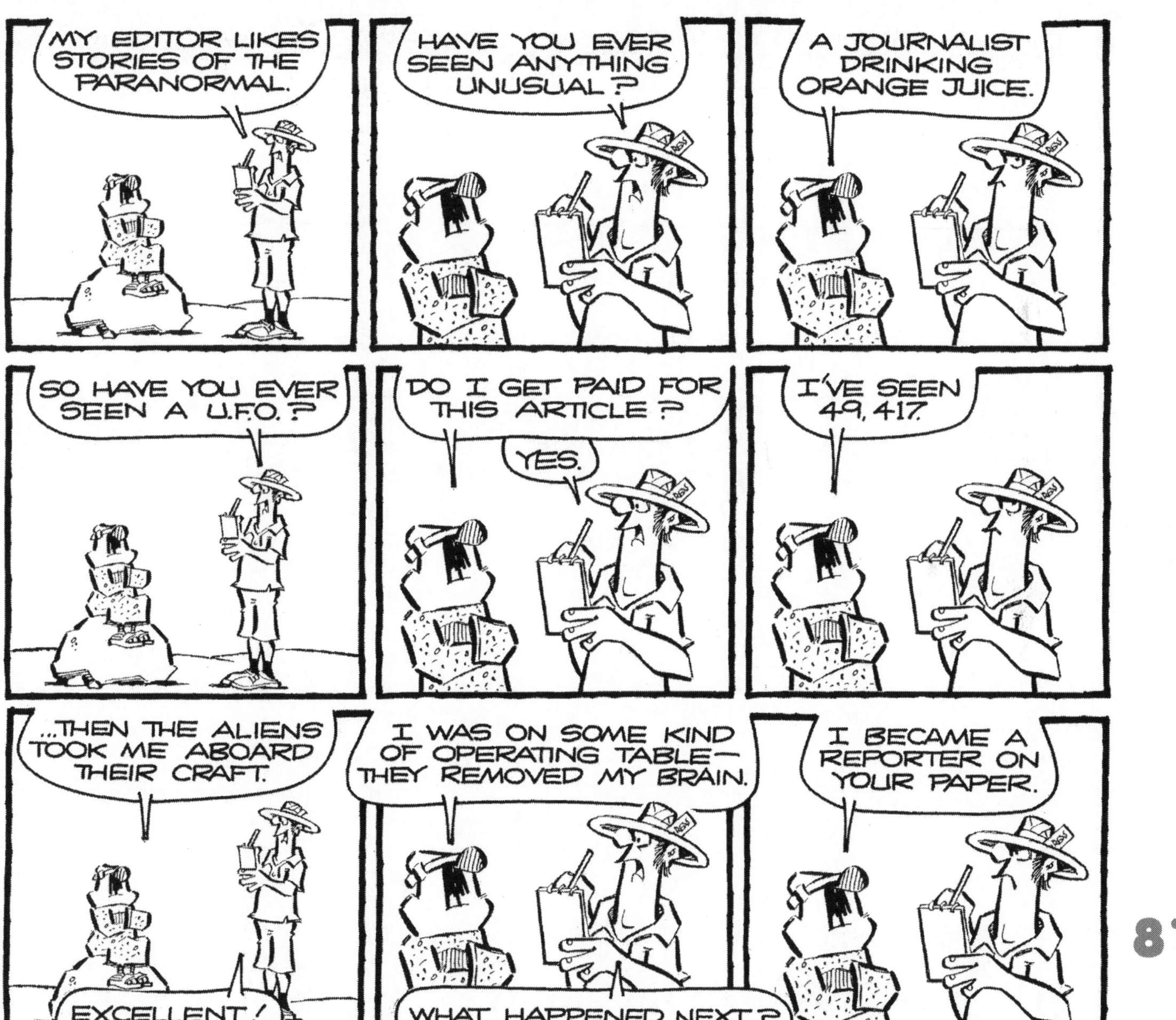
MY EDITOR LIKES STORIES OF THE PARANORMAL.
HAVE YOU EVER SEEN ANYTHING UNUSUAL?
A JOURNALIST DRINKING ORANGE JUICE.
SO HAVE YOU EVER SEEN A U.F.O.?
DO I GET PAID FOR THIS ARTICLE?
YES.
I'VE SEEN 49,417.
...THEN THE ALIENS TOOK ME ABOARD THEIR CRAFT.
EXCELLENT!
I WAS ON SOME KIND OF OPERATING TABLE— THEY REMOVED MY BRAIN.
WHAT HAPPENED NEXT?
I BECAME A REPORTER ON YOUR PAPER.

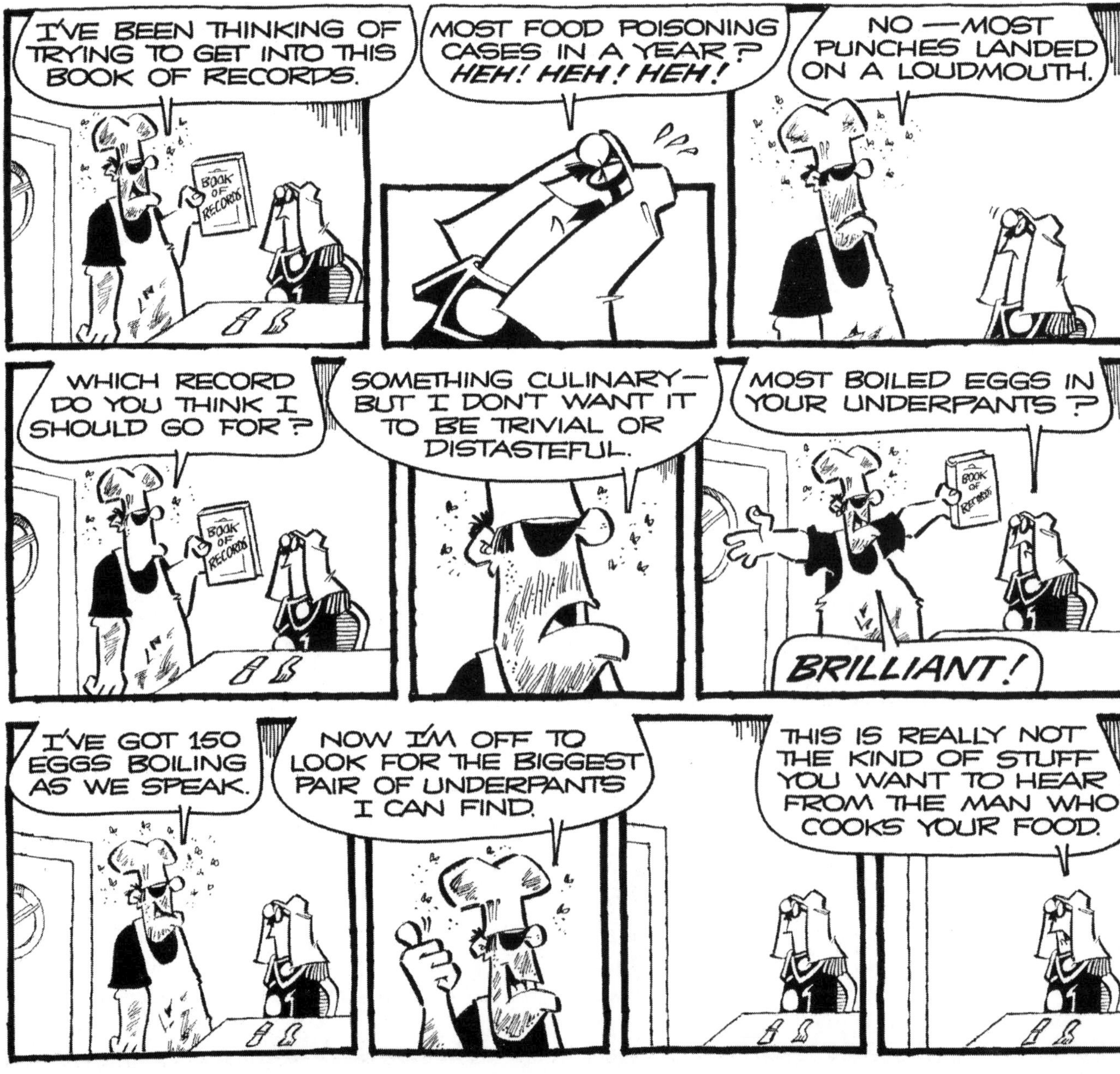
I'VE BEEN THINKING OF TRYING TO GET INTO THIS BOOK OF RECORDS.
BOOK OF RECORDS
MOST FOOD POISONING CASES IN A YEAR? HEH! HEH! HEH!
NO — MOST PUNCHES LANDED ON A LOUDMOUTH.
WHICH RECORD DO YOU THINK I SHOULD GO FOR?
BOOK OF RECORDS
SOMETHING CULINARY— BUT I DON'T WANT IT TO BE TRIVIAL OR DISTASTEFUL.
MOST BOILED EGGS IN YOUR UNDERPANTS?
BOOK OF RECORDS
BRILLIANT!
I'VE GOT 150 EGGS BOILING AS WE SPEAK.
NOW I'M OFF TO LOOK FOR THE BIGGEST PAIR OF UNDERPANTS I CAN FIND.
THIS IS REALLY NOT THE KIND OF STUFF YOU WANT TO HEAR FROM THE MAN WHO COOKS YOUR FOOD.

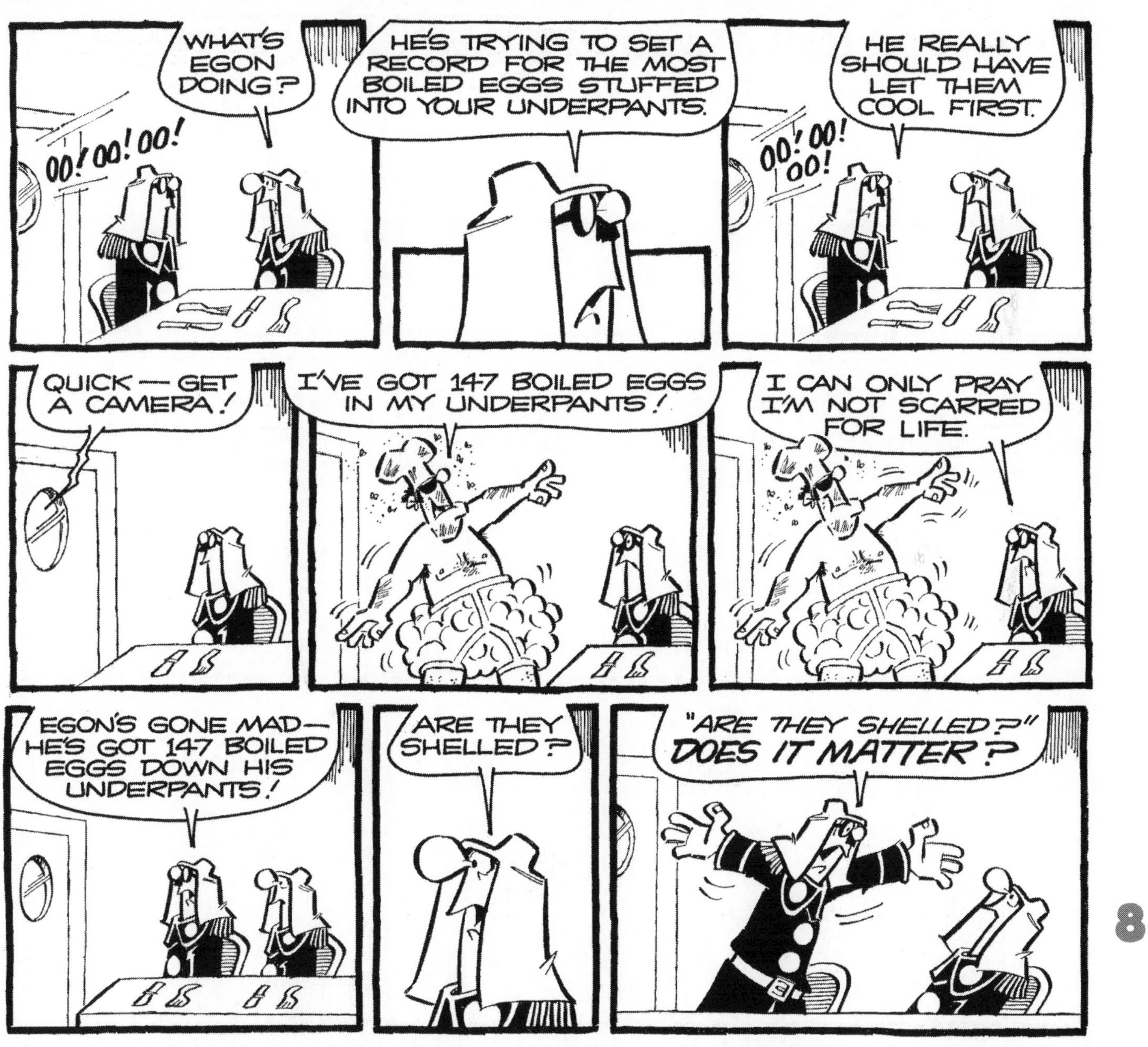
WHAT'S EGON DOING?
OO! OO! OO!
HE'S TRYING TO SET A RECORD FOR THE MOST BOILED EGGS STUFFED INTO YOUR UNDERPANTS.
OO! OO! OO!
HE REALLY SHOULD HAVE LET THEM COOL FIRST.
QUICK — GET A CAMERA!
I'VE GOT 147 BOILED EGGS IN MY UNDERPANTS!
I CAN ONLY PRAY I'M NOT SCARRED FOR LIFE.
EGON'S GONE MAD— HE'S GOT 147 BOILED EGGS DOWN HIS UNDERPANTS!
ARE THEY SHELLED?
"ARE THEY SHELLED?" DOES IT MATTER?

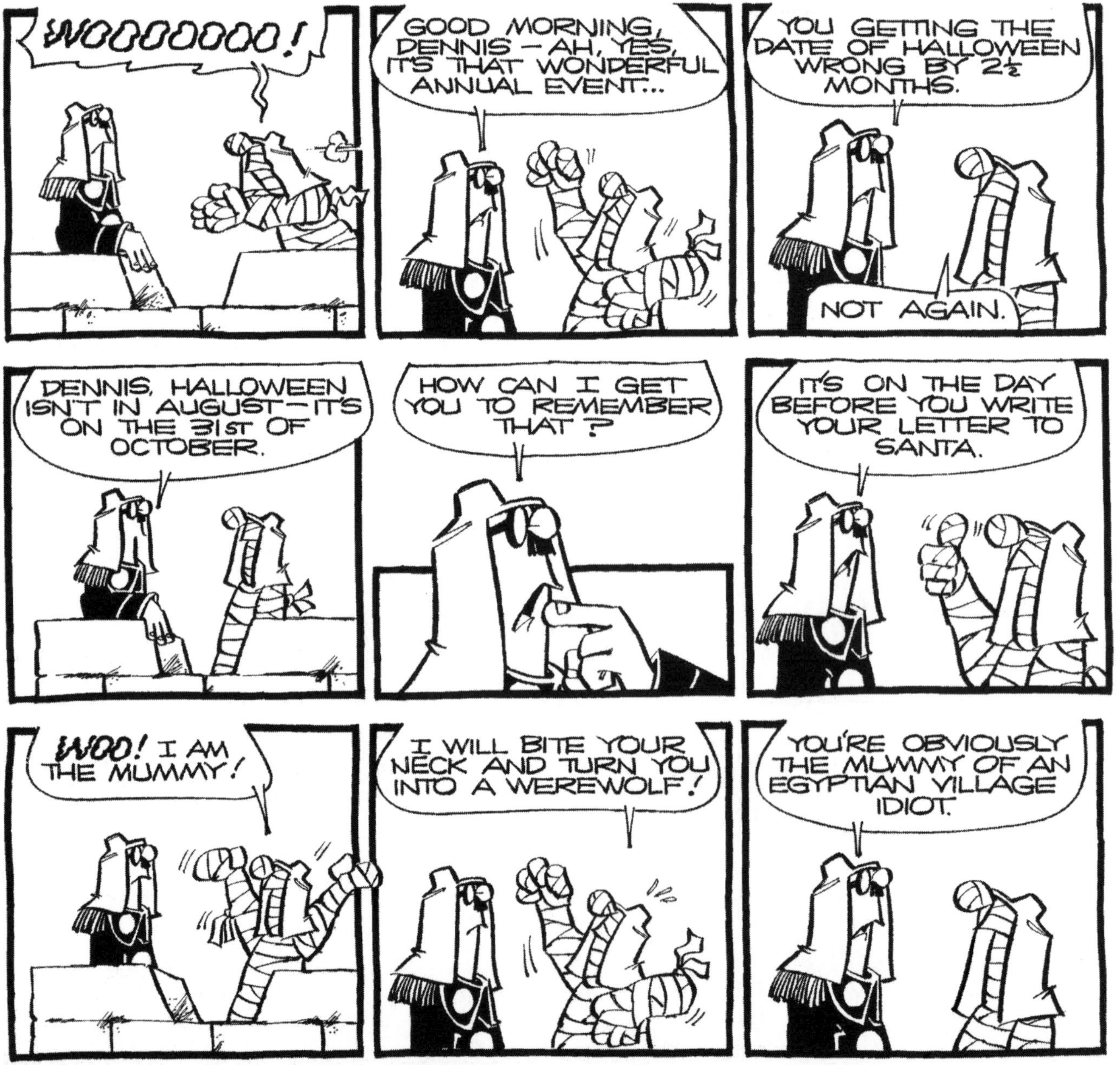
WOOOOOOO!
GOOD MORNING, DENNIS—AH, YES, IT'S THAT WONDERFUL ANNUAL EVENT...
YOU GETTING THE DATE OF HALLOWEEN WRONG BY 2½ MONTHS.
NOT AGAIN.
DENNIS, HALLOWEEN ISN'T IN AUGUST—IT'S ON THE 31st OF OCTOBER.
HOW CAN I GET YOU TO REMEMBER THAT?
IT'S ON THE DAY BEFORE YOU WRITE YOUR LETTER TO SANTA.
WOO! I AM THE MUMMY!
I WILL BITE YOUR NECK AND TURN YOU INTO A WEREWOLF!
YOU'RE OBVIOUSLY THE MUMMY OF AN EGYPTIAN VILLAGE IDIOT.

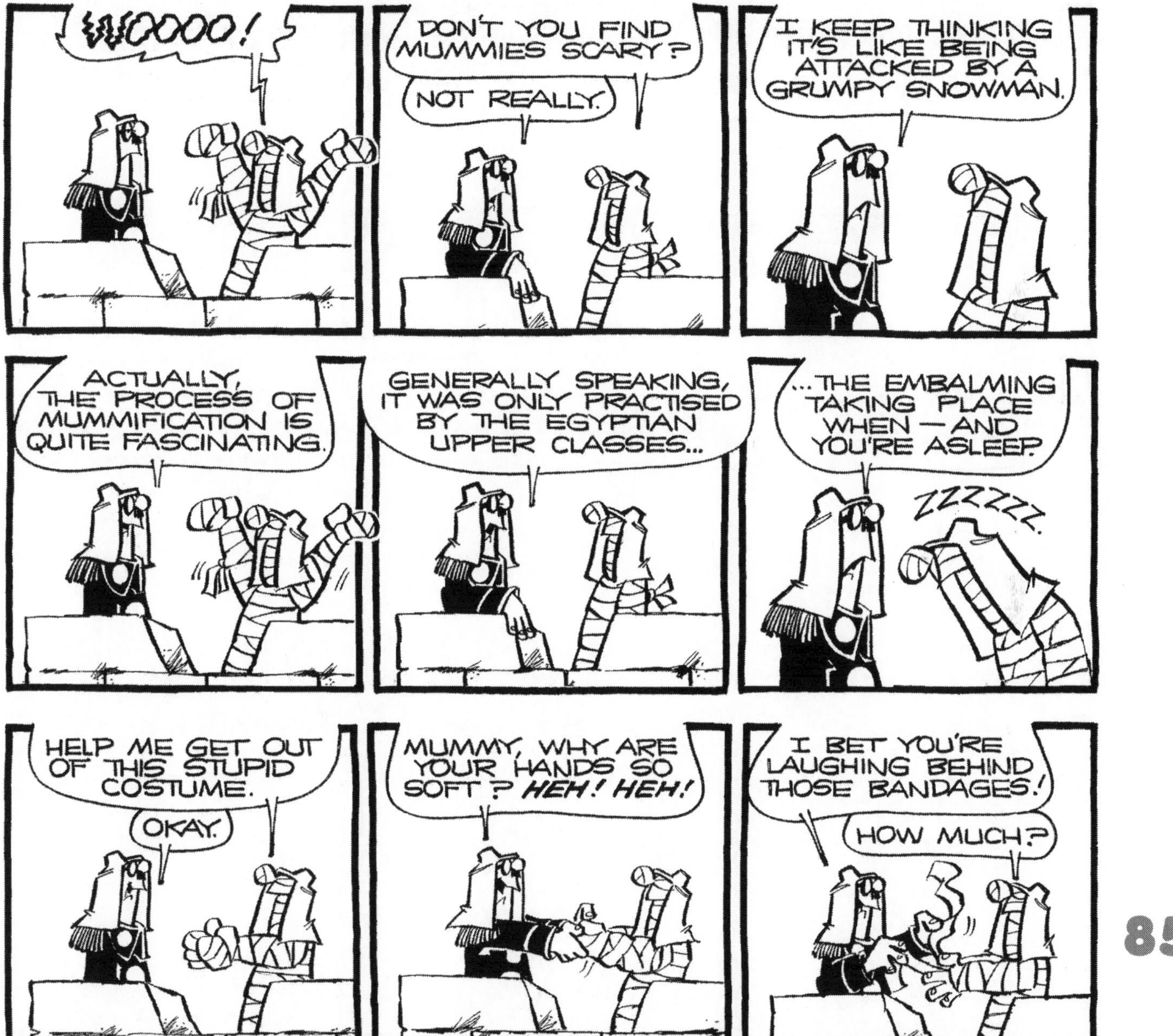
WOOOO!
DON'T YOU FIND MUMMIES SCARY?
NOT REALLY.
I KEEP THINKING IT'S LIKE BEING ATTACKED BY A GRUMPY SNOWMAN.
ACTUALLY, THE PROCESS OF MUMMIFICATION IS QUITE FASCINATING.
GENERALLY SPEAKING, IT WAS ONLY PRACTISED BY THE EGYPTIAN UPPER CLASSES...
...THE EMBALMING TAKING PLACE WHEN — AND YOU'RE ASLEEP?
ZZZZZZ.
HELP ME GET OUT OF THIS STUPID COSTUME.
OKAY.
MUMMY, WHY ARE YOUR HANDS SO SOFT? HEH! HEH!
I BET YOU'RE LAUGHING BEHIND THOSE BANDAGES!
HOW MUCH?

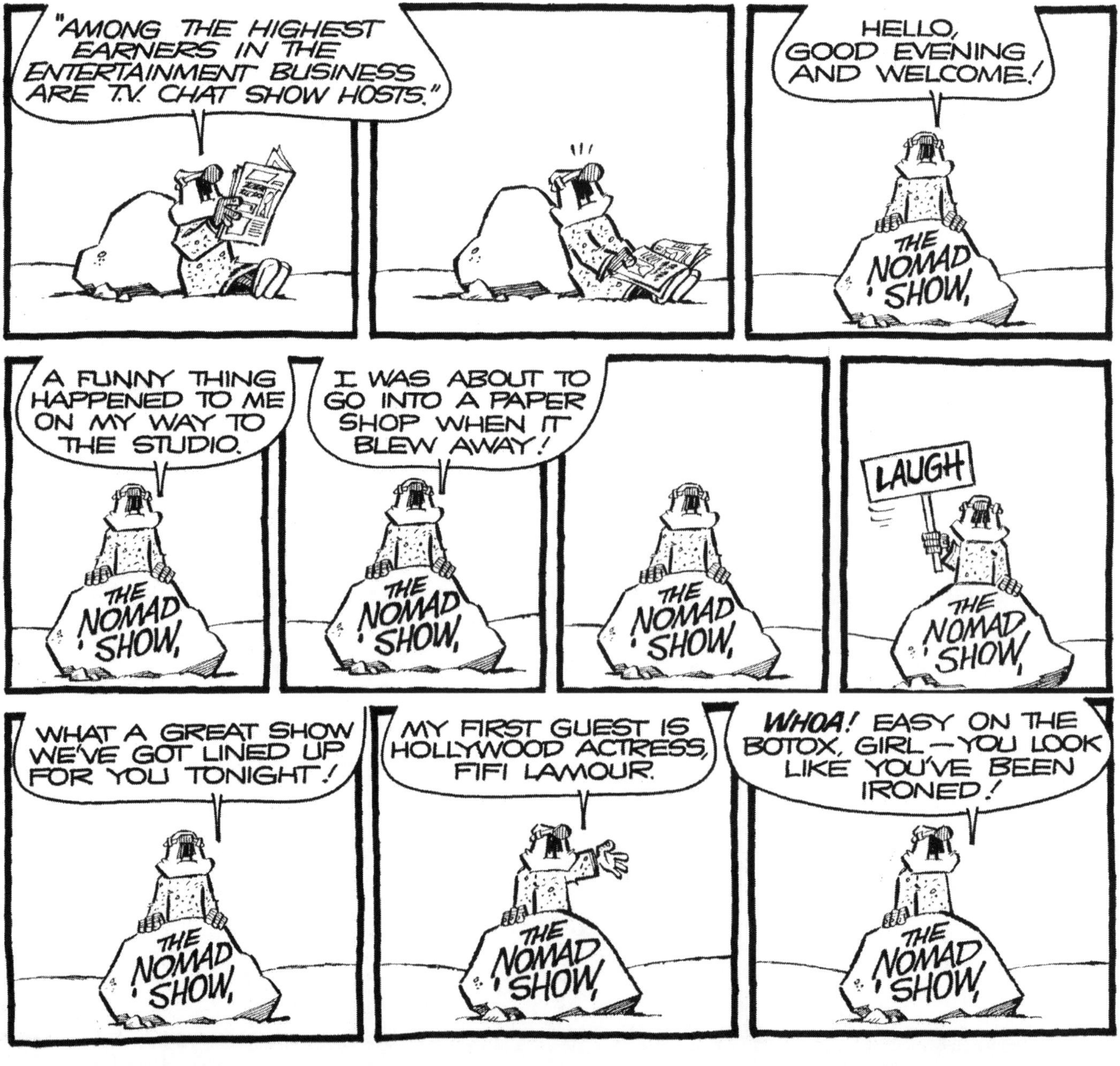
"AMONG THE HIGHEST EARNERS IN THE ENTERTAINMENT BUSINESS ARE T.V. CHAT SHOW HOSTS."
HELLO, GOOD EVENING AND WELCOME!
THE NOMAD SHOW,
A FUNNY THING HAPPENED TO ME ON MY WAY TO THE STUDIO.
I WAS ABOUT TO GO INTO A PAPER SHOP WHEN IT BLEW AWAY!
LAUGH
WHAT A GREAT SHOW WE'VE GOT LINED UP FOR YOU TONIGHT!
MY FIRST GUEST IS HOLLYWOOD ACTRESS, FIFI LAMOUR.
WHOA! EASY ON THE BOTOX, GIRL—YOU LOOK LIKE YOU'VE BEEN IRONED!

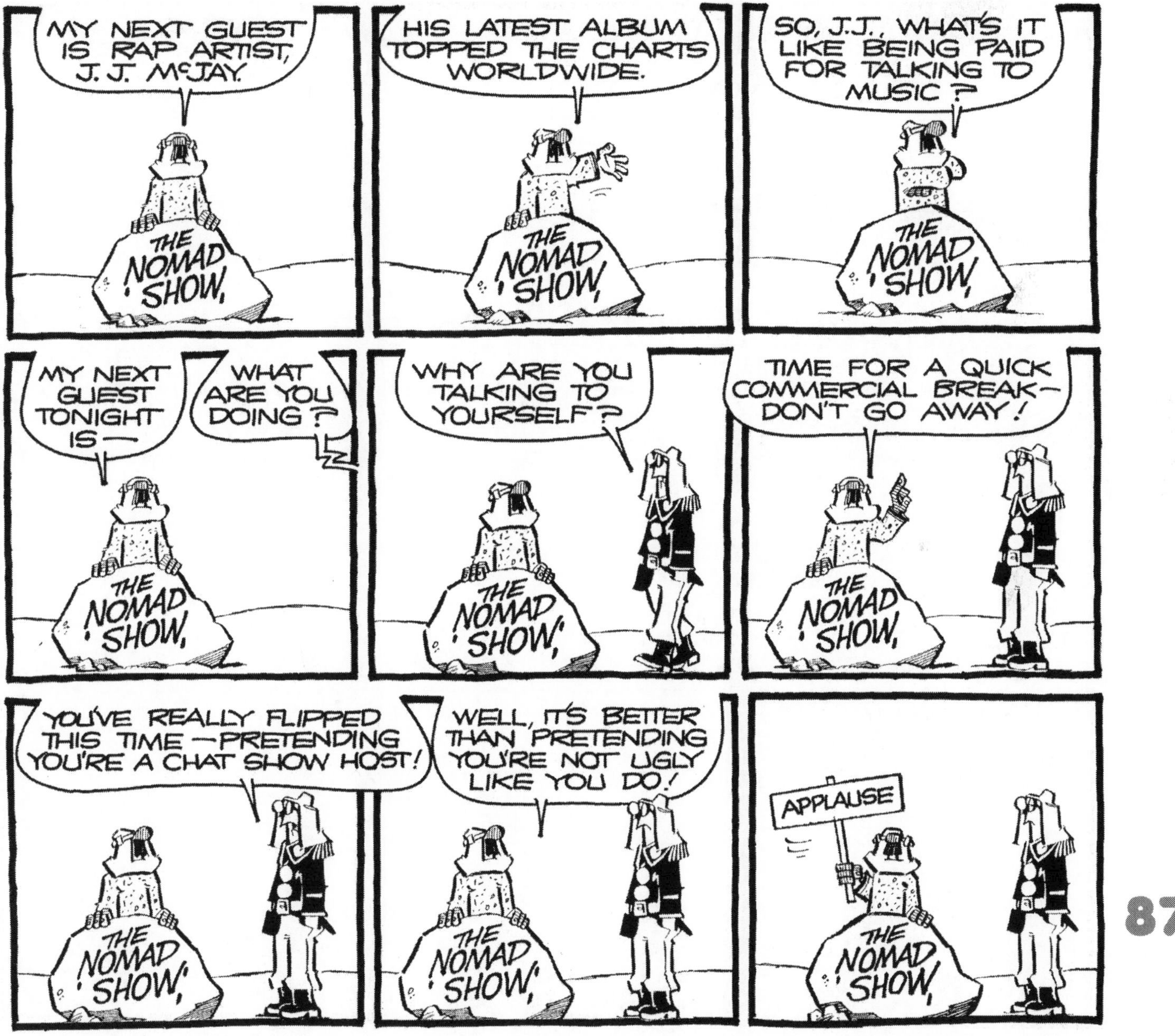
MY NEXT GUEST IS RAP ARTIST, J. J. McJAY.
THE NOMAD SHOW,
HIS LATEST ALBUM TOPPED THE CHARTS WORLDWIDE.
SO, J.J., WHAT'S IT LIKE BEING PAID FOR TALKING TO MUSIC ?
MY NEXT GUEST TONIGHT IS—
WHAT ARE YOU DOING ?
WHY ARE YOU TALKING TO YOURSELF ?
TIME FOR A QUICK COMMERCIAL BREAK— DON'T GO AWAY !
YOU'VE REALLY FLIPPED THIS TIME—PRETENDING YOU'RE A CHAT SHOW HOST!
WELL, IT'S BETTER THAN PRETENDING YOU'RE NOT UGLY LIKE YOU DO!
APPLAUSE

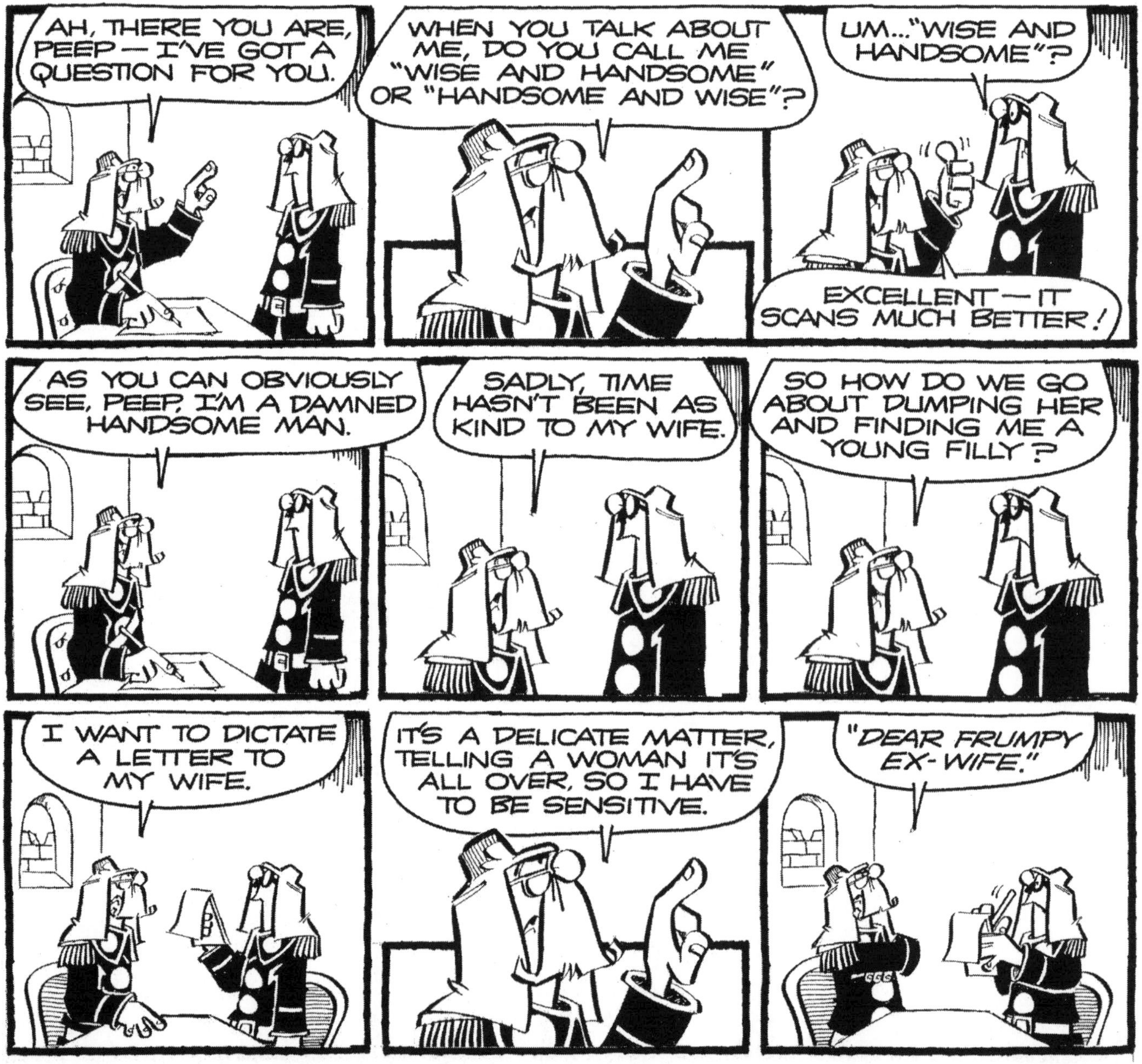
AH, THERE YOU ARE, PEEP — I'VE GOT A QUESTION FOR YOU.
WHEN YOU TALK ABOUT ME, DO YOU CALL ME "WISE AND HANDSOME" OR "HANDSOME AND WISE"?
UM..."WISE AND HANDSOME"?
EXCELLENT — IT SCANS MUCH BETTER!
AS YOU CAN OBVIOUSLY SEE, PEEP, I'M A DAMNED HANDSOME MAN.
SADLY, TIME HASN'T BEEN AS KIND TO MY WIFE.
SO HOW DO WE GO ABOUT DUMPING HER AND FINDING ME A YOUNG FILLY?
I WANT TO DICTATE A LETTER TO MY WIFE.
IT'S A DELICATE MATTER, TELLING A WOMAN IT'S ALL OVER, SO I HAVE TO BE SENSITIVE.
"*DEAR FRUMPY EX-WIFE.*"

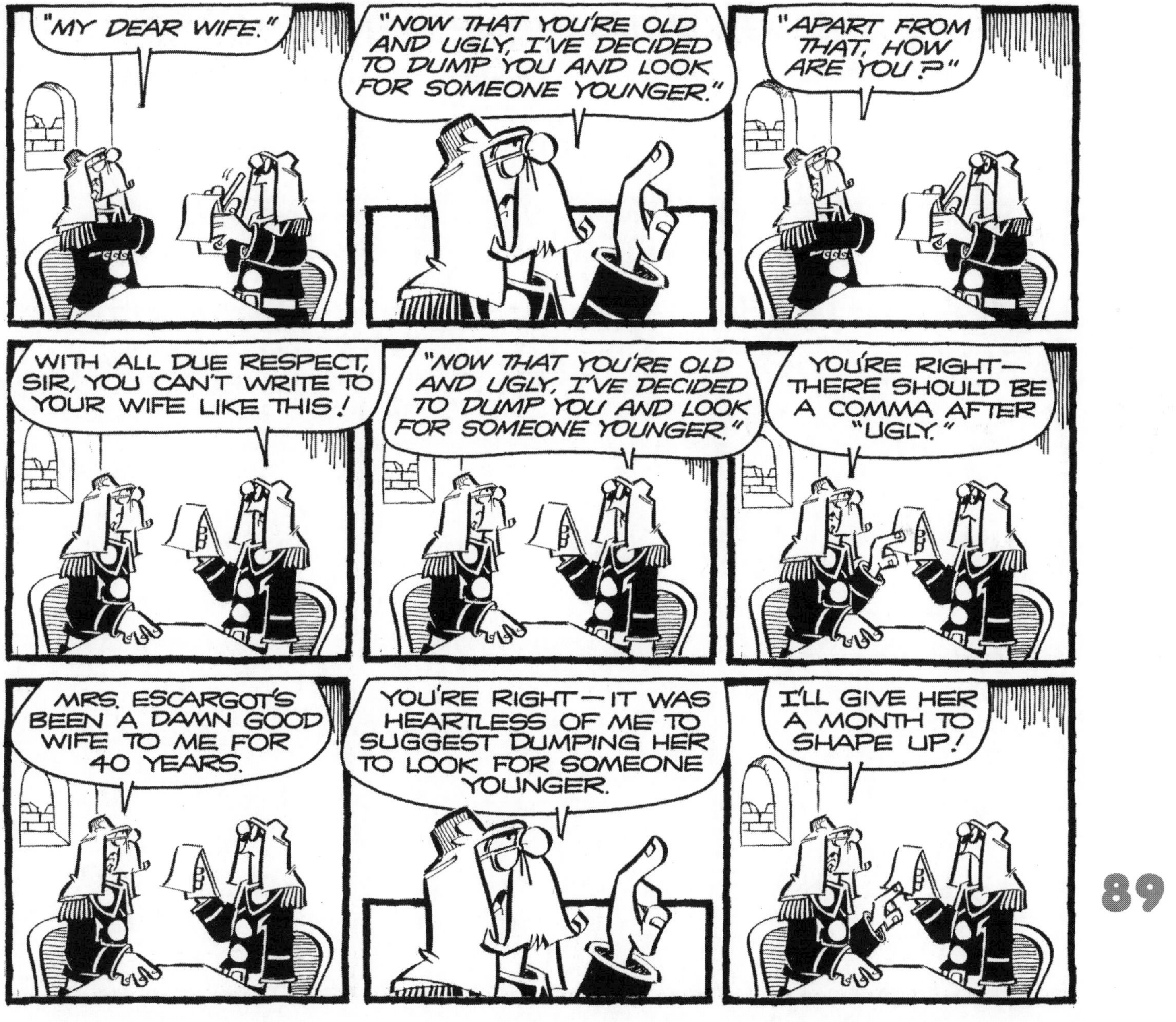
"MY DEAR WIFE."
"NOW THAT YOU'RE OLD AND UGLY, I'VE DECIDED TO DUMP YOU AND LOOK FOR SOMEONE YOUNGER."
"APART FROM THAT, HOW ARE YOU?"
WITH ALL DUE RESPECT, SIR, YOU CAN'T WRITE TO YOUR WIFE LIKE THIS!
"NOW THAT YOU'RE OLD AND UGLY, I'VE DECIDED TO DUMP YOU AND LOOK FOR SOMEONE YOUNGER."
YOU'RE RIGHT— THERE SHOULD BE A COMMA AFTER "UGLY."
MRS. ESCARGOT'S BEEN A DAMN GOOD WIFE TO ME FOR 40 YEARS.
YOU'RE RIGHT—IT WAS HEARTLESS OF ME TO SUGGEST DUMPING HER TO LOOK FOR SOMEONE YOUNGER.
I'LL GIVE HER A MONTH TO SHAPE UP!

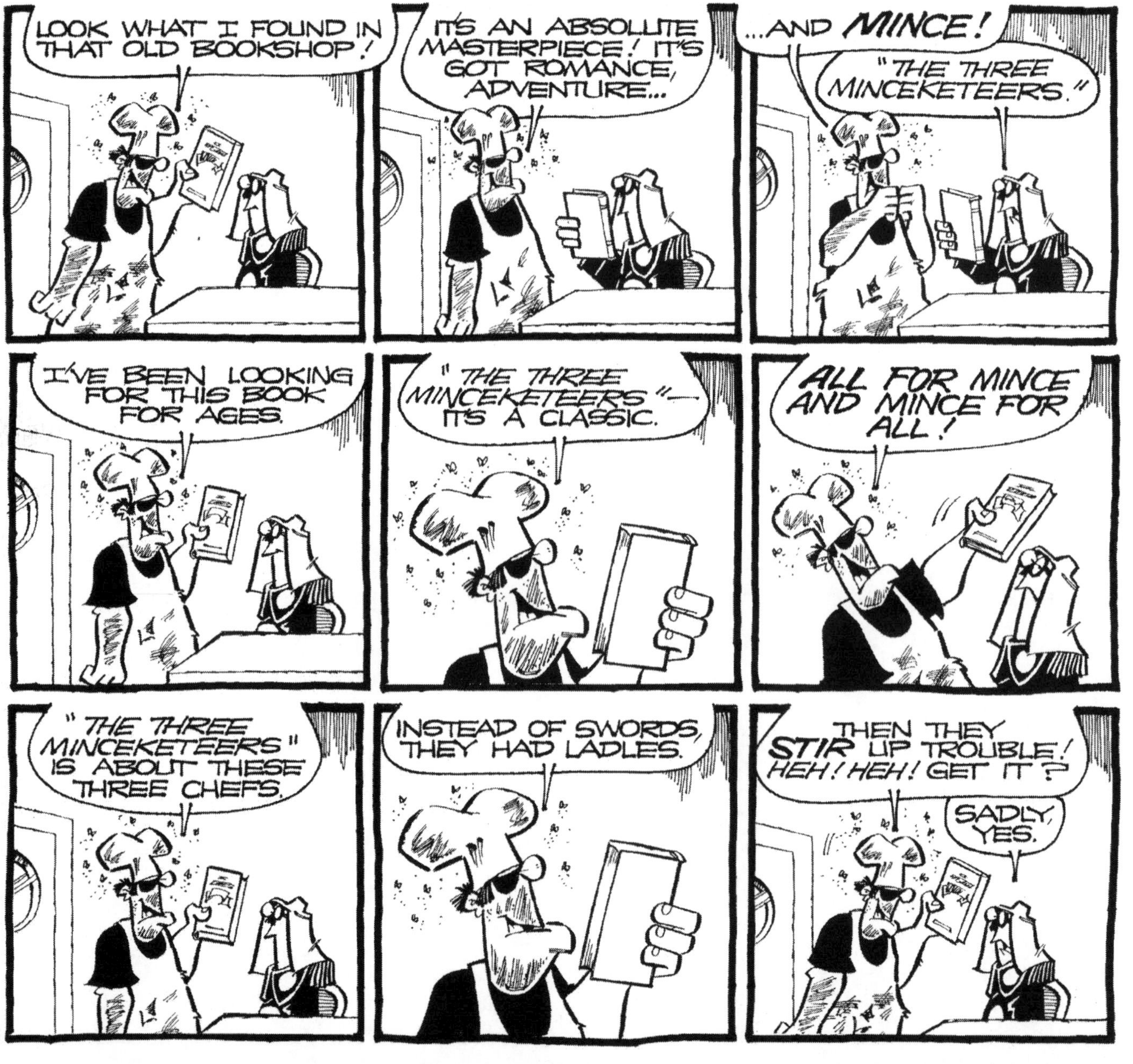
LOOK WHAT I FOUND IN THAT OLD BOOKSHOP!
IT'S AN ABSOLUTE MASTERPIECE! IT'S GOT ROMANCE, ADVENTURE...
...AND MINCE!
"THE THREE MINCEKETEERS."
I'VE BEEN LOOKING FOR THIS BOOK FOR AGES.
"THE THREE MINCEKETEERS"— IT'S A CLASSIC.
ALL FOR MINCE AND MINCE FOR ALL!
"THE THREE MINCEKETEERS" IS ABOUT THESE THREE CHEFS.
INSTEAD OF SWORDS, THEY HAD LADLES.
THEN THEY STIR UP TROUBLE! HEH! HEH! GET IT?
SADLY, YES.

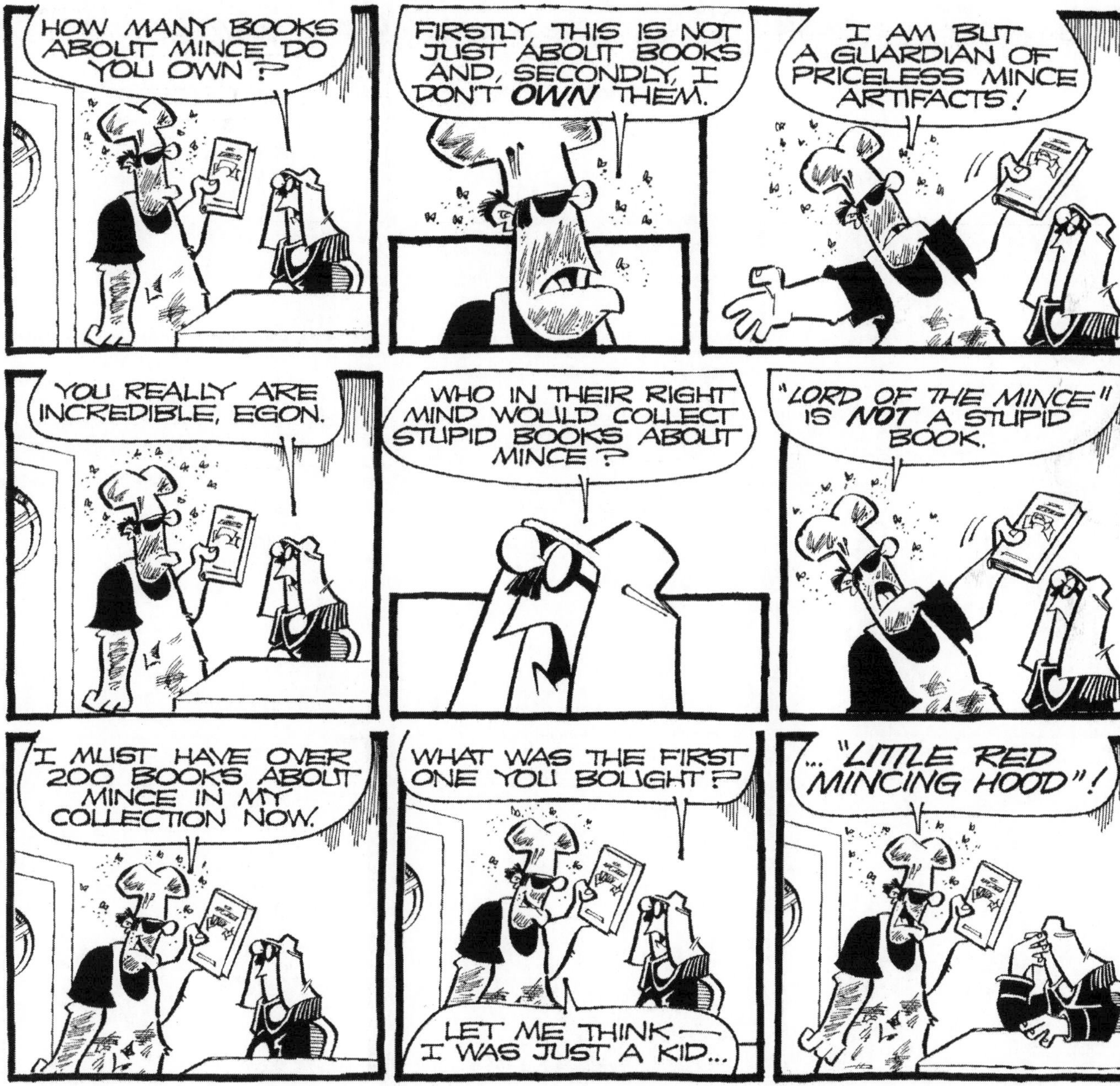
HOW MANY BOOKS ABOUT MINCE DO YOU OWN?
FIRSTLY, THIS IS NOT JUST ABOUT BOOKS AND, SECONDLY, I DON'T **OWN** THEM.
I AM BUT A GUARDIAN OF PRICELESS MINCE ARTIFACTS!
YOU REALLY ARE INCREDIBLE, EGON.
WHO IN THEIR RIGHT MIND WOULD COLLECT STUPID BOOKS ABOUT MINCE?
"*LORD OF THE MINCE*" IS ***NOT*** A STUPID BOOK.
I MUST HAVE OVER 200 BOOKS ABOUT MINCE IN MY COLLECTION NOW.
WHAT WAS THE FIRST ONE YOU BOUGHT?
LET ME THINK— I WAS JUST A KID...
... "*LITTLE RED MINCING HOOD*"!

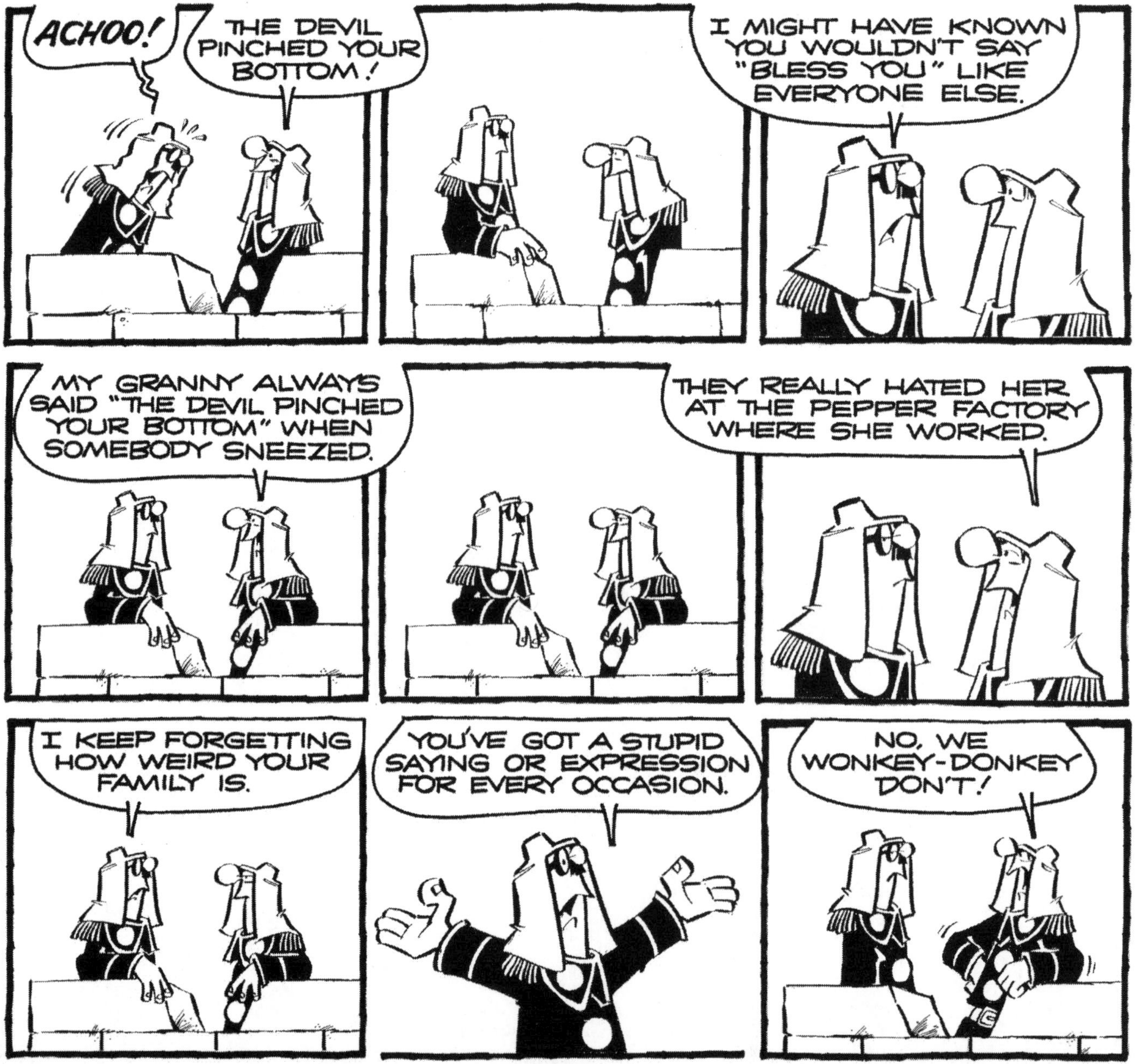
ACHOO!
THE DEVIL PINCHED YOUR BOTTOM!
I MIGHT HAVE KNOWN YOU WOULDN'T SAY "BLESS YOU" LIKE EVERYONE ELSE.
MY GRANNY ALWAYS SAID "THE DEVIL PINCHED YOUR BOTTOM" WHEN SOMEBODY SNEEZED.
THEY REALLY HATED HER AT THE PEPPER FACTORY WHERE SHE WORKED.
I KEEP FORGETTING HOW WEIRD YOUR FAMILY IS.
YOU'VE GOT A STUPID SAYING OR EXPRESSION FOR EVERY OCCASION.
NO, WE WONKEY-DONKEY DON'T!

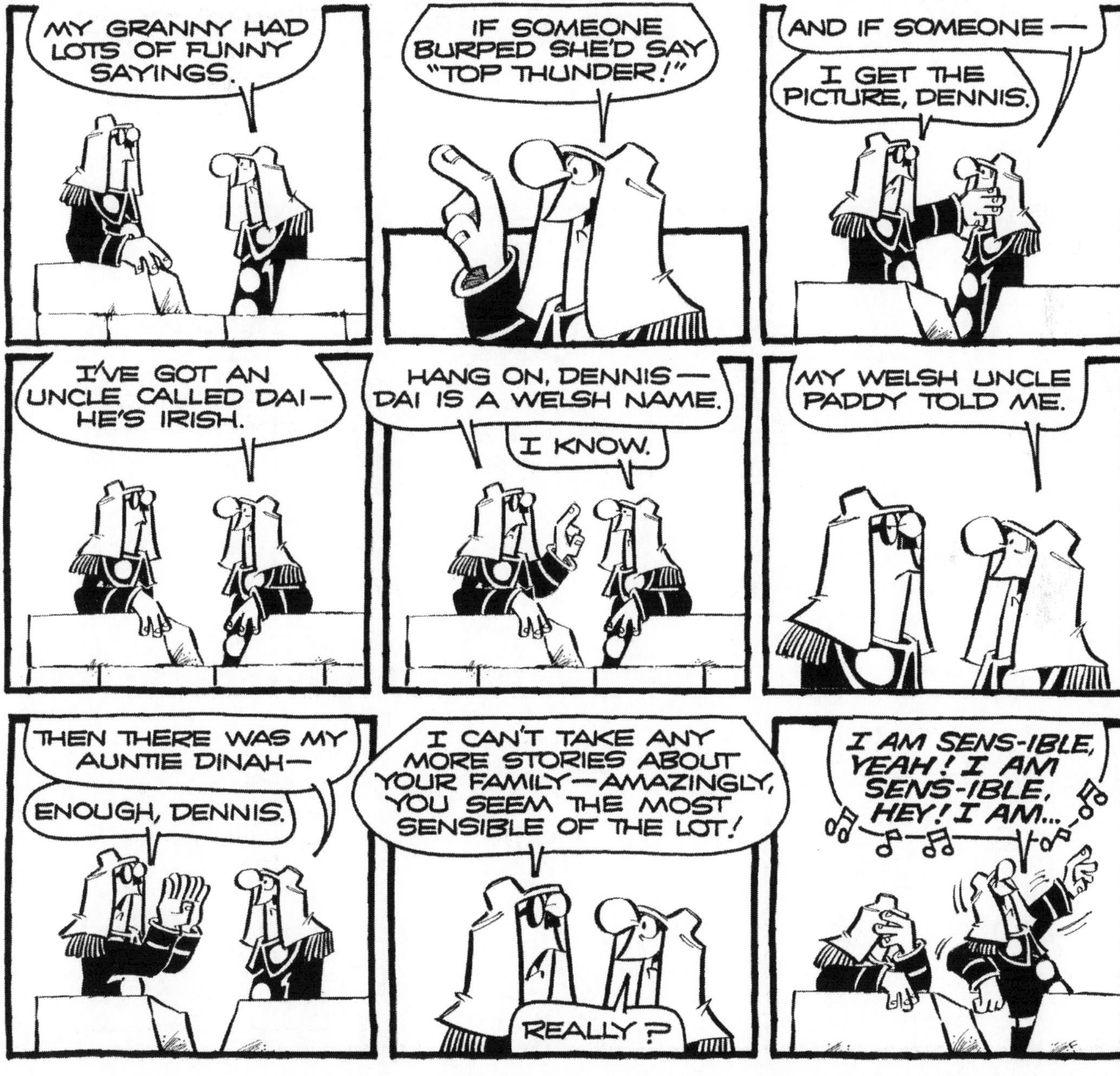
MY GRANNY HAD LOTS OF FUNNY SAYINGS.
IF SOMEONE BURPED SHE'D SAY "TOP THUNDER!"
AND IF SOMEONE—
I GET THE PICTURE, DENNIS.
I'VE GOT AN UNCLE CALLED DAI— HE'S IRISH.
HANG ON, DENNIS— DAI IS A WELSH NAME.
I KNOW.
MY WELSH UNCLE PADDY TOLD ME.
THEN THERE WAS MY AUNTIE DINAH—
ENOUGH, DENNIS.
I CAN'T TAKE ANY MORE STORIES ABOUT YOUR FAMILY—AMAZINGLY, YOU SEEM THE MOST SENSIBLE OF THE LOT!
REALLY?
I AM SENS-IBLE, YEAH! I AM SENS-IBLE, HEY! I AM...

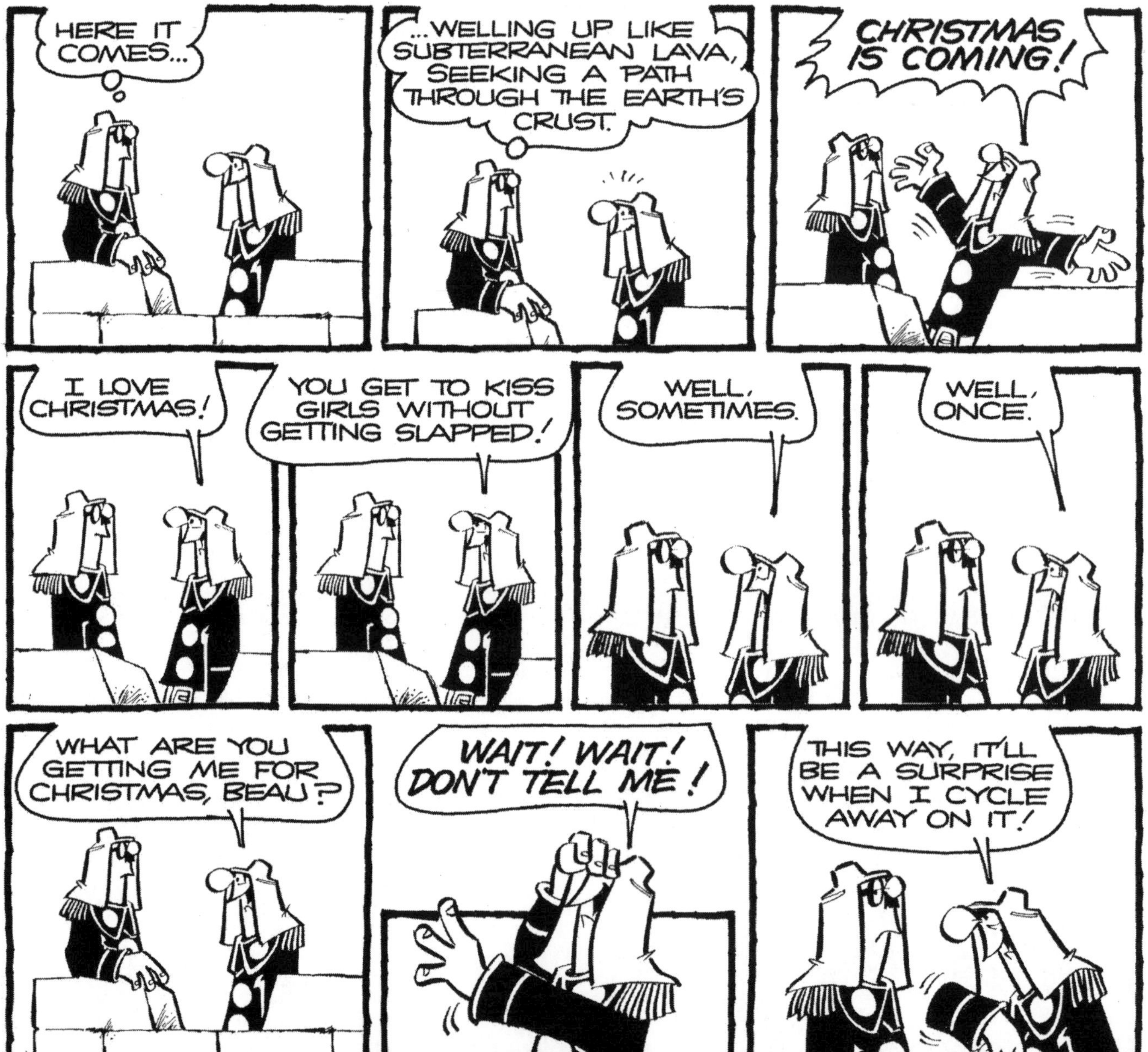
HERE IT COMES...
...WELLING UP LIKE SUBTERRANEAN LAVA, SEEKING A PATH THROUGH THE EARTH'S CRUST.
CHRISTMAS IS COMING!
I LOVE CHRISTMAS!
YOU GET TO KISS GIRLS WITHOUT GETTING SLAPPED!
WELL, SOMETIMES.
WELL, ONCE.
WHAT ARE YOU GETTING ME FOR CHRISTMAS, BEAU?
WAIT! WAIT! DON'T TELL ME!
THIS WAY, IT'LL BE A SURPRISE WHEN I CYCLE AWAY ON IT!

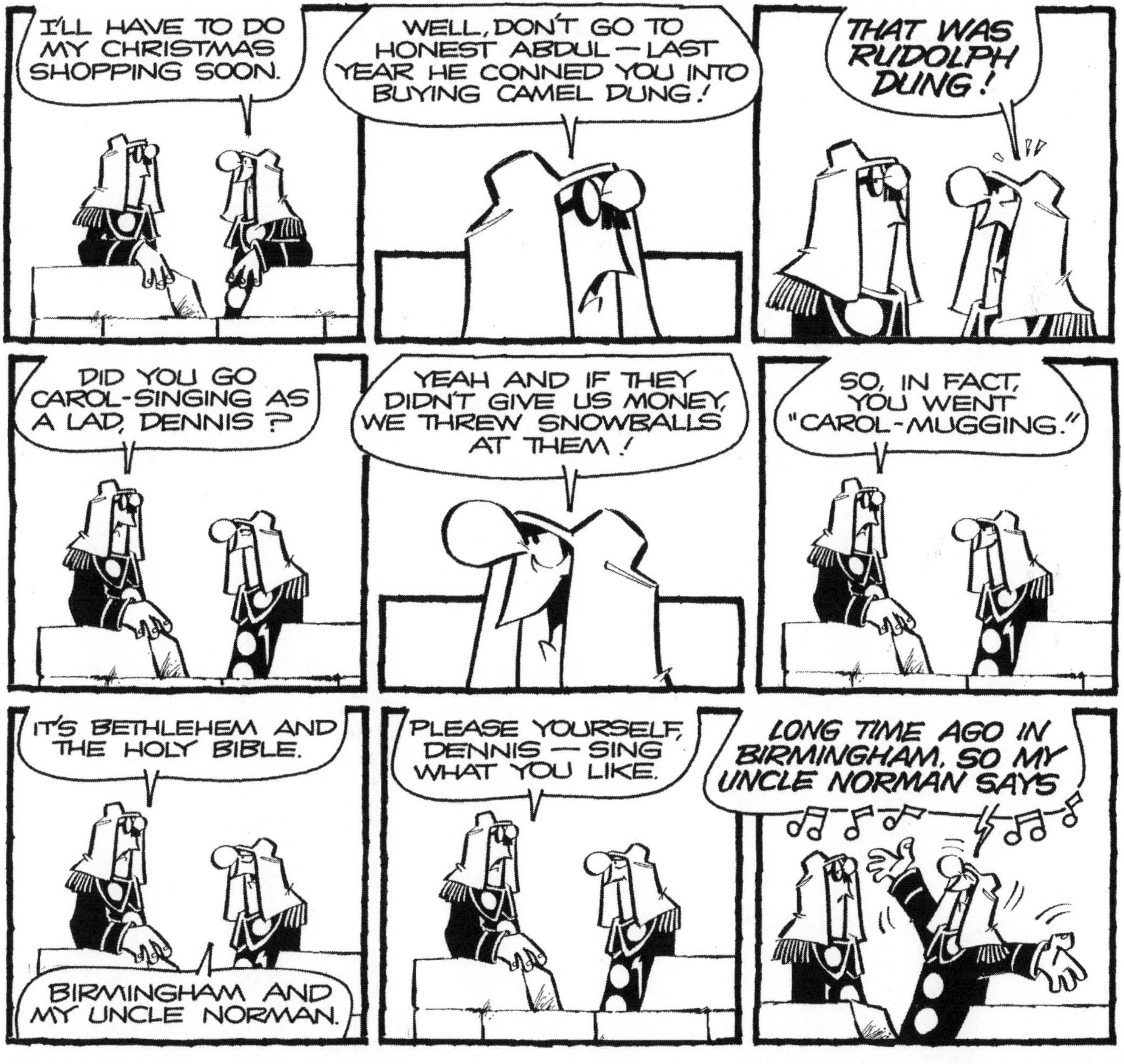
I'LL HAVE TO DO MY CHRISTMAS SHOPPING SOON.
WELL, DON'T GO TO HONEST ABDUL—LAST YEAR HE CONNED YOU INTO BUYING CAMEL DUNG!
THAT WAS RUDOLPH DUNG!
DID YOU GO CAROL-SINGING AS A LAD, DENNIS?
YEAH AND IF THEY DIDN'T GIVE US MONEY, WE THREW SNOWBALLS AT THEM!
SO, IN FACT, YOU WENT "CAROL-MUGGING."
IT'S BETHLEHEM AND THE HOLY BIBLE.
BIRMINGHAM AND MY UNCLE NORMAN.
PLEASE YOURSELF, DENNIS—SING WHAT YOU LIKE.
LONG TIME AGO IN BIRMINGHAM, SO MY UNCLE NORMAN SAYS

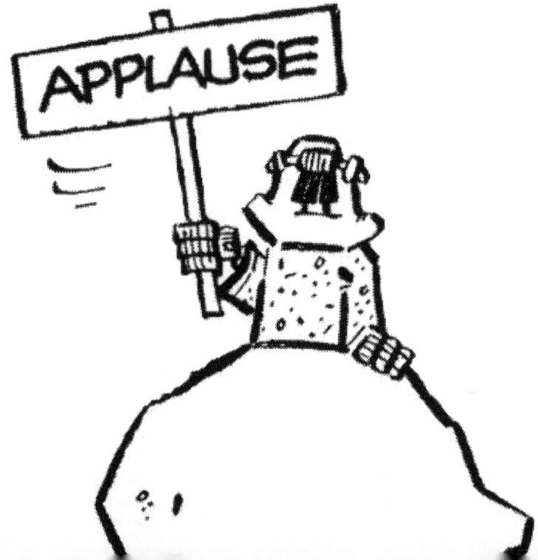
APPLAUSE

Printed in Great Britain
by Amazon.co.uk, Ltd.,
Marston Gate.